License to Harass

THE CULTURAL LIVES OF LAW

AUSTIN SARAT
SERIES EDITOR

License to Harass

LAW, HIERARCHY, AND
OFFENSIVE PUBLIC SPEECH

Laura Beth Nielsen

PRINCETON UNIVERSITY PRESS
PRINCETON AND OXFORD

Copyright © 2004 by Princeton University Press
Published by Princeton University Press, 41 William Street,
Princeton, New Jersey 08540
In the United Kingdom: Princeton University Press,
3 Market Place, Woodstock, Oxfordshire OX20 1SY

Library of Congress Cataloging-in-Publication Data

Nielsen, Laura Beth
License to harass / law, hierarchy, and offensive public speech /
Laura Beth Nielsen.
p. cm. — (The cultural lives of law)
Includes bibliographical references and index.
ISBN 0-691-11985-6 (cloth : alk. paper)
1. Freedom of speech—Social aspects—United States. 2. Hate
speech—United States. 3. Libel and slander—United States.
4. Threats—United States. 5. Public places—Law and legislation—
United States. I. Title. II. Series.
KF4772.N52 2004
342.7308′53—dc22   2003065496

British Library Cataloging-in-Publication Data is available.

This book has been composed in Palatino

Printed on acid-free paper. ∞

pup.princeton.edu

Printed in the United States of America

1 3 5 7 9 10 8 6 4 2

For my parents
David and Judy Nielsen

———————————

and in memory of our friend
Erwin Berliner

CONTENTS

TABLES

ACKNOWLEDGMENTS

THE JOURNEYS OF LIFE teach more than the art of arrival.

The journey that has been *License to Harass*, has taught me more than how an academic book is published. I've learned of the power of ideas, the complexity of subordination, and many, many lessons about how the world is experienced by people not like me.

The most important lesson this journey has taught thus far, however, is that completing this book, like so many other things in life, required the help and support of many people. First and foremost, I thank those people who took the time to tell me about their experiences with street speech. Although they must remain anonymous, I thank each of them from the bottom of my heart.

My ideas began at the University of California, Berkeley, Jurisprudence and Social Policy Program and Boalt Hall School of Law. My dissertation committee, Troy Duster, Angela Harris, and Lauren Edelman, provided countless hours of advice, feedback, and guidance. Most especially, Kristin Luker, my committee chair, supported me in so many ways—she convinced me to stick with this topic when others were derisive, she guided my intellectual development, and she shared her home, her tea, and even some of her baby clothes with me.

My research was supported by the Chancellor's Dissertation Fellowship at Berkeley. While there, I had the pleasure of working with and learning from a number of other faculty and friends including Marge Shultz, Kaaryn Gustafson, Brad Bugdanowitz, Brooke Bedrick, Tom Ginsburg, Anya Binsacca, David Lieberman, Matt Shultz, Margo Rodriguez, Rod Watanabe, and Kathleen Morris. I was fortunate to be part of the *Berkeley Women's Law Journal*, which provided respite and support during the law school years.

Throughout my graduate career and now into my professional career, I have been supported in so many ways by the Law and Society Association. From grants to attend the Graduate Student Workshop in 1994 and the Summer Institute in 1999, LSA has provided opportunities to try out ideas and meet other scholars working in these areas, and it has provided an intellectual and professional home. This work has been presented at more Law and Society Annual Meetings than I care to admit, and the generous comments and feedback I received from other Law and Society Association members, including Michael McCann, Sally Merry, Austin Sarat, Patricia Ewick, Jon Gould, and Susan Silbey, have improved this book dramatically.

Portions of chapter 5 appeared as "Situating Legal Consciousness: Experiences and Attitudes of Ordinary Citizens about Law and Street Harassment," *Law and Society Review* 34 (2000): 1055–90. Portions of chapter 6 were previously published as "Subtle, Pervasive, Harmful: Racist and Sexist Remarks in Public as Hate Speech," *Journal of Social Issues* 58 (2002) 265–80. I am grateful to the Law and Society Association, publishers of *Law and Society Review*, and the Society for the Psychological Study of Social Issues, publishers of the *Journal of Social Issues*.

I consider myself incredibly fortunate to work at the American Bar Foundation, the best place to conduct socio-legal research in the world. But for the financial and intellectual support of the American Bar Foundation, this book simply would not exist. Surrounded by generous and supportive colleagues Carol Heimer, Tracey Meares, Susan Shapiro, Chris Tomlins, Steve Levitt, Michael Greenstone, Jack Heinz, Ann Southworth, Katharina Heyer, Bonnie Honig, Michele Landis Dauber, Terry Halliday, Vicky Saker Woeste, Janice Nadler, Ronit Dinovitzer, and Ron Levy, it is not surprising that I have completed this project. Excellent research assistants, Alva Hayslip, Adriene Hill, and Aaron Biem, contributed enormously to this project. The support for research at the ABF is amazing, and thanks are due to the helpful people who make things happen like Joanne Martin, Lucinda Underwood, and Bryant Garth. Andy Koppelman at Northwestern University School of Law provided excellent assistance with the manuscript as well.

There is a special place in my heart for the two people who actually made this book happen—Austin Sarat, who encouraged me to submit the book as part of the "Cultural Lives of Law" series, and Chuck Myers at Princeton University Press. Their encouragement and enthusiasm for the project has been invaluable.

There is a very small and very special group of people who foster my intellectual development and whom I consider part of my family. It is rare and special to find such a combination in people. Young scholars know that support like this is hard to come by and means so much. We share ideas but we also share friendship, love, and life. I consider myself incredibly lucky to be a part of their lives and intellectual worlds and am honored that they share mine. KT Albiston, Christine Carter, Ben Fleury-Steiner, Robert L. Nelson, and Mary Rose, I cannot thank you enough.

Finally, there is my actual family. My mom, Judy Nielsen, is among the bravest women I know, and she helped me complete this project by providing skilled and loving child care for my sons more hours than can be counted. I could have left my children in only the most loving and capable hands. Thanks for all the trips to the condo, the Kohl Museum, the doggie park, the Acton Park, the Green Park, the Penny

Park, and the fire truck park. My dad, David Nielsen, has always encouraged me to do my best and serves as my twenty-four-hour, seven-
day-a-week computer help desk. My brothers and their families also
have been wonderfully supportive throughout my academic career.
Thank you, thank you, thank you!

There are no words to adequately thank the most important people
in my life, my husband, Eric Sorensen, and our sons, Zach and Skyler.
These three are largely responsible for helping me stay sane throughout this project. Eric is the best partner a person could hope for. He
is an excellent chef, amazing musician, talented artist, and most importantly, a loving stay-home-parent. Zach and Skyler are the sweet-
est and the most wonderfully fun boys ever. Zachary is my sunshine
and Skyler is so beautiful. As Skyler says, "Our family is the best in
the whole city of all." My family makes me what I am. Thank you; I
love you.

License to Harass

Chapter One

INTRODUCTION

This guy says to me, "I hate women, they're all sluts."
(24-year-old white woman, student, interview #10)

And he said, "I love that smile. I would have liked
to have been there this morning when your man
put that smile on your face. What did he do to
put that smile on your face? I'll bet he fucked you
so long you'll be smiling all day."
(field notes 1994)

"Monkey for a dollar!"
(18-year-old African American woman, interview #54)

I get these comments all the time. Mostly because of
the fact that I am a lesbian. When I am walking down
the street with my girlfriend we get lots of comments
like, "Try me and you'll never go back" or "I can
show you things that she can't."
*(19-year-old Hispanic woman, emergency
medical technician, interview #6)*

A man says to me, "[H]ey white bitch, come suck my
dick." *(26-year-old white woman,
unemployed, interview #30)*

WORDS LIKE THESE are spoken on the streets of America every day. To women, such words instill fear as a possible prelude to sexual violence. To people of color, such words bring the sting of racism, a bitter reminder that racial bias lives on and can surface anywhere, anytime, in subtle or blatant forms. To gays and lesbians such words convey a threat of hostility and aggression if they display affection for a same-sex partner or depart from conventional norms of dress and self-presentation. To all these groups, such words are a deep affront to personal dignity. To the courts, such words are protected speech.

This book examines the dilemma that offensive public speech poses for American society, and in that effort probes deeper questions about the relationship between law and society. Why has this society, which has shown increasing sensitivity to the legal protection of traditionally disadvantaged groups, continued to afford constitutional protection to offensive public speech? What does this policy imply about the relationship between law and social hierarchy in the contemporary United States? Is this policy choice shared by all segments of American society, or do judges, traditionally disadvantaged groups, and traditionally advantaged groups hold different beliefs about the legal status of offensive public speech?

This book pursues these questions through a socio-legal investigation of offensive public speech. In addition to examining the official doctrines of courts and public authorities, it analyzes data from interviews with ordinary citizens about their experiences with offensive public speech, their attitudes about the extent to which it poses a problem for American society, and their beliefs about whether the law should be employed to restrict offensive public speech. These interviews allow systematic comparison of the legal experiences and legal consciousness of different social groups—white men, white women, and people of color.

Important insights into how Americans view offensive public speech and the role that law should play in dealing with it emerge from this analysis. Consistent with other research, I find that white women and people of color are much more likely to personally experience offensive public speech than are white men and that street harassment imposes serious harms on these groups. While experience with the phenomenon varies, there is broad consensus among all social groups that sexist and racist comments in public are serious social problems. There also is considerable agreement that the law should not be deployed to attempt to stop such speech. But the reasons that white women, women of color, and men of color give for opposing legal regulation are significantly different from those offered by white men. Beneath a surface consensus against legal intervention, we see that different groups of Americans have very different attitudes about the law, which are rooted in their experience with the law. In the specific context of offensive public speech, white women and people of color are reluctant to turn to law for help, either because they do not believe the law can help them or because they fear the law would be used against them.

These findings have a larger significance for theories of law and legal consciousness in the United States. Contrary to the popular depiction of Americans as overly litigious, we see here that Americans have a pragmatic skepticism about the law as a remedy for offensive public behavior. In part the attitudes of ordinary citizens about offensive public speech may be shaped by judicial doctrines of free speech. Yet these attitudes seem to be anchored in a lay realism about the law and what it can be expected to accomplish. Only a small proportion of the indi-

viduals I interviewed, most of whom are white men, cite freedom of
speech as the principal rationale for exempting offensive public speech
from legal regulation.

Thus there is a disjuncture between the constitutional analyses of the
courts and legal scholars (both orthodox First Amendment scholars
and critical proponents of hate speech regulation) and the views of average Americans. Most of the individuals I interviewed spoke frankly
both about the problem of harassment in public and spoke realistically
about the difficulties of legal intervention to control it. But the courts
have made hate speech decisions with virtually no empirical analysis
of the phenomenon or its effects on target groups. Rather than seriously engaging in an analysis of the costs and benefits to society of
rules that might limit such behavior, American courts have treated
such conduct as "speech," which can be regulated only if the state offers a compelling justification. This doctrinal treatment in effect grants
a license to harass. The judicial protection of offensive public speech
works to normalize and justify such behavior. Without acknowledging
it, courts have placed a significant burden on traditionally disadvantaged groups in our society. Moreover, the judicial treatment of offensive public speech is not consistent across all forms of offensive public
comments. The courts have been more tolerant of legal restrictions on
begging than on other forms of public speech. Because begging is the
one form of public speech that most often confronts more privileged
members of our society and because it often is opposed by merchants
and property owners, this inconsistency appears to reflect a class bias
in judicial doctrine.

It is only through a combination of legal and sociological analysis
that it is possible to consider the relationship between the legal consciousness of ordinary people, the judicial treatment of offensive public speech, and the racial and gender hierarchies that offensive public
speech reinforces. Through that inquiry we gain new insights into the
relationship between law and social hierarchy in the contemporary
United States.

THE LOGIC OF COMPARING DIFFERENT TYPES OF OFFENSIVE PUBLIC SPEECH: BEGGING, SEXUALLY SUGGESTIVE SPEECH, AND RACIST SPEECH

I study "offensive public speech." For theoretical reasons, I chose to
ask respondents about begging, sexually suggestive speech, and race-
related speech between strangers in public places. The decision to ask

about sexually suggestive and race-related comments is straightforward, given the salience of this kind of speech in urban areas and their clear connection to race and gender hierarchies. The decision to compare begging to sexist and racist speech requires more comment.

By including begging with sexist and racist speech, I do not intend to make a normative judgment about its relative harm or offense. Rather, because the law gives serious treatment to the harms associated with being the target of aggressive begging, begging raises a number of theoretically driven but empirically unexamined questions. First, do people consider begging to be "offensive" public speech? (The answer largely is no). Second, insofar as they do consider it offensive or troubling, do they consider it problematic in the same way that they think of racist and sexist street speech as problematic? (Again, the answer is no—even those who do find begging troublesome think of it as far less "offensive" than racist and sexist street harassment). Third, by including begging, I am able to ask: How is simply being in public different for members of different social groups? If I did not include some form of unsolicited street speech that frequently targets white men, such a comparison would not be possible. Including begging in the study brings out important doctrinal and empirical comparisons about the nature of "offensive" public speech and how that category is constituted in law and in the everyday lives of individuals.

One could make similar arguments about "harmless compliments" made to women on an everyday basis. Some women may find such comments pleasant or flattering. These difficulties associated with defining "offensive" were among the primary reasons that I chose a subjective approach to the phenomenon. That is to say, the category of "offensive public speech" is defined by respondents' answers to questions about interactions they had with strangers in public places. In the interviews (described in greater detail in appendixes A and B), I prompted respondents to describe pleasant, benign, and offensive interactions. What they reported as offensive is what I counted as offensive. What is offensive to one target may not be to another.

Indeed, my interviews and observations demonstrate that there is a wide spectrum of interactions that are considered problematic by targets and that there is disagreement about what is troubling. One woman may be offended by the same comment that is considered complimentary and flirtatious to another woman. Sexually suggestive banter or flirting may be deemed appropriate when the speaker is of a certain social status or race but deemed inappropriate when the intended suitor is of lower social status or another race. Therefore, conscious and unconscious biases, including racism, that are inherent in targets' analysis of such interactions, are captured rather than controlled for in the definition of offensive public speech for the purposes of this study.

I made the explicit choice to study the targets, as opposed to perpetrators, of hate speech. This approach to hate speech or any other form of prejudice shifts the concept of prejudice from an objective one to a "subjective phenomenon with differences in perceptions and interpretations occurring between observers and actors, among target groups, and even within target groups" (Swim and Stangor 1998, p. 5). The study of targets' perceptions of discriminatory acts (as a subjective phenomenon) is said to necessitate "greater emphasis on descriptive and qualitative data," including "observational approaches in order to fully understand different groups' perspectives" (p. 6). My interviews were constructed to elicit a fuller understanding of the experiences of offensive public speech.

THEMES

This book addresses three interrelated themes. First, it examines the role that offensive public speech plays in how different social groups experience "being in public." A second theme of the book is legal consciousness. The study of "legal consciousness" explores individuals' experiences with and knowledge of the law and legal norms, as well as how this legal experience and knowledge translate into actions and decisions (Ewick and Silbey 1998). Finally, this book engages with debates about free speech and hate speech. The debates of legal scholars, critical race scholars, and even members of the judiciary have been largely uninformed by empirical data about offensive speech and its effects. This project provides needed empirical data about the contours of this debate and the positions of the parties most directly affected by harassing speech.

Being in Public

One objective of this work is to better understand social hierarchy as it is created, produced, and reproduced in public. The stories recounted by my respondents demonstrate that the anonymity people enjoy in crowded public places makes the public sphere an arena that is uniquely amenable to street harassment. As racism and sexism increasingly are becoming socially unacceptable (at least superficially), public places provide an opportunity for the expression of such comments without reprisal both because the target fears further violence and because the speaker and the target do not know one another.

The book demonstrates how simply being in public is raced, gendered, and classed. That is to say, simply being in public is different for white women, people of color, and those in poverty. My findings show how social hierarchies are reinscribed everyday through racist harassment, sexist harassment, and even through begging.

In its broader social context, hate speech is but one mechanism of subordination that "usually includes a complex, interlocking series of acts, some physical, some verbal, some symbolic" (Lederer and Delgado 1995b, p. 5), and creates "an atmosphere of fear, intimidation, harassment, and discrimination" (p. 5). Modern scholars of prejudice understand that prejudice involves more than individual negative stereotypes and actions. Prejudice involves "most centrally a commitment to a relative status positioning of groups in a racialized social order" (Bobo 1999, p. 447). If prejudice is about relative group position, then public hate speech provides a clear example of one of the ways in which such social hierarchies are constructed and reinforced on a day-to-day basis.

The effects of street harassment are significant. It is not simply a reminder of lower status for the target. Instead, as the respondents articulate, street harassment results in precautions people take to avoid being made a target. Taken together, the study of racist street speech, sexist street speech, and begging provide the basis for a sociological inquiry into the nature of being in public.

LEGAL CONSCIOUSNESS

In addition to a study of being in public, this also is a study of the sociology of law generally and of legal consciousness more specifically. The sociology of law traditionally has been concerned with the legitimacy of law, which ultimately is rooted in individuals' belief in and acceptance of the legal order (Unger 1985). Legal consciousness recently has become an important topic in socio-legal research because it represents the intersection of law as an institutional force and individuals as knowing agents. The contemporary concern with legal consciousness moves away from this traditional emphasis on the acceptance of official power by individuals to the notions of justice, rights, and power carried in the minds and applied in the everyday lives of individuals. Thus, scholars have begun to inquire whether and why people invoke the law in disputes (Bumiller 1988; Conley and O'Barr 1998; Merry 1990; Yngvesson 1985) and in social movements aimed at broader social change (McCann 1994).

The shift in concern among socio-legal scholars reflects a broader shift within social theory. Durkheim, Weber, and Marx were, in different ways, struggling to explain the rise and consequences of modern industrial society. Leading contemporary theorists such as Bourdieu, Scott, and MacKinnon have moved the debate to an examination of the relationship between modern institutions and the fate of individuals and groups. They look at how institutions shape modern life, including the worldviews of members of society. They theorize about the complexity of these interactions, as some groups and individuals develop strategies to improve their position within the social order while others resist it.

How do individuals come to possess knowledge of and opinions about the law and legal norms, and how does this knowledge shape their decisions about their life? This book seeks to move beyond the study of attitudes and opinions about law to examine the cultural schemas available to individuals as they attempt to make sense of the social world. Working from the context of offensive public speech, I attempt to analyze the role that law plays (or does not play) in how individuals conceive of a phenomenon that often deeply affects them.

This project concerns the interplay between race and gender hierarchies, law, and attitudes about the phenomenon of offensive speech. I explore citizen attitudes in depth and ask how their experiences have shaped these attitudes—experiences with the law and experiences in public places. Ewick and Silbey write that "legality [or law] is an emergent feature of social relations rather than an external apparatus acting upon social life" (1998, p. 17). The heart of this project is to understand precisely how this interactive understanding of legality (the personal understanding of law) filters, affects, constructs, and defines individuals' perceptions of these particular social interactions.

What is legal consciousness? Sally Merry defines legal consciousness as "the way people conceive of the 'natural' and normal way of doing things, their habitual patterns of talk and action, and their common-sense understanding of the world" (1990, p. 5). For my purposes, I might add, *their commonsense understanding of the way law works.* Put simply, legal consciousness is how people think about the law. It is prevailing norms, everyday practices, and common ways of dealing with the law or legal problems. It is the product of experience with the law and ideologies about the law.

Offensive public speech is an apt arena in which to study legal consciousness. Notions about law are intimately connected to ideas about offensive speech, although not in a simple or straightforward way. These respondents continually interpreted their experiences through the lens of law even before I posed questions about the law. That is to say, the law shapes people and their ideas, and people shape the content of law. While it is almost a cliche to talk about the constitutive power of law, this seemed to be the case in my interviews. Yet that did not necessarily mean that respondents favored the use of formal law to regulate offensive public speech. Rather, I found that legal consciousness is contradictory and contingent. The law is present in the everyday thinking of average citizens, and it affects what falls into the categories of redressable social harm versus the private burdens one must endure for a civil society.

The study of legality emerges from and contributes to the study of law in everyday life (Sarat and Kearns 1995), which is specifically designed to "encourage legal scholarship to bridge the separation between the instrumental and the constitutive perspectives and to recognize more fully the interactive character of law's relationship to society" (p. 21). My project seeks to close this gap because neither an instrumental nor a constitutive perspective provides an adequate approach to the problem of harmful public speech. An instrumental view treats the law simply as a "tool for sustaining or changing aspects of social life" (Sarat and Kearns 1995, p. 23) and is not helpful in the case of offensive public speech because an instrumentalist conception primarily is concerned with law's effectiveness in resolving a social problem. Since offensive public speech and its effects in reinforcing hierarchies of gender and race domination are not widely recognized, it would be difficult to measure the effectiveness of the law in this area. In other words, because the law renders the problem "invisible," it is extraordinarily difficult to uncover. Moreover, the instrumentalist perspective simply explores the law as an external social institution and fails to explore the meaning of the law as understood by citizens.

My empirical research demonstrates that street harassment is, in fact, a problem of the magnitude that many scholars claim. The instrumentalist's next question is how the law can correct this problem. But given the bias in favor of extra protection for speech in public, it is unlikely that this particular form of subordination through speech will be remedied by law. Instead, I turn my attention to people's conception of social problems to explore how their legal consciousness—that is, their understanding of the law—affects their determination of what is or is not a social problem and when the law is an appropriate medium to address a social problem. Some First Amendment scholars might argue that how people understand the law is not important given the magnitude of the democratic principle at stake. Yet the normative claim should not foreclose the legal sociologists' interest in the legal consciousness of ordinary citizens. It is interesting and important to learn whether there is a consensus among ordinary citizens about the legal status of offensive public speech, and further to determine whether their views are consistent with First Amendment doctrine, their own experiences, or something else.

To reveal the contradictory and contingent nature of legal consciousness requires that the researcher view law not as a monolithic institution, but rather in the context of the "entire social environment" (Silbey and Sarat 1987). Law must be "defined less as discrete rules and official decisions than as various modes of knowledge—as specific cultural conventions, logics, rituals, symbols, skills, practices, and processes that citizens routinely deploy in practical activity" (McCann and March 1996, p. 210). To capture this complexity, I asked respondents not only about their experiences with offensive public speech, but also about their experiences with the law, their understanding of the principles that underlie the First Amendment, and how that affects their response to and understanding of offensive public speech.

These data demonstrate that subjects have strong normative reactions against most offensive public speech. They are willing to say that they find it offensive and morally wrong to make racist or sexist comments to strangers in public. Despite this, most people are not in favor of limiting such speech. What explains this apparent contradiction? The answer lies in varieties of legal consciousness: that is, differing attitudes about the law. Some respondents hold staunch First Amendment ideals. Others distrust the state. Still others are unwilling to be defined as victims, which they think would happen if they invoked the law to "protect" them. Moreover, I find that these attitudes are correlated with race and gender. Thus, behind an apparent consensus against attempting to regulate offensive public speech, I find significant variations in legal consciousness about offensive public speech, depending on the race and gender of the respondents.

My results thus lead to a somewhat different perspective on legal consciousness than emerges from previous work. Ewick and Silbey, for example, talk about the capacity to render some information less important than might otherwise be the case as the "hegemonic power of law" (Ewick and Silbey 1992, p. 727). According to a strong model of legal hegemony, the dominant model of legal thought with respect to offensive public speech—the First Amendment model—would control the attitudes of ordinary citizens across categories of race, gender, and class. I find, instead, that there is not so much widespread support for the First Amendment theory of street speech as there are conflicting perspectives on the value of using law to redress the problem of offensive public speech. The First Amendment model controls the law of the street, but more as a product of elite control of judicial doctrine and the police powers of the state, and less out of mass conformity to First

Amendment values. White women and people of color do not appear ready to mount a campaign to use the law to restrict racist and sexist street speech. This position is premised on and reflects skepticism about the law as a remedial tool, based on personal prior experiences with the law, legal institutions, and legal actors, broadly defined. A rejection of law also reflects political realism—the First Amendment theory of street speech remains firmly in control of legal and political institutions.

These systematic variations in legal consciousness that I found have methodological implications for studying legal consciousness. It is important that studies of legal consciousness are crafted to allow us to observe and measure variations in legal consciousness across social groups. To date, studies primarily have focused on the legal consciousness of a particular group such as welfare recipients (Ewick and Silbey 1992) or working-class people (Merry 1990). Instead of limiting my research to particular groups who traditionally have borne the burdens of particular problems (white women or people of color in my case), I interviewed people from different social groups, including white men. As a result, I was able to offer a broader theory of legal consciousness concerning offensive public speech.

A motivating theme in research on legal consciousness is resistance. How do ordinary people resist the imposition of power and the creation of hegemonic stories power imposes on subordinates? Elements of resistance to dominant ideology drive much of this research. My analysis of resistance in this book focuses on resistance to the imposition of race and gender status hierarchies in public places. If racist or sexist street harassment is designed to (re)inscribe social hierarchies based on race and gender, then what do targets do to reject the imposition of these constructions when such incidents occur in public places?

Free Speech

Racist and sexist speech generate much debate about the proper balance between freedom of speech and the protection of historically disadvantaged groups from verbal abuse. First Amendment absolutists argue that speech cannot and should not be legally restricted (Post 1990, 1993; Strossen 1995). Critical race theorists argue that racist speech results in substantial harms for its victims (Matsuda, Lawrence, Delgado, and Crenshaw 1993), perpetuates inequality, and must therefore be legally limited to realize the equality guaranteed by the Fourteenth Amendment (Lawrence 1990). Cultural theorists contemplate how the performative aspects of speech translate into harms (Butler 1997). Feminist scholars identify sexist street harassment as a source of women's disempowerment (West 1987), investigate the harms associated with sexually suggestive public speech (Gardner 1980, 1995), explore potential legal remedies (Bowman 1993; Davis 1994), and question if pornography is a legally actionable harm (MacKinnon 1993).

Classic studies in public opinion, as well as more recent replications show a correlation between class, education, public participation, and support for the First Amendment (McCloskey and Brill 1983; Stouffer 1992). Concerned about the fate of civil liberties in a democracy, this research focuses on political tolerance. The studies of political tolerance have been large-scale empirical endeavors that survey attitudes and opinions toward the political speech of communists, socialists, and organized hate groups such as the Ku Klux Klan (McCloskey and Brill 1983; Stouffer 1992; Sullivan, Piereson, and Marcus 1982). This work provides a set of hypotheses about attitudes toward the legal regulation of individually directed hate speech, but leaves open questions about how individuals think about and understand the law with respect to everyday incidents of targeted hate speech. Moreover, because it relies on structured attitude and opinion data, it does not capture the more complex and subtle character of legal consciousness that in-depth interviews may provide.

My project builds on this work but differs in several important respects. I sought to investigate the relationship between experience with offensive public speech and legal consciousness. Therefore, instead of asking about organized political speech, I asked individuals about their experiences with and understanding of sexually suggestive speech, racist speech, and begging in public areas, allowing respondents to define what they considered offensive or problematic speech. Interviews were replete with subjects' reports of incidents in which they were made the target of offensive, sexually suggestive public speech, racist speech, and begging.[1] Many of these comments are considered offensive and problematic by at least some of their targets. All have been subject to attempts at legal regulation. Chapter 2 elaborates attempts and failures of regulatory regimes for dealing with these forms of speech.

Although most average citizens have not been party to a First Amendment lawsuit, they have opinions about the First Amendment and what types of speech should (or should not) be limited. The First Amendment and debates about regulating speech attract much attention in the popular media. For example, think of recent debates regarding flag burning, "political correctness," and media coverage of controversial stories. Indeed, even when one is the target of street harassment, the law may be present in one's interpretation of the event. In other words, the way in which average citizens make sense of these sorts of interactions involves ideas about the law. The language of law may be a powerful force in the mind of the individual (Conley and O'Barr 1998).

In addition to saying what this book *is*, it may be useful to say what this book *is not*. This book *is not* an attempt to make a constitutional argument either in favor of or in opposition to the restriction of the forms of speech that I examine. My purpose is to develop a sociological analysis of the experience of being a target of sexist and racist speech, of the attitudes of ordinary citizens about the legal regulation of such speech, and of the official legal status of such speech. One of the lessons of that analysis, however, is that, as a society, we need to understand that the legal regulation (or lack thereof) of offensive public speech is a policy choice. When we make that choice we should do so in light of the empirical data about the nature of the burden borne by those who are frequently made targets. With a detailed understanding of the nature of the harms associated with allowing such speech, legal scholars may remain in favor of allowing such speech. But, these data require recognition that the burden of free speech is dramatic and largely is borne by white women and people of color.

Another lesson of the study concerns the relationship between law and power. The law celebrates "free speech" in public places as a cornerstone of democracy, as a protection from undue concentrations of power. Yet in protecting offensive public speech, the law protects a social practice that reinforces and actualizes hierarchies of race and gender. And, traditionally disadvantaged groups—white women and people of color—are well aware of the reality of the relationship between law and power. These groups already know not to look to the law for help. Thus, my analysis suggests that in its current form, the law grants a "license to harass" white women and people of color in public. At the same time, the law offers formal and informal protection to targets of begging. It is clear that the relative social status of the target of offensive public speech makes a difference in how different types of offensive public speech are legally managed.

NATURE OF THE STUDY

Given my theoretical concerns, I combined field observation, in-depth interviewing, and closed-ended interviewing. The ethnographic component of this study is based on over 120 hours observing street interactions in a variety of public settings (for more on methods, see appendix A). There also is a narrative component to my research method. I attempted to preserve the integrity of the stories that respondents told me by tape recording and transcribing the accounts of street harassment given in the targets' own words. While these modes of data collection follow previous studies of legal consciousness, my research design differs from prior work in a few important respects. First, I conducted semistructured interviews with one hundred people. Second, I chose to interview people from a wide variety of backgrounds, rather than exploring the legal consciousness of particular groups of citizens. This combination of observation, in-depth interviewing, and semistructured questions put to a range of social groups allowed both a qualitative and quantitative inquiry into the legal consciousness of respondents and preliminary testing of hypotheses about the relationship between group characteristics/membership, experience with different varieties of offensive public speech, and attitudes about legal intervention.

An important element of the research design was the use of field observation as a distinct methodology. I conducted planned, systematic observations of interactions between strangers in public places designed to provide me with a better understanding of the nature of such interactions. One of the major advantages of field observation is that the researcher is privy to "unfiltered" information. Indeed, I was able to observe many street interactions prior to and during my efforts to construct and recruit a sample from the streets.

I selected three Northern California cities in which to conduct observations and recruit subjects. I conducted my research in San Francisco, Orinda (a very wealthy suburb of San Francisco), and Berkeley (using Oakland as a substitute during school months so as not to oversample people affiliated with the university). After observing interactions for some time, I used a careful selection process to determine which individuals to approach and ask if they would be willing to participate in an interview. The selection process (described in greater detail in appendix A) was designed to ensure that everyone in the location had an equal chance of being selected to participate in the interview.

Selecting subjects from public places had several advantages. First, I knew that the people I approached were consumers of public space. That is to say, they were willing to venture into public places and had, more likely than not, been party to the interactions about which I would be asking. Second, by "going where the data are" I was able to observe interactions as verification for the stories I was told in the interviews. Third, by approaching people in person, I could establish rapport in a way that would be impossible if contact were initiated via telephone. Finally, potential respondents were less threatened being approached in a crowded public place than they might have been in some other context.

The dataset analyzed herein has strengths and limitations. The data were collected, analyzed, and presented in accordance with accepted practices for qualitative research. I chose depth over breadth in this qualitative research, but took care to construct a sample that was large enough to include members of different social groups. This allows for simple statistical comparisons across these groups. The data also are confirmed because they comport with findings by several scholars in a variety of disciplines using different methodologies. Finally, the patterns in my data are clear in many respects. Without replication, we cannot be sure they will hold across time and place. Yet they are a plausible account that may well prove robust in other contexts. These and other methodological questions are discussed at greater length in the methodological appendix, appendix A. The limitations of the data lie in the small numbers of subgroups of respondents. The quantitative data about the subgroups are intended to be descriptive for comparison and should be taken primarily as suggestive.

Plan of the Book

In the chapters that follow, I study offensive public speech, not just as a social problem, but as a particularly interesting context in which to examine the interrelationship of race, gender, class, and legal consciousness. The primary focus of my data collection was on ordinary citizens moving in public space, particularly those groups who most often are targets of offensive public speech. The questions I put to these ordinary citizens were informed by ongoing debates in law and among legal scholars.

In chapter 2, I elaborate on the theoretical debates that inform my approach to offensive public speech and document the current state of the law regarding offensive speech of all varieties. Chapters 3, 4, 5, and 6 contain empirical results and analysis. Chapter 3 analyzes how frequently people of different races, genders, and classes are the targets of offensive public speech. This chapter elaborates the "detailed calculus for being in public" and demonstrates that those who are not the targets of offensive public speech of a particular variety systematically underestimate how frequently these sorts of interactions occur, as well as their effects on their targets.

In chapter 4, I address three important questions. First, do people consider offensive public speech to be a personal problem? Second, do

people consider the various forms of offensive public speech to be social problems? Finally, I ask if they think the law should intervene to
remedy these problems. The answers vary across social groups based
on experience. Although a majority of subjects think that offensive
public speech is a serious personal and social problem, they do not
think it is a problem that should be addressed by law. This pattern is
especially striking among women. Women often are the targets of sexist speech, yet they are no more likely than men to favor legal regulation of such comments. Similarly, people of color are no different from
whites in whether they favor the legal regulation of racist comments.

Chapter 5 probes the discourses people use in talking about the phenomenon of offensive public speech and its legal regulation. I find that
there are four basic paradigms that people invoke when they oppose
the legal regulation of offensive public speech. The paradigms vary
significantly by race and gender.

Chapter 6 explores reactions and responses to offensive public speech
in public places. If, as the respondents suggest, offensive speech is a
serious personal and social problem but one that the law should not
address, how do targets handle such situations in the moment? As they
denounce the use of law, respondents suggest that this is a problem that
can be dealt with on the spot. But their own stories suggest that most
targets (probably rightly) are fearful and do not address the discriminatory messages during an actual encounter. In examining these various
paradigms, I explore themes of resistance and counterhegemonic ideology. In contrast to some other studies (McCann 1994; Merry 1990), in
which a protean rights consciousness figured prominently in the minds
of ordinary citizens, my informants show surprisingly little interest in
using the law as an instrument of resistance against racist or sexist public speech. Indeed, the aspect of law which is more often invoked is the
First Amendment. Thus law is referenced in defense of a status quo that
does little to regulate offensive public speech.

In chapter 7, the conclusion, I draw out the theoretical and methodological implications of my findings. I suggest that a more complete
understanding of legal consciousness requires that we take account of
how ideas about the law vary by the experiences and attitudes of individuals, and by the nature of the issues involved. Legal doctrine may
not accurately reflect the experiences of various groups in our society.
Yet it has practical and ideological effects. In the context of offensive
public speech, First Amendment doctrine rejects an inquiry into the
effects of such speech on various groups or the relationship of such
speech to hierarchies of gender and race in our society. For white
males, this is a normative position. Thus, there is a correspondence
between legal doctrine and the most privileged position in public

spaces. A First Amendment approach reflects and ratifies white male experiences on the street. Indeed, the only area in which there has been a softening of the First Amendment model concerns begging—the one form of street harassment faced by white men.

While women and people of color would deny that formal doctrine captures their experience, neither do they seem particularly interested in seeking law's protection for this harm. Their reluctance appears to be rooted in their experience with law and with their broader experiences as women or persons of color, rather than in a belief in the value of applying First Amendment protection to offensive public speech. The complexity, indeed the reasoned wisdom of these groups, suggests that it is too facile to assert that there is a pool of rights consciousness among less privileged groups that can be mobilized for legal and social change. White women and men and women of color do not mindlessly accept the harms they face from offensive public speech. Perhaps correctly, they see the law as offering no recourse or worse, as posing an added threat of legal repression. Instead they struggle, as individuals, to resist, avoid, or accommodate to the acts of racist and sexist speech they encounter as a part of their daily lives. Finally, in the conclusion I speculate about law and its limits for social reform.

CONCLUSION

Conventional wisdom suggests that gender harassment in public places is a harmless nuisance that women simply must tolerate as one price for a "free" society. The courts take a similar position in striking down limits on racist speech on constitutional grounds. Feminist and critical race scholars attack this approach, arguing that such speech is intimately connected to broader systems of gender and race inequality that place a special burden on members of subordinated groups. Yet the theoretical and doctrinal debate remains uninformed by empirical data on the nature of this phenomenon and its effects.

Inequality and social hierarchies of race, gender, and class are produced and reproduced everywhere in any number of ways. Unlike the workplace, the family, and in violent encounters such as rape and domestic violence in which scholars have paid careful attention to these processes, public space is mentioned in passing or not at all. Street harassment becomes a site in which to study processes of subordination in raw form. In doing so, this book advances our understanding of hierarchy, power, legal consciousness, and resistance.

Chapter Two

LAW AND POWER IN SIDEWALK ENCOUNTERS

CONFLICTING PERSPECTIVES ON OFFENSIVE

PUBLIC SPEECH

OFFENSIVE PUBLIC SPEECH is contested terrain. It is contested on the street. Those who utter racist or sexist comments may be consciously asserting a dominant role. The targets of such comments are faced with a choice about what to do in the face of such comments. Do they flee, do they fight, do they ignore, do they resist? Part of the contest on the street is a matter of interpretation. Is a crude comment a harmless compliment? Is it an inevitable occurrence in a diverse, sexually liberated society? Is it a hurtful offense? Or is it a threat?

Offensive public speech is contested terrain in the courts. As universities, municipalities, and other public authorities have attempted to regulate various kinds of offensive public speech, these efforts have generated constitutional litigation over whether such regulations unduly infringe on First Amendment freedom.

Offensive public speech is contested terrain in the academy. Critical race and feminist scholars assert that racist and sexist speech are linked to broader hierarchies of race and sex, that such comments do serious harm to individual targets and vulnerable groups in society, and make no serious contribution to the exchange of ideas that is the underlying value of the First Amendment. Scholarly advocates of free speech sometimes agree but respond that even well-meaning controls on speech in public places could undermine free speech and are not constitutionally permissible.

The contested character of offensive public speech is precisely why it is such a promising area for socio-legal inquiry. Because it is the subject of extensive judicial analysis, it provides a window into how courts analyze the legal status of such speech. Because it is the subject of extensive scholarly debate, there are a series of empirical and theoretical questions about offensive public speech and its relationship to law and social hierarchy that have only begun to be examined. Because it is a prominent aspect of social interaction, it has been the subject of sociological theorizing about its meaning and significance. And because it is a part of so many individuals' everyday experience on the street, it provides an occasion to examine the consciousness of ordinary citizens about offensive public speech, social hierarchy, and law.

The phenomenon of offensive public speech must be located in the jurisprudential context in which it is embedded. Understanding how the First Amendment applies (or does not apply) to offensive public speech is crucial for understanding individuals' responses to such interactions as well as the possibility for legal intervention and judicial response. At the same time, it is not useful to reify the categories of the First Amendment if those categories constrain empirical examination of the phenomenon. Fundamentally, this book concerns how ordinary people understand being the target of offensive public speech and whether and how their understanding of the First Amendment plays into their understanding of these experiences. Thus, while this chapter provides analysis of some First Amendment jurisprudence, it is not meant to be an exhaustive review of relevant case law on the matter. Rather, it is meant to give the reader a basic understanding of what courts say about the legal regulation of such speech and demonstrate the necessity for an empirical understanding of what happens on the street.

This chapter begins to examine the contested terrain of offensive public speech in the courts with a brief analysis of the legal doctrine about the regulation of begging, racist speech, and sexist speech in public places. This analysis reveals seeming inconsistencies in how the law treats restrictions on different kinds of troubling public speech. Although restrictions on racist speech are struck down as content-specific, restrictions on begging are upheld in some jurisdictions as reasonable time, place, or manner restrictions. I propose two related explanations. The first is simple power dynamics. Where the target of offensive public speech is a member of the dominant group (as in begging), courts recognize the harm imposed and are amenable to regulation. A second, related theory is that courts respond to the notion of threat. Where courts recognize threat as part of offensive public speech, they are willing to uphold restrictions. This leads to important questions about what is happening in these interactions on the street. The final section of the chapter develops a socio-legal theory of power in sidewalk interactions based on contemporary social theories.

LEGAL DOCTRINE

Hate speech poses a fundamental jurisprudential problem in American society. The law itself, in the form of judicial opinion and political debate, and most legal scholars largely view the problem of street harassment out of its street context. They ask, "Should hate speech enjoy the same constitutional protection as other forms of expression?" This issue has taken on new significance in the last twenty years, as members of historically disadvantaged groups have attempted to use the law and the rules of private organizations to gain protection from verbal abuse, especially due to race. The attempt to reframe the jurisprudential debate is based on showing that racist hate speech inflicts serious psychological and social harms without contributing to genuine freedom of discussion. Attempts to regulate race-related speech generally have met unsympathetic responses by the courts and by advocates of free speech. Restrictions on sexually suggestive or explicit speech largely are accepted in the workplace and in education, but are not considered viable for public spaces. Meanwhile, restrictions on begging in public places are constitutionally ambiguous. These conflicts continue to unfold in legal battles over hate speech codes, restrictions on begging and loitering, as well as other restrictions on public speech and behavior.

The American liberal legal model posits that speech is nearly always outside the boundary of law and speech that is merely offensive certainly is outside the zone of activities the state may regulate, especially when it occurs in public places.[1] Indeed, a fundamental tenet of freedom in the United States is the freedom of speech. While it is important that this project be firmly grounded in an accurate understanding of First Amendment doctrine, my purpose is not to invent a doctrinally sound argument for regulating begging, racist hate speech, or sexist harassment. Such an effort likely will be futile, would not necessarily advance socio-legal or feminist theory concerning street harassment, and has been attempted by a number of legal scholars. Nonetheless, it is interesting to treat First Amendment doctrine as a set of empirical propositions about street harassment. By comparing judicial construction of the phenomenon to laypeople's experience with and interpretation of the phenomenon, we may be able to see if there is a link between doctrine and the legal consciousness of everyday citizens. In addition, the doctrine provides a rich source of data worthy of sociological analysis about what types of speech (and speakers) garner protection in the United States.

In this section, I provide a brief overview of relevant First Amendment doctrine. In short, courts largely allow (with some notable exceptions) the regulation of begging but strike down restrictions on racist speech. This section demonstrates the reasoning of the courts that allows this seemingly contradictory state of speech regulation to exist and hypothesizes about what actually may be motivating the courts in some of the cases.

The Legal Status of Street Speech: A Brief Overview

All three forms of speech that I am centrally concerned with—racist hate speech, gender hate speech, and begging—have been the subject of legal regulation in one location or another. While each has been the subject of legal intervention, begging and racist hate speech have been subjected to the most serious doctrinal analysis by the courts in recent years. Although the presumption in the United States always is in favor of allowing even offensive speech (*Cohen v. California*, 1971), there are limited exceptions. For example, the Court upholds regulations on speech when the speech is libelous, is part of committing another crime such as conspiracy, or is commercial in nature.

Speech in public spaces enjoys the highest degree of First Amendment protection by the courts (*Hague v. CIO*, 1939). This project emphasizes speech that occurs in public places precisely *because* it is the least likely to be successfully legally regulated. This is a study of a problem that offers no real legal solution. Indeed, the law provides a powerful normative justification, of which many respondents were aware, for allowing speech no matter how offensive.

But what about threatening speech? Even the most committed free speech advocates concede that when speech reaches the level of a threat, it can be legally regulated. And some racist and sexist speech certainly is threatening. How do the courts treat the distinction between "mere offense" and "threat"? And, how can there be such a doctrinal inconsistency?

THE AMBIGUOUS LEGAL STATUS OF BEGGING AND LOITERING

Despite the Supreme Court's ruling that solicitation on behalf of charitable organizations is protected speech for First Amendment purposes (*Village of Schaumburg v. Citizens for Better Environment*, 1980), a number of cities and states have laws on the books that prohibit begging and/ or loitering that have successfully withstood judicial challenge. The ACLU, along with several other legal scholars, argues that begging should be a fully protected form of speech (Hershkoff and Cohen 1991). The Supreme Court has not definitively ruled on the question of begging restrictions, so the constitutional status of legal restrictions remains determined by the jurisdiction in which these regulations are passed.

Federal circuit courts currently are split regarding the extent to which begging is protected speech. Restrictions on begging in "public" places have been upheld in the Second,[2] Seventh,[3] and Eleventh Circuits.[4] In the Sixth Circuit there has been no ruling, but an indication by the court that an ordinance restricting "reckless interference with pedestrian or vehicular traffic" likely would be upheld.[5] Restrictions on begging have been struck down in the Ninth[6] and Second Circuits.[7]

To understand this split requires analysis of the cases in greater depth. In *Perry Education Association v. Perry Local Educators' Association* (1983), the Supreme Court attempted to set out rules about the regulation of speech in public forums. In that case, the court said there are three types of public forums: (1) "quintessentially public forums" (such as streets and parks) that by tradition or government fiat have been sites for communication; (2) "limited purpose" forums (such as university facilities and school board meetings), which are used for expressive activity; and (3) public property that is not by tradition or fiat used for communicative activity. These sites lie on a spectrum with the most stringent speech protection for "quintessentially public forums" and less protection on down the line.

This forum-based approach is not the end of the jurisprudential story, however, as any restriction on speech in public places requires analysis along a three-part test. In a public forum, any restriction on speech must be (1) content-neutral, (2) serve a significant government interest, and (3) leave open adequate alternative channels for communication (*Consolidated Edison v. Public Service Commission*, 1980). Analysis of speech restrictions always begins with the question, "Is the restriction content-based or content-neutral?" Content neutrality requires that the "government regulation of expressive activity is . . . justified without reference to the content of the regulated speech" (*Gresham v. Peterson*, 2000, p. 905) and depends on the government's justification for the restriction (*Ward v. Rock against Racism*, 1989; *Hill v. Colorado*, 2000).

"Content-neutral" restrictions on speech can be upheld if a "substantial" government interest can be shown and the mechanism for achieving that interest that does not burden "substantially more speech than necessary" (*Gresham*, p. 906, citing *Ward*). "Content-based" restrictions require that the government interest be "compelling" and the fit between the restriction and the interest "narrowly tailored." In practice, it is nearly impossible to justify a content-based speech restriction in public places. Thus, the determination of content-neutrality is vitally important to the ultimate outcome in any case.

For example, consider *Young v. New York City Transit Authority* (1990), in which the Second Circuit Court of Appeals upheld a Transit Authority regulation prohibiting begging within the confines of the New York City Transit Authority (including Grand Central Station). In *Young*, the court determined that the Transit Authority's regulation of begging was content-neutral. The *Young* court also said that begging is a source of too little information to merit First Amendment protection because "[i]t seems fair to say that most individuals who beg are not doing so to convey any social or political message" (*Young*, p. 153). Moreover, the court determined the subway to be an "instrumental forum" as opposed to a quintessentially public forum. Despite the Court's determination that begging is not speech that merits the maximum level of protection and it is occurring in a place that does not require maximum First Amendment protection, the court went on to say that, even assuming for the sake of argument that begging merits full First Amendment protection, the Transit Authority's restrictions on it are permissible because the regulations are reasonable "time, place, or manner" restrictions (p. 156).

According to the *Young* court, the compelling state interest for limiting this speech in subways is to protect commuters who must use this space for transportation. Relying on a survey conducted by the Transit Authority, commuters felt annoyed and sometimes threatened by the beggars in "the *very real* context of the New York City subway," in which people with *legitimate* business are intimated, harassed, and threatened (*Young*, p. 159; emphasis added). In a populist appeal, the Court asserted that the subway is the "primary means of transportation for literally millions of people of modest means, including hard-working men and women, students and elderly pensioners" (p. 153). The Court uses this reasoning to justify its classification of the New York City Subway (including Grand Central Station) as an "instrumental space" in which concerns about restrictions on speech are less severe. Moreover, ample alternative channels were left open to beggars in New York City, according to the *Young* Court, because panhandlers could beg in any of the streets and sidewalks of the city.

After the *Young* decision, however, the Second Circuit Court of Appeals overturned a loitering law in New York City which explicitly prohibited "wander[ing] about in a public place for the purpose of begging" (*Loper v. New York City Police Department*, 1993, p. 699). Distinguishing *Young* on the grounds that the statute at issue in *Young* left open ample alternative channels for speech, the *Loper* court struck down the ordinance in that case because it prohibited begging in all public places. Had the statute at issue in *Loper* been upheld, there would have been no legal place to beg in New York City.

Similarly, in the other jurisdictions that have allowed the regulation of begging in public places, appellate courts have relied on the state's interest in "providing a safe, pleasant environment and eliminating nuisance activity on the beach" (*Smith v. City of Ft. Lauderdale*, 1999, p. 956), and "ensuring public safety and order, in promoting the free flow of traffic on public streets and sidewalks" (*Madsen v. Women's Health Cen-*

ter, 1994). More or less restrictive, the ordinances at issue in these cases allowed alternative means of communicating the message of begging.

The split among circuit courts means that the questions of whether or not begging is a form of protected speech for First Amendment purposes is still being actively debated even as restrictions on begging are upheld in many public places. Crucial in this debate is the content-neutrality determination, which, as the next section demonstrates, also is the case with restrictions on racist speech.

UNCONSTITUTIONAL RESTRICTIONS ON SPEECH: RACIST SPEECH

Laws, ordinances, and codes aimed at restricting racist speech have been passed in a variety of settings. Hate speech regulation has been written into city ordinances (see St. Paul, Minn., Legis. Code § 292.02, 1990), workplace environments (Post 1990), as well as both public (*Doe v. University of Michigan*, 1989 or *UMW Post Inc., v. Board of Regents of the University of Wisconsin System*, 1991) and private institutions of higher learning (*Corry v. Stanford University*, 1995). Only restrictions on racist speech in the workplace have been upheld, although not every situation has been legally tested. Restrictions on racist speech in institutions of higher learning and city ordinances have been struck down on the grounds that they are content-based, which the courts treat as a fundamental constitutional flaw.

Racist speech may be the most obvious example of speech that constitutes the "fighting words" that "by their very utterance inflict injury or tend to incite an immediate breach of the peace" (*Chaplinsky v. New Hampshire*, 1942). According to *Chaplinsky*, these utterances could be constitutionally regulated. Yet courts never have applied this doctrine to racist hate speech. In fact, the Court's failure to allow *Chaplinsky* to justify the prosecution of hate speakers has led some commentators to speculate that *Chaplinsky* has been sub rosa overruled, although it has never been formally overturned (Note 1993). Those charged with drafting city ordinances and university hate speech codes have attempted to use the language of *Chaplinsky* in order to satisfy constitutional requirements. Nonetheless, the Supreme Court has determined that using the exact language of *Chaplinsky* is not sufficient to justify speech restrictions at public and private universities.

In perhaps the most famous of opinions on the subject, *R.A.V. v. City of St. Paul*, the Court overturned a St. Paul, Minnesota, ordinance that prohibited "fighting words" that provoked violence "on the basis of race, color, creed, religion, or gender" (1992), including cross burning. The statute was carefully crafted to comply with existing case law by invoking the very standard elaborated by the Court in *Chaplinsky*. The problem, according to the Court, was that the statute specified particular subsets of fighting words and was therefore content-based. The Court reasoned that this made the statute an underbroad, content-based prohibition on some forms of speech, but not all. By adding the language about race, the city had narrowed the scope of "fighting words" on the basis of content, making the statute unconstitutional. The Court makes the same argument in the context of public and private universities (for more on this issue, see Gould 2001).

More recently, the Court ruled that an ordinance prohibiting cross burning was not a violation of the First Amendment if the cross burning was done "with the intent to intimidate" (*Virginia v Black,* 2003). In a relatively unnoticed Supreme Court opinion, *Black,* six justices agreed that the component of intimidation transformed the regular communicative cross burning protected in *R.A.V.* into something that could be legally prohibited. The only disagreement among the six-justice majority was whether or not cross burning could presumptively be said to be threatening. Interestingly, the only African American Supreme Court justice was also the only one who thought that cross burning could be presumed to be threatening. Nonetheless, a statute prohibiting cross burning done with the intent to intimidate is constitutionally valid so long as a judge or jury makes the determination about the intent to intimidate.

The constitutional status of laws restricting racist hate speech is clearer than the constitutional status of laws prohibiting begging. It is definitely *not* permissible to prohibit certain forms of hate speech, though it *may* be permissible to prohibit all forms of hate speech, and it certainly *is* permissible to restrict hate speech when done "with the intent to intimidate."

SEXIST SPEECH

Of the three types of public discourse that make up this project, gender hate speech is the least doctrinally developed. Although verbal harassment on the basis of gender is prohibited by federal antidiscrimination laws in the workplace by Title VII of the Civil Rights Act of 1964, restrictions on sexist hate speech in public have not been passed or challenged at the Supreme Court level. Limitations on speech that harms women concern the workplace, where antidiscrimination law mandates that women should not face unreasonable barriers. Although speech restrictions in the workplace now are widely accepted (but see Volokh 1992), the idea that women should not suffer unreasonable sexual advances by people with power over them was, until very recently, not widely accepted. Sexual harassment in the workplace was a novel legal claim just twenty years ago. But in recent years, prohibitions on sexual harassment in the workplace have become accepted in the law and in society more generally. This concept may readily carry over to academic contexts, where gender hierarchies are pervasive. But sexual harassment in public remains a novel and untested legal issue.

Considering Doctrine

First Amendment doctrine about offensive and harassing speech in public places is ambiguous. The determination about which doctrinal test to apply to any given ordinance or statute will significantly affect the outcome of the proposed regulation, and yet these are not natural distinctions. Begging restrictions (at least sometimes) are upheld (as content-neutral and appropriate time, place, and manner restrictions), but restrictions on racist speech are universally struck down (as content-based and therefore unjustifiable). Why? Why aren't laws prohibiting begging considered content-based?

There are at least three possible explanations for this. First, it may be that the doctrine is sensible and coherent. Or, it may be simply about the perceived social value of the target of the speech. Where the target of offensive speech is a member of a privileged group being targeted because of that privilege, restrictions are upheld. Finally, there is an argument to be made that what underlies these decisions is a recognition of threat, with the courts allowing restrictions on what they see as threatening speech and rejecting restrictions on speech that seems nonthreatening from their perspective. In what follows, I treat each of these hypotheses in turn.

The forum-based approach explained above should mean that restrictions on speech in public places are subject to the same analysis. But, while the courts find that restrictions on racist speech are content-based, many courts find that restrictions on begging are content-neutral. It is difficult to understand how a penal law that provides a "person is guilty of loitering when he . . . loiters, remains or wanders about for the purpose of begging" (*Young,* p. 151) is content-neutral. The law specifically mentions the content of the speech—begging—making it difficult to understand how a court could interpret such a restriction as content-neutral. Other courts agree that singling out begging is a content-based restriction. As the *Gresham* court points out, one could also "solicit passers-by for their signatures, time, labor, or anything else" (*Gresham,* p. 905). Only a determination based on the *content* of the speech allows a determination of whether or not the ordinance has been violated.[8]

In contrast, consider the Supreme Court's finding that the St. Paul ordinance prohibiting cross burning was content-based. That city ordinance prohibited placement of objects, "including, *but not limited to*, a burning cross or Nazi swastika, which one knows or has reasonable grounds to know arouses anger, alarm or resentment in others on the basis of race, color, creed, religion or gender" (*R.A.V.*, p. 380, emphasis mine). The constitutional flaw with this ordinance, according to the Court, was the specification of the content of the speech. Just mentioning that the law was intended to restrict certain content (racist and anti-Semitic speech) made this ordinance content-specific.

The determination of content-specificity is, at best, ambiguous and, at worst, subterfuge. Would the statute at issue in *R.A.V.* have survived constitutional scrutiny if the phrase "on the basis of race, color, creed, religion, or gender" was eliminated from the statutory language? Would the statute then have been considered content-neutral? And, what kind of statute prohibiting begging would be considered content-specific? Why doesn't the mention of begging (as opposed to other speech between strangers in public places that may disrupt the flow of traffic) make a statute content-based? Learned appellate court judges, Supreme Court justices, legal scholars, and commentators cannot seem to agree on what is required for a finding of content-neutrality.

Based on the Supreme Court's rulings regarding hate speech and the increasingly conservative composition of the Supreme Court, it seems unlikely that prohibitions on racist speech will be upheld, although it is easy to imagine an analysis that parallels the begging cases—a restriction on speech designed to threaten or terrorize individuals (content-neutral), justified on the state interest of maintaining order, that prohibits terrorizing speech (according to the reasonable person standard). Such a statute could be considered a reasonable time, place, and manner restriction on racist and sexist speech because it leaves open ample channels for communication such as harassing people in public, crowded places during daylight hours, or burning crosses in the same circumstances. The law proposed here would eliminate the forms of speech that are, as the respondents articulate in the chapters that follow, the most threatening and frightening, such as when they are spoken to in places with no place to escape (like the subway riders in *Young*), or when there is no one else around (presumably to come to the rescue or call authorities if the situation escalates).

Given the doctrinal ambiguity, a legal realist-style analysis of what happens in fact is illuminating. What happens in fact is that speech that targets people of higher social status (begging) is successfully regulated and speech that targets people on the basis of their race or gender is struck down. The perhaps simplistic, but factually accurate, analysis of the current state of the law is that the law protects people from harassment and annoyance when they are of a certain social status.

The law favors the powerful, and courts are hostile to the claims of people of color.

A related explanation for the outcomes in these cases is that courts respond to threats they recognize. Courts seem to be responsive to efforts to restrict speech (1) where there is empirical evidence (as in *Young*) about harm, (2) where they have an intuitive sense that people are being threatened, and (3) when threat is an element of the crime (*Black*). But courts do not seem to believe that there is threat or other harm associated with being the target of offensive public speech regarding race, and they highlight the harms associated with being the target of begging.

Considering racist speech, courts tend to fail to recognize the fundamental attack on a person that words like "nigger" pose. In *UMW*, the appellate court writes that "it is unlikely that all or nearly all demeaning, discriminatory comments, epithets or other expressive behavior which creates an intimidating, hostile, or demeaning environment tends to provoke a violent response" (*UMW*, p. 1173). The court is speculating about the effects of racist comments in order to argue that the regulation is unconstitutional because *Chaplinsky* allows for the prohibition of "fighting words." Underlying the analysis is the idea that a threat might be legally regulated.

Even when the harms associated with offensive speech are taken more seriously, concerns about free speech overwhelm concerns of targets and potential targets of offensive public speech. In striking down campus hate speech codes aimed at preventing a hostile, demeaning, or intimidating learning environment on the basis of race and sex, a U.S. District Court noted that "it is an unfortunate fact of our constitutional system that the ideal of freedom and equality often are in conflict" (*Doe*, p. 853). This is one of the most serious treatments by a court of the harms associated with racist speech. The court recognizes that such speech erodes another constitutional right—the right to equality. But the court rules in favor of "free speech," without a mention of the threat that a target of racist speech may feel.

Consider the different, more serious treatment of the harms that accompany problematic speech by a court that rules in favor of restricting speech. The *Young* court recognized that "begging in the subway often amounts to nothing less than assault, creating in the passengers the apprehension of imminent assault" (p. 157). In the campus hate speech code cases, the facts of the cases often were of graffiti on dorm doors and other situations in which threat seemed less imminent. The speaker was not in the face of the target.

To observe that courts tend to give cursory treatment to some harms or subjective experiences of threat and not others is not necessarily to advocate for the opposite outcome. If the courts gave credence to the power of these remarks in a real way, instead of simply asserting that some words that are *merely* offensive and cannot be proscribed by law, it would not necessarily dictate that the balancing task would come out differently. Rather, I mean to demonstrate the cursory treatment of important yet unexamined empirical questions about what it means to be the target of various forms of offensive public speech.

Legal Scholars on Legal Doctrine

Most legal scholars do not consider the relative positions of power among those involved in speech interactions. The terms of the legal debate about offensive public speech are fairly circumscribed. Traditional First Amendment scholars argue about what constitutes legitimate restrictions upon speech. Historically, a number of formal and informal mechanisms have limited women and minorities' ability to exercise their First Amendment rights in public. The U. S. military employed the threat of prosecution for prostitution to silence women who sought to exercise their right to political speech in the eighteenth century (Ryan 1990). Informal social control through street harassment has worked to exclude women from public space (Bowman 1993). Street harassment is said to be a more insidious problem for women of color (Davis 1994).

Conventional theoretical accounts about how free speech works rarely confront this history. Rather, they hold that when offensive speech occurs, it will be combatted with more speech. By this account, the "truth" will emerge in the debates between people with divergent opinions. The common notion about free speech is the metaphor of the "marketplace of ideas" in which ideas are like products. Good ideas will survive the market and bad (or false) ideas will lose out to truthful ones. Like a good product in a "free" market, the truth will triumph.

Some First Amendment scholars argue that traditional principles should be applied to questions about restricting racist hate speech, gender-based hate speech, and begging, although there is disagreement between those who argue that the First Amendment's purpose is to protect democratic deliberation (Post 1993), and therefore should prohibit almost all restrictions on speech, and those who believe that the purpose of the First Amendment is not to protect all speech, but to foster productive political debate (Meiklejohn 1948). According to the latter view, the First Amendment need not protect speech that undermines productive political debate, meaning that offensive speech may fall into an unprotected category.

In the first model, the First Amendment represents the values of democracy (Post 1993); speech is an end in itself, and it follows that speech should almost never be restricted. Restricting speech is tantamount to restricting the will and autonomy of people. In the context of offensive public speech, proponents of this view would argue that the speech should be protected not just to fulfill speakers' wishes to speak, but also because there are no false ideas. Those who propose to move toward a more racist and sexist society should be allowed to put those ideas on the public agenda. The main benefit, according to democracy theorists, is a more well informed public that will reject the move toward racism and sexism with full knowledge of all the "good" arguments in favor of moving toward racist and sexist society.

A second theory of freedom of speech holds that speech is not itself a goal, but, rather, is a means toward achieving the goal of intelligent self-governance. According to this model, only that speech that is important to the public discussion of self-governance merits the special protection of the First Amendment (Fiss 1986; Meiklejohn 1948). Whether or not begging, racist hate speech, and gender harassment are forms of speech that merit First Amendment protection is a matter of debate within the model. Critical theorists could argue within this model that gender and race hate speech should not merit First Amendment protection, because they actually interfere with public debate by excluding members of certain groups. But critical scholars largely reject this model entirely, leaving only a few traditional scholars to argue this "community based" notion of free speech.

A third camp in the free speech debate represents a more fundamental critique of the boundaries of debates about free speech and emerges from the Critical Legal Studies and Critical Race Theory movements.[9] Critical race theorists argue that free speech, like other areas of substantive law, operates in a seemingly neutral way that serves to reproduce existing social hierarchies. Contesting the idea that more speech can effectively combat offensive speech, critical race scholars point out that the liberal legal conception of free speech presumes equality where none exists. As in most markets, systematic advantage falls to certain members of society, and the ability to speak and the ability to be heard are differentially distributed. Moreover, critical race scholars argue that tolerating hate speech (regardless of the rationale) undermines equality because the act of hate speaking is an injustice that both perpetrates and reinforces inequity. Failure to protect people of color from racist hate speech is thought to violate the Fourteenth Amendment's guarantee of equal protection.

Critical race scholars argue that the liberal legal model effectively excludes the perspectives of some people. Typically, targets of sexist and racist hate speech are precluded from talking about the incident or the nature of the speech. Asking the First Amendment question places some people's story outside the realm of legally relevant stories. As Richard Delgado explains, "[t]hese dialogues-about-dialogue will be heavily weighted in favor of the current regime" (Delgado and Stefanic 1994, p. 857).

Critical race scholars criticize the "more speech" model because the liberal legal conception assumes that all speech is equally harmful or harmless. Catharine MacKinnon suggests that the problem is that "[t]he position of those with less power is equated with the position of those with more power, as if sexual epithets against straight white men were equivalent to sexual epithets against women, as if breaking the window of a Jewish owned business in the world after Kristallnacht were just so much as breaking glass"(MacKinnon 1993, p. 105), as if burning a cross in the yard of an African American family at night were just so much as burning two pieces of wood. The premise is that when equality is perpetuated in the name of some, it is perpetuated in the name of all. This perspective is mandated by the requirement of the First Amendment that regulation of speech be "content-neutral." The difficulty is that this removes speech from its context. But regulation divorced from context may not promote equality; critical race legal scholars argue that it privileges the speech of the dominant majority.

Recognizing that the ideology of the First Amendment is powerful, Charles Lawrence says that "unconscious racism causes us (even those of us who are direct victims of racism) to view the First Amendment as the 'regular amendment'—an amendment that works for all people" (1990, p. 475). The Fourteenth Amendment "is no less a part of the constitution than the First" (Gale 1990, p. 55).

These debates about the value of free speech often center on speech events in the abstract: Can a law prohibit racist graffiti? Can an ordinance meet constitutional standards if it prohibits cross burning on private property? One area of overlap between staunch First Amendment scholars and critical race scholars may be in the arena of face-to-face encounters in public places. If everyone can agree that threats are not protected speech (and they are not), then we have to more closely examine what types of speech are considered threatening by ordinary people.

This reading of First Amendment doctrine about public speech brings to the surface important empirical and theoretical questions about offensive public speech. How often do such interactions occur? Do people think of them as minor inconveniences that are momentarily annoying? Or is offensive public speech viewed as a serious personal and social problem? Are life activities constrained by the fear of being made a target? Are such interactions perceived as threatening? Do targets connect these interactions with broader social systems of race, class, and gender hierarchies?

Socio-legal scholars are interested in a broader set of issues. Do people think the law should intervene in such interactions? Do average citizens balance the costs and benefits of regulation in the same way as First Amendment doctrine that insists that law has no place in such interactions? Alternatively, do they think the law should not intervene but for different reasons? Or do they resist the law's terms of the debate and favor laws that prohibit offensive public speech?

Those are the questions that drove my research. Critical race and feminist scholars assert that there is a price to be paid for free speech, and it is borne by white women and people of color. But what do we really know about what happens in public places?

The Sociology of Public Space

Much of what we know about face-to-face interactions between strangers in public places comes from the work of sociologists. Sociologists who study public interactions typically examine street harassment as a microinteraction, but fail to connect such events to a broader social theory, observing that street harassment is an interaction that violates social norms. Three sociologists stand out in the area of public harassment. Erving Goffman, Carol Brooks Gardner, and Mitchell Duneier document the experience of being on the street. Each makes important contributions to our understanding of interactions between strangers in public, but questions remain.

Classic studies of interactions between strangers in public places are the work of Erving Goffman, who tells us that the normal relationship between strangers on the street is that of "civil inattention" (1963). Civil inattention is the practice employed when strangers pass by one another and politely ignore each other. He also investigates the interaction of men speaking to women with whom they are unacquainted (Goffman 1959, 1963, 1971). Certain male-female interactions such as "requests for the time of day, for a light, for directions, and for coin change" constitute legitimate breaches of civil inattention, "although, given a choice in the matter, the accoster is under obligation to select the individual present whom he is least likely able to exploit" (1963, p. 130). In certain settings, such as bars and cocktail lounges, comments by men directed at women with whom they are unacquainted are legitimate because of a presumption of "openness" of the women there. Heterosexual men may use the contact system in society for the purposes of making romantic contact with a woman, according to Goffman. When homosexual males do the same, however, they are, "abus[ing] the contact system in the society" (p. 130).

Although his account of public behavior is detailed and nuanced, the primary flaw in Goffman's analysis is his failure to link the practice of "breaching civil inattention" with a broad social theory. This may be due, in part, to the era in which Goffman conducted his observations, but the metatheory that underlies Goffman's accounts is not about the exercise of power and domination in public. Instead, he develops a theory about social interaction that seeks to highlight and explain anomalies therein.

More recently, Carol Brooks Gardner and Mitchell Duneier have explored sexually suggestive speech in greater detail (Duneier 1999; Duneier and Molotch 1999; Gabel 1981; Gardner 1980, 1995). Gardner describes and categorizes forms of street harassment based on brief, on-the-spot interviews with over five hundred people. Gardner's work about street harassment stands out because she explores the interaction itself, having women tell her their stories of public harassment. She also treats street harassment as its own problem, connecting the practice of gender public harassment to a theory of gender domination. Although she engages in some analysis about how women think about these interactions, Gardner primarily emphasizes the individual harms of shame, embarrassment, fear, and inconvenience that accompany the remarks. Gardner's impressive work catalogues the ways in which men accomplish street harassment, the ways in which women seek to avoid offensive interaction (by wearing headphones, by avoiding certain areas of town, by wearing sunglasses), and women's responses (or, more accurately, nonresponses) to offensive public remarks.

Gardner's work provides an interesting and thorough account of the type of harassment women encounter in public, but her work is limited in three ways relevant to this project. First, she does not address the relationship between law and offensive gender harassment. She does not probe whether her subjects feel they should be legally protected from such intrusions, much less whether they think such speech should enjoy legal protections under the First Amendment, although some of her subjects mention these issues. Law provides the primary institutional and cultural justification that mandates tolerance for sexist street speech. Thus, while the phenomenon of street harassment connects our work, the theoretical problems that animate our research are different. Her emphasis is the role of street speech in creating and maintaining systems of gender hierarchy. My emphasis is on the relationship of law in the same.

Similarly, Mitchell Duneier's ethnographic study of street vendors in New York accurately captures much of what it is like to be in public, and he documents street harassment with great detail (Duneier 1999; Duneier and Molotch 1999). While his interest is on the street vendors he studies who are perpetrating (fairly mild) street harassment, he does capture some of the range of responses women/targets offer and reports the seeming displeasure of some targets.

Interactionist approaches to offensive public speech are a good starting point for understanding the dynamics of these interactions. However, without a theory that explicitly links legal attitudes to these experiences, observation and interviews do not uncover the complex ways that people view these interactions, the way that the interactions affect their ability to access and utilize public space, or the role of the law in legitimizing the practice.

A Socio-Legal Understanding of Hierarchy, Power, and Privilege in Public

Empirical social science provides a glimpse into what happens in public places. But how, if at all, does this connect to a broader understanding of relationships of power and privilege? Contemporary social theory has begun to address these links. It suggests that phenomenon like street harassment and the hierarchical systems reinforced by it are accepted as "social facts"—real, uncontestable, and inevitable. In this framework, assumptions and ideologies about gender relations, the law, and street harassment become naturalized and taken for granted. Social norms about law, gender, and public interactions work together to create and reinforce these interactions as "normal." Law works with existing systems of hierarchy (based on race or gender) to render these interactions invisible and uncontestable.

Perhaps the most influential statement of this conception is Bourdieu's theory of practice. In this view, individuals interpret the social world in ways that tend to reproduce existing hierarchical social relationships (Bourdieu 1977). Social relations are reproduced rather than contested because norms and customs can be rendered invisible and therefore unquestionable. This field of shared "doxa" consists of unarticulated assumptions that ultimately shape the individual's understanding of the world (p. 168). Just short of doxa is "orthodoxy," in which assumptions are rarely articulated and concepts here are considered self-evident. Bourdieu explains, "[b]ecause the subjective necessity and self-evidence of the commonsense world are validated by the objective consensus on the sense of the world, what is essential *goes without saying because it comes without saying"* (p. 167, emphasis in original). "Dominated classes have an interest in pushing back the doxa and exposing the arbitrariness of the taken for granted; the dominant classes have an interest in defending the integrity of doxa or, short of this, of establishing in its place the necessarily imperfect substitute, orthodoxy" (Bourdieu 1977, p.167).

The "force of law," according to Bourdieu, is facilitated through "miscognition," or "induced misunderstanding . . . by which power relations come to be perceived not for what they objectively are, but in a form which renders them legitimate in the eyes of those subject to the power" (1987, p. 814). Systems of race and gender hierarchy as well as ideas about the freedom of speech have become subject to miscognition. They are part of this body of unarticulated norms, rules, and systems that drive this culture, and they constitute each other in a way that makes street harassment seem at best only vaguely problematic and at worst something that members of dominated classes must tolerate as a price for freedom.

Gender Domination

Dominance theory, as elaborated by Catharine MacKinnon, argues that women are so accustomed to being dominated by men on an individual and institutional level that we fail to fully comprehend the nature of gender hierarchy (1987, 1989). Domination theory contends that women are not simply unequal in society, but that they continue to suffer the domination of men in many ways. Like Bourdieu's concepts of doxa and miscognition, MacKinnon argues that power in gender relations is hidden and therefore uncontestable. Given this theoretical insight, street harassment seems easy to understand. Street harassment becomes one more way that women are sexually objectified; one more way that women's sexuality is constructed; and one more way that men reinforce the idea that "all women live all the time under the shadow of the threat of sexual abuse" (1989, p. 149).

Street harassment certainly is a form of gender domination, but it represents a more complicated process because multiple hierarchies are in play at the same time. All people are situated at the axes of multiple identities (Harris 1990; Spelman 1988) including race, gender, sexual orientation, and socioeconomic status, to name just a few. In other words, an individual may be at once, a woman, African American, heterosexual, and wealthy. Along each of these axes, an individual may be privileged or disadvantaged. Street harassment is complex because it serves to both reinforce and re-create hierarchies along certain axes as well as to upset certain hierarchies.

Invoking race or gender to indicate that the speaker is advantaged along either of these axes is to invoke and reinscribe status inequality. When a white person makes a racist comment to a person of color they invoke a hierarchy to illustrate their privilege. When a man makes a sexually suggestive or threatening comment to a woman, he does so to assert his status, power, and domination over the woman. The woman is reminded of her lower social status as a woman and her physical/sexual vulnerability at once. In this way, street harassment is simple: the person with privilege asserts it over the person that is less privileged.

At the same time that this simple power play is being enacted, other systems of hierarchy may be transcended. Consider the paradigmatic conception of street harassment between a construction worker and a well-dressed professional woman. Despite his (presumably) less privileged social class, he is invoking the identity category in which he is superior to her. This interaction reinforces gender hierarchy and transcends socioeconomic status hierarchy in which people of "lower" social status should demonstrate respect to those more privileged than they. Consider the story of an African American man, well dressed, walking on the street in a rainstorm. As he approaches a particularly pitiful homeless fellow, the African American professor is reminded of his status when the white homeless man looks up from his rain-soaked cardboard shelter and says, "At least I'm no nigger." This interaction transcends socioeconomic status hierarchy through the invocation of race.

There is a way in which these stories (and those in the chapters that follow) are both simple and complex. Invoking race and gender despite the more privileged position of women and people of color along other identity characteristics demonstrates the power that hierarchies of race and gender still embody. Despite all our attempts to be colorblind and to give women equal opportunities, it is still better to be a white male, and as the position of white males in society is challenged, threatened, eroded, street harassment (because it is accomplished anonymously and outside the settings in which women may be making strides, like work and the family) may become more, rather than less, frequent.

The pervasiveness of gender hierarchy also leads women to downplay the harms associated with such interactions. Problems of sexual subordination are not seen as related to street harassment. Women are taught to accept some of the blame for sexist interactions. My skirt was too short, I should not have walked in that neighborhood, and I could have crossed the street. Women internalize gender norms, rendering them seemingly natural.

Sexist Hate Speech?

Although I use the term "sexist hate speech," the phrase "hate speech" typically is used with regard to racist and homophobic speech. Indeed, the use of the term "sexist hate speech" to describe even extremely offensive sexually suggestive speech is met with some resistance because it seems not to contain a message of hate. I contend the opposite; a message that reduces a woman to nothing more than a sexual object available to any man is a message of hate. Dismissed perhaps as "crude" or "inappropriate," apologists for perpetrators argue that at root, the message is one of sex or, even more benignly, of flattery. Such messages can be viewed this way only if the subordination of women is not seen in its entirety.

Women are raped, murdered and beaten by intimates and by strangers *on the basis of their sex* on an appallingly regular basis. Sexual subordination, in its various forms, is accomplished when women are thought of as less than full human beings. Of course, being subjected to an offensive, sexually suggestive comment cannot be equated with being the victim of date rape or domestic violence. But these forms of sexual subordination exist on a spectrum and are related to one another. In the same way that a burning cross and a history of lynching are connected in the minds of those who call such expressive activity "hate speech," I contend that sexual suggestions, threats, and directives are linked to the history of violent sexual subordination of women.

Racism and sexism are not the same phenomena. However, the inability to connect some forms of sexual subordination viewed as relatively benign (like sexist street speech) to broader systems of gender hierarchy is itself sexist. This failure is based on the idea that women somehow are to blame for receiving sexual comments (she wore inappropriate clothing or traveled alone), for being battered by their partners (she knew he was violent and *chose* not to leave him), for being date raped (she shouldn't have led him on), for being stranger raped (she shouldn't have been in that part of town), and even for their own murder (she should have obtained a restraining order, she should have called the police, she shouldn't have been involved with that type of man). Feminism has begun to reverse some of this thinking, revealing the absurdity of blaming the victim for the violent actions of others. With sexually suggestive speech, however, women are supposed to be flattered (someone finds me attractive) and grateful that it was not worse (he didn't rape me) rather than viewing such treatment as symptomatic of the pervasive system of gender hierarchy at work all the time. Sexist speech is just one of the ways that hierarchy is manifested in public places.

Law's Dominance

The problems associated with street harassment may be underestimated not just because of a failure to fully understand gender domination, but also due to the legitimizing effects of law in the form of the First Amendment. Here I do not speak strictly of First Amendment doctrine. Rather, I refer to the cultural tradition or customary rules and assumptions about freedom of speech. These norms may be so ingrained as to be invisible and rarely articulated. Yet they may shape how individuals understand and excuse street harassment, especially gender street harassment.

The liberal legal model, with its veneer of fairness and neutrality, may work against the interests of women in a variety of contexts and is rejected by many feminists as the way to solve gender inequalities. Similarly, traditional First Amendment theory fails to consider what role the law may have in "normalizing" street harassment. The law minimizes the significance of the problem in both legal doctrine and in the legal consciousness of individuals. MacKinnon elegantly illustrates how the First Amendment may appear "neutral" but has a differential impact on women (MacKinnon 1993).

Other studies suggest that the law has the power to constrain (or at least affect) how people view and interpret events in their everyday lives. A number of socio-legal scholars point out that there is a misalignment between the imposition of legal categories and concepts on the lives of white women and people of color (Bumiller 1988; Ewick and Silbey 1992, 1998). As an example, Ewick and Silbey point to the fact that "many black respondents described situations in which they believed they had experienced discrimination. But they expressed reluctance to claim the situation was discriminatory" (1998, p. 237).

As compelling as contemporary theories are about the invisibility of connections between law and hierarchy, they pose methodological challenges for empirical work. Indeed, in part in response to theoretical challenges, socio-legal scholars have begun to examine consciousness about law in a more critical vein.

Conclusion

This review of legal doctrine, sociological studies of street interactions, and contemporary theories of legal domination lay the basis for the empirical analysis that follows. The legal doctrine of offensive public speech is bottomed on a traditional analysis of free speech questions. As such it is heavily weighted against regulation. Yet if one pushes on the doctrinal analysis, it becomes apparent that it fails to address basic empirical questions about the actual costs and harms of offensive public speech. Moreover, because it offers more protection to sexist and racist speech than to begging, a form of speech that more often offends the privileged, it is subject to the accusation of being biased in terms of race, gender, and class. The concept of "threat" that permeates the decisions remains unexamined empirically, with the courts treating some threats as more valid than others.

The lack of systematic empirical analysis of offensive public speech is not limited to the courts, but also characterizes the debate between critical and orthodox legal scholars. Neither camp employs meaningful data on the experiences of the targets of offensive public speech or on the content of what is spoken in these encounters. Sociological studies of public interactions are empirically rich, but fail to link observations about interaction with theories about social hierarchy, including the role that law plays in legitimating such a social practice. Contemporary social theory has drawn a connection between these social practices, theories of consciousness, and institutional forces like the law. Recent efforts by socio-legal scholars that focus on the legal consciousness of individuals have attempted to bring these theoretical insights to bear in empirical work.

With these questions in mind, we turn to an empirical analysis of the experiences and attitudes of ordinary citizens about offensive public speech.

Chapter Three

EXPERIENCING OFFENSIVE PUBLIC SPEECH

THE DETAILED CALCULUS FOR BEING IN PUBLIC

WITH FEW NOTABLE exceptions (Feagin 1991; Gardner 1995; Garnets, Herek, and Levy 1992; Landrine and Klonoff 1996), little empirical evidence exists about experiences with offensive public speech. Although some scholars advocate its legal regulation (Delgado 1993; Delgado and Yun 1995; Lawrence 1990; Matsuda, Lawrence, Delgado, and Crenshaw 1993), it is a social problem that remains largely invisible to members of privileged groups, perhaps because they less often are targets of such speech. Despite this invisibility, being the target of hate speech is a problem that members of traditionally disadvantaged groups share.

In this chapter, I present data about the frequency and nature of offensive street encounters. All of the subjects who participated in the research were asked about their experiences with three forms of offensive public speech I study.[1] The first section of this chapter uses respondents' own words to recount commonly experienced interactions and to provide descriptive statistics about the frequency of these sorts of interactions.[2] In this section, I show that simply being in public is different for people of different races and genders. The second section of this chapter demonstrates the invisibility of the problem of offensive public speech by comparing estimates of frequency by members of target and nontarget groups. Members of groups not targeted by offensive public speech systematically underestimate the frequency with which it occurs. The third and final section of the chapter offers an in-depth study of a particular reaction to offensive public speech—the development of an ongoing calculus regarding one's own safety in public places. When in public, most people report warily paying attention to both their physical surroundings and the people in their personal zone; I refer to this as the "detailed calculus for being in public." Both men and women report that they go through a calculus routinely when they are passing through public places, but these data demonstrate that women's detailed calculus is far more complex, conscious, and articulable than that employed by men.

WHAT HAPPENS IN PUBLIC?

Critical race scholars such as Richard Delgado (1997; Delgado and Yun 1995) and Patricia Williams (1991) argue that racist or at least race-related interactions between strangers in public places occur with some regularity. These comments often occur outside the earshot of all but the intended victim, rendering them invisible to whole groups of people—namely, white people. These claims are not based on systematic empirical research, however, but on the experiences of these authors. Feminists, such as Robin West (1987) and Carol Brooks Gardner (Gardner 1980, 1995), make similar claims about sexually suggestive or sexist speech. Brooks Gardner presents by far the most ambitious attempt to document this phenomenon; she observed and analyzed hundreds of incidents of street harassment (1995). In a study that did not even specifically inquire about racist verbal attacks in public places, Feagin found that nearly half (45%) of randomly-selected, middle-class African American subjects had been the targets of such attacks (1991). Similarly, Landrine and Klonoff found that 50% of African American subjects reported being called a racist name in the previous twelve months (1996). Gardner (1995) describes large numbers of instances of sexist speech, but offers no baseline estimate about its frequency. The difficulty is that she presents no baseline data to help judge the frequency with which various groups experience harassment. Other research shows that the problem of harassing speech is pervasive for gays and lesbians as well (Garnets, Herek, and Levy 1992).

Like these scholars, I found that simply venturing into public places carries with it the risk of being subjected to offensive public speech of one form or another. But how often does it happen? And how often does it go beyond annoying to degrading or even threatening speech?

Begging

As table 3.1 demonstrates, at least in the San Francisco/Bay Area, begging is pervasive. It is not surprising that when asked, all subjects indicated that they had been asked for money while in a public place. Almost half (46%) reported that they are asked for money every day and 82% reported being asked for money every day or often. But what is the nature of these interactions? While a few people recount stories in which begging escalated to name calling or threatening and/or following, most subjects reported that panhandling is benign. The following two accounts provide a good general idea of the spectrum of begging activities. One subject recounted a typical interaction:

TABLE 3.1
Frequency of Respondents' Experiences with Offensive Public Speech
by Race and Gender

	Everyday/Often	Sometimes/Less	Total (N)
Begging			
All	87%	13%	100% (91)
Gender			
Men	82%	18%	100% (33)
Women	90%	10%	100% (58)
Race*			
Whites	93%	7%	100% (44)
People of Color	81%	19%	100% (47)
Sexually Suggestive Speech			
All	45%	55%	100% (83)
Gender***			
Men	14%	86%	100% (29)
Women	61%	39%	100% (54)
Among Women			
White Women	55%	45%	100% (29)
Women of Color	68%	32%	100% (25)
Race-Related Speech			
All	26%	74%	100% (85)
Race***			
Whites	5%	95%	100% (41)
People of Color	46%	54%	100% (44)

Chi-square significance * p ≤ .10, *** p ≤ .01

The last time it happened to me that I could remember was outside of Blockbuster Video, and a man said you know, "Can you spare some change?" and I said, "Yes, on my way out." So I went back out and gave him some change. (29-year-old white woman, lawyer, interview #16)

A more invasive form of panhandling was reported by this subject:

Probably the most recent thing is a window washer at the Emeryville [gas] Station who's pretty aggressive. He'll just come up and start washing your windows without asking and sort of stand around until you give him some change. So in the beginning I felt pretty obligated. It just was sort of almost threatening in a way, but it was also you know, not a big deal because there are people around and he's there all the time. (24-year-old Asian/Polonaise woman, financial auditor, interview #100)

This interaction, reportedly "no big deal," for the target was in answer to the question "Can you think of a time when someone you did not know asked you for money in a way that made you uncomfortable or afraid?" While many respondents could not recall such an encounter, she does. But, this is, by her own account, the most threatened she ever has been made to feel by a panhandler.

Many participants reported knowing, or at least recognizing on sight, the panhandlers with whom they come into frequent contact. Knowing the panhandler provides an added measure of comfort for the target of the interaction. Numerous respondents with routine travel patterns reported something like this:

You know, any city I've ever lived in, where there's a college, it's happened, and the experiences vary a little bit. I mean, when I was in college . . . there was a guy, and there were like two or three regulars around campus, and they always sat in the same place, and they tried to befriend students so they would have a regular supply of money. . . . He was a pretty good-natured guy, and he would talk to you, and you could have a conversation with him. Um, you know, cause he sat on the walkway that everybody walked back and forth on every day. And he got to know people and people got to recognize him and realize he was nonthreatening. (29-year-old white man, student, interview #3)

Frequent contact with a particular panhandler reduces the level of threat because the panhandler becomes a known commodity. Having passed by a particular panhandler many times without incident makes targets more secure in assuming nothing will happen this time.

Nonetheless, begging can be more threatening. The following interactions were frightening for the targets and seem to border on crimes.

He asked me for money, and . . . he was walking toward me and then suddenly asked me for money, and I said, "No, I'm sorry" and kept walking, and he said "Yeah, I'm sure you're really sorry" like yelling after me. . . . He's been a little more aggressive with other people, and, um, like sworn at them before, but he didn't do that to me. (27-year-old white woman, unemployed/homemaker, interview #4)

I was approached by somebody who—the line was "I need some money to get on BART," and I said, "I don't have any change." And the implication, well, I can't remember the exact words, but the implication was

TABLE 3.2
Frequency of Comments about Appearance Directed at Women

	"Polite" Remarks about Appearance	Offensive or Sexually Suggestive Remarks
Every Day	16%	19%
Often	38%	43%
Sometimes	21%	28%
Rarely	20%	11%
Never	4%	0%
Don't Know	2%	0%
N	56	54

"Well, I wasn't looking for change." And I got nervous. And fortunately, there was a lot of people there, but I sort of felt uncomfortable. (52-year-old white man, part-time worker, interview #24)

I think I was on College Avenue, and it was very early in the morning, I was walking to work, and I had to go to—it was probably like 6:30 in the morning, and somebody asked me for money, but it was like not safe, and I just gave him like twenty dollars, and said, "Leave me alone" and kept walking. (45-year-old white woman, school counselor, interview #48)

These stories represent the most threatening accounts of begging reported. While they were reported as frightening, they also were reported as very rare. For the most part, panhandling is common, expected, and typically not very intimidating when it occurs.

Sexist Speech

In addition to begging, women routinely face the added problem of sexually suggestive or explicit speech from strangers in public places. Women overwhelmingly and disproportionately are the targets of this type of speech. Indeed, almost three-quarters (74%) of the men in this study reported hearing polite comments about their appearance "rarely" or "never." Similarly, about two-thirds of men (66%) reported hearing offensive or sexually suggestive comments directed at *other* people (including women) "rarely" or "never."

As table 3.2 demonstrates, women are more likely to report that they hear sexually suggestive comments "every day" or "often" than they are to report hearing polite comments about their appearance. Fully

16% of the female respondents hear polite comments about their appearance "every day." Almost 38% hear these polite comments "often." Only a tiny handful—under 5%—never heard such comments. At the same time, among these respondents, 19% reported that they hear offensive or sexually suggestive remarks from strangers in public places *"every day."* About 43% report hearing these remarks "often," 28% "sometimes," and only 11% report hearing them "rarely." Every woman asked reported hearing sexually suggestive or offensive comments at one time or another.

Notably, women of color report more sexually suggestive or offensive speech from strangers in public places (see table 3.1). Nearly 68% of women of color report that they hear offensive or sexually suggestive remarks from strangers in public places every day or often, as opposed to only about 55% of white women. One of the reasons may be the myth of heightened sexuality about women of color, especially African American women (Albiston and Nielsen 1995; Collins 1990; Davis 1994).

What is the nature of these experiences? Women reported a wide variety of experiences with sexually suggestive speech in public places. At one end of the spectrum are comments that might be classified as polite compliments or relatively harmless pickup lines. Some women are receptive to these sorts of comments and view them as pleasant or flattering, but many women report that any sort of speech from a stranger in a public place, no matter how well intended, is perceived as offensive and/or threatening. At the other end of the spectrum are the more vulgar or offensive sexually suggestive remarks that women endure on a regular basis. Not infrequently, women are the victims of illegal activities. Although some of these incidents fall outside the realm of speech, because they occur in public, in tandem with offensive talk, they are related to offensive public speech.

Starting at the most unsavory end of the spectrum, many women reported actual crimes such as flashing, following, groping, and witnessing masturbation by men they did not know in public places.

I've had gentlemen, well, I wouldn't call them gentlemen, men do um, like sexual, you know, behavior—

Q: Why don't you tell me about that?

A: That's happened to me three times. Once in the AC Transit System [bus] and twice on BART [train], and they will just be sitting there, and sort of trying to get my attention, and then normally, at least because it happened to me at least once before, I sort of just ignore, but I can see out of the corner of my eye that they're doing—something really bizarre. So . . . the first time this ever happened to me—I got up, and the person followed me. So [now] I just sort of sit there and make like I'm not seeing what's going on, and then normally they just continue whatever they're doing. But it's really disgusting. . . .

Q: And you mean that they're exposing themselves?

A: Yeah. And like, one guy had some lotion or something, and it was making this really gross sound—

Q: And you just stay there and pretend not to see?

A: Yeah. Because it happened to me once, I was actually on AC transit, but when it happened that time I got up—I moved from my spot, and the person followed me. So I've always been afraid now to move, because I think they may follow me, so I just sit where I am. (35-year-old African-American woman, manager, interview #80)This story is interesting not just because it has happened to this woman more than once, but also because this respondent has a predetermined response, based on past bad experiences, to stay where she is. For her, the prospect of being witness to a stranger masturbating nearby is less frightening than the threat of having a perpetrator follow her, even in the well-lit and crowded public transportation system.

Another woman told of being followed by a stranger after some "polite" conversation:

I know one time I was coming from the BART and we were conversating on the train, and once it stopped, he kept going—I was like, "Okay, that's the end of the conversation."

Q: You can't follow me home—

A: Right. And I don't want anybody following me to my car.

Q: Right.

A: So he kept on talking, and I was like, "Okay, I'm not going to go to my car, I'm gonna go somewhere else," and then he went on his way— but that's when I kind of felt, you know— (18-year-old African American woman, unemployed, interview #54)

Two women reported seemingly polite interactions with strangers that resulted in more serious stalking. Both ultimately required police intervention.

The first day it happened, I was standing by [my aunt's] door . . . and this really good looking fellow stopped his car and got out of his car and he said, "Well, hi, can I help you?" And I was taking stuff out of my car, and I thought it was one of [my aunt's] neighbors, and he looked vaguely familiar, and he was just really nice and I said, "Oh, no thanks, I don't need any help." I never thought about it. . . . And then as I was going home, I remember I looked in the rearview mirror, and a car was behind me. And for a second it just sort of surprised me, but I never really thought about it. And to make a really long story short, he started following me, and um, this went on for about two weeks. And then I got really scared and I was afraid to tell [my husband] because I thought maybe I'd done something to create this problem.

So I would drive home, and he would be right behind me, and then I would get out of the car with [my son], and we'd walk into the house, and sometimes he would stop the car and watch me walk in the house. And sometimes he would just continue to drive by. So I knew I was being followed, so that's when I told [my husband].

[One time, my husband] followed him in the car, and came back, and called the police. And then the police came out. So by now, it had been going on for over a month, and it was like every day, every day. And sometimes we would find him sitting outside the house, just looking in the house, and I wasn't going anywhere. It was just like he was outside. It was just really scary. And the really unusual thing about it was he never said anything that was menacing. He was just always this—a movie star looking guy—with this beautiful smile, just being nice, but just being there—

Q: Way too much.

A: *Way* too much. And um, and then. Not backing down after [my husband] went after him. He came back the next day. I think he came back two or three times after that before the police finally came out to take a report. . . . And there were several people that felt that there was really something wrong with me for being afraid of this man that was following me. Because they thought, "Oh, that is so cute." You know, it was really insulting. "But oh, he is such a good-looking man, how could you be afraid of him?" (53-year-old white woman, property manager, interview #21)

Finally, this man was arrested and he eventually moved from the area when his family and work associates were told of his activities. The impact of this interaction is significant for this woman. This experience affects her assessment of even seemingly normal interactions. She learned that even "normal" interactions with "normal" people can lead to something more insidious. Even seemingly benign speech can lead to stalking or violence.

Unfortunately, assault also was reported by a number of women. Sexual assaults in public places tended to be in crowded areas so the target was not sure who had actually touched her, or they were done in a location where the perpetrator could get away very quickly, as in this woman's experience:

The one I was thinking of is uh, I was like—where was I? I think I was in high school, either late high school or early college, and it was summertime, and I was walking down the street with a friend of mine and we were both wearing like bathing suits and shorts. . . . Hanging out at the beach—I think we had our beach bags over our shoulders or something like that. We were walking either to or from the beach. And these kids were probably like three years younger than us, rode by on bicycles, and one rode up like really, really close to me, and I wasn't really paying attention, and suddenly, he grabbed my breast. And it was a great shot; he got full hand coverage of my breast, and rode away laughing and yelling something. And I was so pissed because there was absolutely nothing I could do. (27-year-old white woman, student, interview #67)

Even though the above stories do not center on—indeed, some do not even involve speech—these incidents inform women's interpretations of other, seemingly more benign encounters. Women's experiences, either their own or those recounted by friends and relatives, affect how they respond when men speak to them. Such interactions provide the framework through which women interpret other interactions, even "polite" remarks. These sorts of incidents serve as reminders that "polite" remarks from strangers in public places can be followed by less polite and sometimes even criminal behavior.

Women also are subjected to implied sexual threats when they are in public places. While not illegal, these comments nonetheless leave the target unsettled and fearful.

And a man sort of walked—I think I was talking to her about certain issues having to do with my partner, who is a woman, and he sort of like, like as he was walking by me screamed "fucking lesbians" and kept going. Or "fucking dyke" I can't—probably "fucking dyke" I can't remember which one, but after the fact I was . . . afraid because I was like, "Oh my God, there's these people out there who want to beat me up." (29-year-old white woman, lawyer, interview #16)

Even though she claimed not to be afraid of this particular perpetrator, his comments served as an implied threat to her. Whether or not it was the perpetrator's goal, this woman was reminded of her "lower" status as both a woman and as a lesbian. She also was reminded of her heightened vulnerability to random violence.

All of the women in the sample reported comments that center on appearance, dress, physical bodies, and even include sexual propositions. The following interactions are typical of those reported as commonplace for women:

I was walking to BART, and this man sort of slowed down to—so that I could catch up with him, and he says, "Do you want $10?" And at first I didn't really know what he was talking about and then he did it again, and the only reason I could think of why he would say that to me was 'cause he was trying to proposition me. (22-year-old white woman, journalist, interview #13)

I guess just walking down the street—in San Francisco again.

Q: Mm hm. And what did that person say to you?

A: Um. Like "nice ass." (22-year-old Hispanic woman, human re-sources professional, interview #36)

Although the comment may include a compliment or statement of admiration regarding a woman's appearance, the vulgar presentation and use of foul language makes it clear that the perpetrator does not seek to engage his target.

There are men who make comments in a more polite fashion with a similar message—that the target is beautiful or that he has an amorous interest in her:

I was walking to work, or my bus stop a couple of weeks ago, and there was an older Caucasian man, who—he's a homeless man—he came up really close, in fact was right up against my side. And um, he kind of uh, made eye contact. I was startled because I turned around right into his face and he said, "You're a very pretty girl, very pretty girl." (24-year-old Asian/Polonaise woman, financial auditor, interview #100)

Back when I was probably eighteen, and I was working for a savings and loan on Market Street, they were doing construction next door, and all the construction workers were just awful. And it wasn't only me, but at lunch time, when all the women tellers would leave the bank, it was just . . . it got to be that we hated to leave because they would just yell things like, "Hi honey, gonna have lunch with me?" I mean, nothing really degrading, but just enough to make it really uncomfortable to walk out of the bank. I hated it. (53-year-old white woman, property manager, interview #21)

Q: You were getting your BART ticket . . .

A: Yeah. And this man was sitting there on the floor and he told me that I had nice feet. (21-year-old Asian American woman, student, inter-view #17)

Um. I was—in a restaurant with um—someone I was with for a long time, and uh—a stranger came over to me. He was fairly well dressed, with his wife. He was walking out of the restaurant and he came over and in front of my friend said, "You know, you're the most beautiful girl I've ever seen," and left. (49-year-old white woman, business owner, inter-view #49)

Something about my legs. "Nice legs." Real loud. (43-year-old African-American woman, project manager, interview #45)

More polite comments happen everywhere in public, in restaurants, on public transportation, and when women are simply walking on the street. Almost every woman asked reported receiving these sorts of compliments at one time or another. Only two women reported *never* hearing polite remarks about their appearance in public places.

Even those women who could not recall a specific instance of sexual harassment in a public place could recall such events generally.

> I don't have any particular recollection but I am sure that just, I've been very mildly harassed. Just because I'm a woman, you know, comments like "Hey baby" like that, but nothing that would really stand out in my mind. (24-year-old white woman, student, interview #10)

This woman illustrates an important point about women's reaction to these sorts of interactions. She can't recall specific instances of harassment and she characterizes it as "mild." This type of response, which was not uncommon, is explored in more detail in chapter 6.

These accounts reveal what women have known for many years, but about which many men are only vaguely aware: women are subjected to a wide array of invasive public speech. Some appears to be complimentary and nice. Much is vulgar, sexually suggestive, or even involves criminal activity. When women choose to be in public, being the target of such speech, or simply fearing being made the target of such speech, is the price they pay.

Racist Speech

Racist, or race-related, speech is another type of offensive public speech to which people of color are subjected when in public. Although people of all races report hearing racist comments from strangers at times, not surprisingly, people of color report far more instances than do whites. Fewer than 5% of whites report hearing remarks about their race "every day" or "often" whereas almost two-thirds (63%) of African Americans report such experiences (see table 3.1). Not a single African American subject reported that they had "never" heard remarks about their race from strangers in public places.

Respondents describe a wide variety of racial epithets in our interviews, ranging from race-related jokes and quips, to subtle hinting that a person of another race should "go back where they came from," to whispers, shouts, and even physical altercations.Some race-related remarks are quite benign and even are welcomed by the target:

> On account of my race? I know some things have been said to me—well, yeah. I guess uh—I guess somebody like . . . the Muslims. "Hey sister, you wanna buy a paper?" "Sister" meaning black woman. (43-year-old African American woman, project manager, interview #45)

Some comments and interchanges were reported as more strange and annoying than patently offensive. Nonetheless, the comments often were reported to be troubling because of a sense that strangers should not be discussing what is viewed as personal or private:

> Um. There's a repeated pattern that I've already mentioned, related to my third world child. . . . The most common comment that we received when he was a young, young child in arms, was—or when he was a little toddler, was "Who's your mommy?" or "How come you're black and she's white?" . . . And I got it so much, I got pretty used to fielding it from all races. A lot, it came from blacks. And that's the one that was the most common. (51-year-old Hispanic woman, laborer, interview #43)

> I was probably like twelve. Um. At a supermarket shopping center, and some like guys in a truck said like "Oh look—Cheech and Chong" or something like that. I don't know.
>
> Q: Mm hm. And how did you respond to that? At the tender age of twelve?
>
> A: I didn't know who Cheech and Chong were. At first, I thought, "Well, do they think that's my last name or what?" (21-year-old Asian American woman, student, interview #17)

Another category of racist comments does not include racial epithets but is suggestive of a message about race. These suggestions include encouraging a person of another race to "go back where they came from," that people of other races are not human beings, and other, subtle messages of racial inferiority. Consider these examples:

> I was at a gas station where we came to a point where two cars were trying to get into the same pump. We had made a U-turn to get the pump, and he wanted to pull in, [but] my friend pulled in really fast and got it. And the guy jumps out and he's like, "Well that's my pump, and you guys better move." And we're like, "No." And he's like, "You fucking people need to go back where you came from. I'm sick of this, you guys come over here, think you can take everything away from us." . . . He made sure he kept most of the racial, racial slurs to himself [except] when he was away from us. We could still hear them, but he wouldn't say them directly to our face. (29-year-old African American woman, account representative, interview #79)

> Well, it wasn't—it wasn't outright, it was just kind of suggesting, and um, let's see, what was it —oh yeah, it was three friends and I were all walking, and then this guy said "Oh, one more of you and you're a gang." (18-year-old African American man, gas station attendant, interview #31)

The comment "one more of you and you're a gang" clearly is meant to invoke a negative stereotype about young African American men as lawless and dangerous.

> I was at work one time [at a camera store in a largely white neighborhood] . . . there was a guy who came in there, and I guess by that being in a white area, like kind of money and stuff like that—the guy came in there, and he didn't have his I.D. for his check. And I told him I couldn't accept it if he didn't have any I.D. so he got upset and said, "Well, they know me here" and this and that—and something. And then he looked at me and said, "Things sure aren't the way they used to be." And he just looked at me real mean. And I said, "Oh yeah, I know exactly what you're say-ing." And he said, "Do you?" And I said, "Oh, believe me, I know exactly what you saying." And he was like "good" and he walked off. But I know what he was saying—you know. I knew what he was saying. (23-year-old African American man, office manager, interview #37).

> I was in Placerville. And I was at a gas station, and a guy came out, didn't talk to me directly, but I knew he was talking about me. I was seated in the car, and the driver who was beside me was white, and the guy just said, kind of in the air, "I can see the driver's the only human being around here." Implying I was not a human being. (21-year-old Filipino American woman, student, interview #75)

> There was one time, but I don't know if they were directing it at us, but me and my friend at the BART train, and this crazy guy was sitting there, and just kept talking about Asians, just like Asians this or that—and he was talking to himself. But there were other people on the train—other Asians on the train.
> Q: And what was he saying?
> A: Something about going back to your own country. (34-year-old Fili-pino man, technology support services, interview #50)

These suggestions seem somewhat strange; they are not overt threats or even epithets but are clearly intended to insult, harass, and upset the target of the speech. One respondent explicitly said that he has no-ticed a change in recent years from the more blatant racial comments and epithets to these more suggestive comments that the target is sup-posed to understand:

> People used to just call me "nigger" or "boy" or stuff like that, but now people are more afraid of black men. You know, because of the young black kids. You never know what they're gonna do. So now it's more sub-tle. Like one day last week, this white guy sits next to me on BART and just starts humming "Swing Low, Sweet Chariot." It's not obvious, but I

knew what he meant. (32-year-old African American man, business professional, interview #89)

He went on to hypothesize why the racist speech directed at him
has taken a turn to the more subtle variety:

Yeah, and the reason they [meaning explicit epithets such as "nigger"]
don't happen much anymore is because the young black kids are not letting it happen. They don't care. Young black kids just won't let that kind
of shit happen anymore. They're afraid of the black kids. They don't know
what the kid might do to them, so they don't say that stuff anymore. (32-
year-old African American man, business professional, interview #89)

Despite this subject's theory about racist harassment being subtler
nowadays, several people reported overtly racist comments directed
at them from strangers in public places.

I think this was actually my first racial slur. I was going through one of the
buildings that connects outside [at San Francisco State University]. And
there were these guys—I think it was a white fraternity—and they were
selling muffins. And one guy had—I think he said, he was saying, "M*uffins*
for a dollar." And once I passed, I thought he said, "M*onkey* for a dollar."
(18-year-old African American woman, unemployed, interview #54)

At the most serious end of the spectrum, there are physical altercations:

Actually one time when I was very young. I was, I would say, like four-
teen or fifteen, and I was actually at the Laundromat washing some
clothes for my family, and there was an older Caucasian, homeless
guy . . .
    Q: And what did he say?
    A: Actually, I was actually trying to get into the Laundromat with my
clothes, and he actually blocked the door. . . . I asked him to get out of the
way, and he said no. And there was actually people around, and um, he
actually pushed me. And um, actually I had to push him out of the way,
and actually it was a little struggle that we had, and actually, luckily, there
was like some older adults there at the time that actually kind of shooed
him away. And actually, while I was in the Laundromat the entire time,
he was pretty much talking a lot of derogatory remarks toward me and
my race. That was probably—probably one of the worst interactions I ever
had with someone.

    . . . I can't remember actually what he was saying, um. It was so long ago,
I just remember, *what really stands out in my mind is that he actually pushed
me, put his hands on me.* (22-year-old multiracial man, business owner, interview #52)

Although people of color reported comments about race and racial slurs on a far more regular basis, a number of white subjects reported being targets of race-related comments by strangers in public places:

I think the only personal, or sort of personal, comments that I've gotten are about my race from an African American.
    Q: Like what?
    A: Well, it's forms of address, sort of like, "Hey whitey" or something like that to get my attention, but address me in terms of my race. Instead of like, "Hey buddy," it's like, "Hey whitey." Something like that. (29-year-old white man, student, interview #3)

[T]here was an elderly black lady dressed in a bright yellow pantsuit of some vintage and she was walking across the—approached you know, the driveway, effectively, so I stopped [the car] and um—waited for her, and she turned around without stopping, and just ranting—calling us all kinds of—I think something about Jews or Jew lovers. . . . And this was an '87 Honda, this was nothing fancy—it was just out of the blue. (45 year-old white man, project manager/construction, interview #33)

I had an experience of walking down the street on my way to work one morning, it was fairly early, and I didn't hear what the person said, but there was a very tall black man, sort of talking to himself, and he came over to me and said something about being a "white bitch" or something and he spit in my face. (49-year-old white woman, business owner, interview #49)

Occasionally, the creative street harasser combines racist and sexist comments.

And sometimes if you get—if you get sexual harassment that's cross-racial, then it will be mixed with some kind of you know, like "white bitch" kind of stuff. Um. Other than that I can't think of any. (29-year-old white woman, lawyer, interview #16)

We were on a walk, and we were coming home on a bus, and it wasn't a black man, it was a bunch of black kids that were on the bus, and . . . this guy said to [my husband], or to his friends, "Oh, look at the way he shelters her, it's like she's his pet, it's just sick." And he said to me, "You're nothing but a flat assed white bitch." And that scared me. Because I mean he wasn't funny, you know. (53-year-old white woman, property manager, interview #21)

They say stuff like "What are you looking at, white bitch?" (35-year-old white woman, unemployed/homemaker, interview #34)

As is evident both by the stories recounted by subjects and the rates that subjects report, street harassment is common and perhaps more severe than many people think. Although begging is reported as the most common form of speech, sexually suggestive and racist speech are experienced almost as frequently by women and people of color as begging is experienced by the general population. Thus, less-advantaged groups face a strikingly different reality on the street than do members of privileged groups. White women and people of color consistently experience offensive public speech as they conduct their day-to-day activities.

WHO KNOWS WHAT HAPPENS IN PUBLIC?
ESTIMATES AND REPORTS OF FREQUENCY OF HATE SPEECH

These quantitative results and qualitative accounts document a range of encounters with public speech and the depth of feelings it generates in targets. As the accounts reveal, racist and sexist assaults often are designed to be out of earshot of others, leaving those who are not the intended targets unaware that these interactions even occur. One woman explicitly spoke of this. Without realizing how late it was, she entered a deserted BART station at 10 o'clock at night.

> [A]s I came down the escalator, and the platform came into view, I realized, "This was a mistake." But you don't turn around on an escalator. . . . [T]here was one man and . . . he wasn't dressed for business, except for what I thought was his business, which I thought was to be a thief. . . . And he started walking toward me, very deliberately, looking at me, and it scared me. And I ran around the corner and found some other people. And I didn't know them at all but I went up to them and said, "Can I stand with you? That man frightens me." It was a man and a woman. *The man seemed surprised, but the woman seemed completely understanding of my situation.* . . . "You stand here with us," that sort of thing. (54-year-old white woman, interview #05, emphasis mine)

This woman alludes to what these data demonstrate systematically. Men are somewhat less aware of the extent to which women are the targets of offensive or sexually suggestive remarks than actually is the case (see table 3.3). About 19% of women reported that they hear these sorts of comments "every day." But when asked to estimate, only 13% of men thought that women hear these comments "every day." At the other end of the spectrum, almost 20% of men think that women receive these comments "rarely," compared to only 11% of women report hearing them rarely Although men are closer to women in the "some-

TABLE 3.3
Offensive or Sexually Suggestive Comments to Women:
Men's Estimates and Women's Reports

	Every Day	Often	Sometimes	Rarely	Never	Total
Men						
Percentage	13%	42%	26%	19%	0%	100%
Estimated Frequency	4	13	8	6	0	31
Women						
Percentage	19%	43%	28%	11%	0%	100%
Reported Frequency	10	23	15	6	0	54

times" and "often" categories, it is interesting that there is more disparity at the extremes.

Similarly, as table 3.4 shows, white people underestimate the frequency with which African Americans are the targets of racist hate
speech in public. Only 8% of whites think that African Americans hear
comments about their race "every day," whereas 38% of African Americans report that they hear these comments "every day." The estimates
by the nontarget groups are farthest off at the extremes. A majority of
whites (53%) think that people of color hear racist comments "often."

Differences in reactions to different types of offensive speech are theoretically interesting. Although racist and sexist hate speech are both
threatening and offensive to the targets in some respects, sexist speech
presents a different sort of problem in that targets of sexist speech often
internalize the blame for such comments. This results in the probably
erroneous belief that by conducting a thorough detailed calculus for
being in public, she can avoid such speech altogether. The target of racist
hate speech is less likely to internalize the blame for such an interaction.
In these communities, in this age, racist comments are broadly thought
of as deviant (albeit common) behavior that can never be justified. Still,
stories of people of color reveal how they find racist comments pro-
foundly disturbing. Interestingly, begging, the one form of speech that
courts occasionally allow to be regulated, appears to be the least trau-
matic and most widely shared experience by all members of society.

THE DETAILED CALCULUS FOR BEING IN PUBLIC

Everyone knows what it is like to be "on guard" in a public place.
Some people may always feel on guard, while others may feel this way

TABLE 3.4
Respondents' Categorization of Offensive Speech by Race and Gender

	Every Day	Often	Sometimes	Rarely	Never	Total
Whites						
Percentage	8%	53%	28%	10%	3%	100%
Estimated Frequency	3	21	11	4	1	40
African Americans						
Percentage	38%	25%	21%	17%	0%	100%
Reported Frequency	9	6	5	4	0	24

only when entering an unfamiliar scene, when it is late at night, or when there are seemingly dangerous strangers around. Being on guard means being aware of one's surroundings and not taking safety for granted. It is this insecurity that leads potential targets of offensive public speech to develop a detailed calculus for being in public.

The detailed calculus for being in public may be the most significant consequence of offensive public speech, because it represents the way that offensive public speech translates into real-life limitations for its targets. As the previous two sections of this chapter showed, and the next chapter confirms, the risk of verbal abuse in public is a burden disproportionately borne by white women and people of color. People of color report almost unanimously that there is little one can do to avoid hearing racist comments in public places.

The Detailed Calculus for Avoiding Begging

Although some people find begging somewhat annoying and offensive at times, very few people report altering their behavior to avoid places where begging is prevalent. This is probably due to the fact that very few people find begging truly threatening. Those who do report altering their behavior say they do so only in the most minor ways:

> Yeah. There's like this particular block where lots of homeless people hang out, and they seem like not just homeless people but also—like, you know—teenagers who—who want to rebel, and um. I often will walk on the other side of the street. Because they don't just ask for money—but they'll like say things or whatever. And I just don't want to deal with it sometimes. If I'm alone—I'll often walk on the other side of the street. But if I'm with someone else, especially my husband, then I don't alter my route. (26-year-old white woman, unemployed, interview #30)

The people likely to make changes in their behavior to avoid begging are the same ones likely to change their behavior to avoid sexually suggestive speech—women. Women are far more likely than men to report that they change their behavior to avoid panhandling. Part of this may be due to the fact that some panhandlers incorporate sexist hate speech into the interaction after a woman has refused or ignored a panhandler. The finding that few people take care to avoid panhandling is particularly striking given the number of panhandlers in the San Francisco/Bay Area.

The Detailed Calculus for Avoiding Sexually Suggestive Speech

Considering one's safety simply is prudent. To bring out the factors that are involved in women's detailed calculus is not to critique women for having one. Rather, analysis of all the factors that go into the detailed calculus and an examination of how women's differs from men's illustrates one of the many ways that everyday hierarchies of gender affect seemingly innocuous aspects of daily life. Gender theorists interrogate sexism in the workplace in the forms of sexual harassment and earnings differentials. There also is a rich feminist literature on sexism in the (heterosexual) home, in the forms of disparity in caring work, housework, and domestic violence. Scholars also examine how sexism plays out in stranger relationships that can lead to violence, such as rape and domestic violence. But little attention has been paid to how simply being in public is gendered. Being in public is gendered in that women are effectively excluded from certain locations, but it also is gendered in that women experience being in public qualitatively differently than do men.

Women report being on guard significantly more often than do men. Moreover, women report a far more complex and nuanced detailed calculus for being in public than do men. This may be due to women's greater vulnerability to physical attack or the risk of sexual assault that women must consider. Whatever the reason, women's detailed calculus involves assessing myriad factors. The elements of women's detailed calculus are so numerous that it is almost impossible to list them all. Consider this woman's detailed calculus for being in public:

> When I'm alone and walking around in a public place, I'm very—standoffish, I think. I'm very closed in my body language, and I walk very fast and I look like I have a purpose and I need to get somewhere, and I don't catch eyes with people. I don't give them indications that I want to chat, and uh . . . I would be approached much more often than I am if I didn't have that. I feel like it protects me.

Q: Mm hm. Do you ever do things like change the route you take or plan a different time of day to go to a particular place?

A: Oh, all the time if I'm in a city. If I'm in [the small town where I live], then no, not ever. But like, when I was just traveling alone . . . I didn't do things I would have [done] if I had a companion, whether it was a woman or a man.

Q: Hm. Like what?

A: Like go to dinner at a couple of different places that were farther away from my hotel where I had to walk through neighborhoods that weren't super well traveled at night. And at dusk, I walked to the restaurant that I wanted to go to for dinner, actually, it was dark, it was the time that I wanted to go to dinner, and I walked to the restaurant. And I felt pretty safe walking there, but I figured that I wouldn't feel safe in a couple hours walking back, and so I didn't go there, I just kept going and went somewhere else. I made a circular route and went back toward the hotel and found another place to eat. (27-year-old white woman, student, interview #67)

In a few moments conversation, she mentions consideration of her location, time of day, appearance, companion (or lack of companion), body language, the distance she must travel, her familiarity with the neighborhoods, and what time she will return. And those are just those factors she mentions with reference to this particular incident. This woman is not alone. Her remarks are particularly striking because they show how integrated the detailed calculus is into her everyday life. In the analysis that follows, the elements of the detailed calculus are presented as separate and distinct, but in its everyday operation, the elements are interrelated. More simply put, a woman is safer in a risky outfit when she is traveling with friends by car and will be dropped off at the door than if she is commuting through an unknown part of town alone.

In addition to these factors, some women also analyze their ability to "escape," should a bad situation arise. The plan for escape is based on an analysis of both the physical space surrounding them and their own attire (i.e., cannot run fast in this skirt and these shoes) as well as characteristics about the (potential) perpetrator (his distance from her, attire, demeanor, etc.). In what follows, I use respondents' own words to describe women's four primary behaviors designed both to avoid offensive sexually suggestive speech and other undesirable interactions with strangers in public places. These behaviors include: (1) being attentive to body language; (2) altering physical appearance; (3) altering route; and (4) assessing the interaction and the perpetrator.

BODY LANGUAGE

Sociologists long have understood that people carefully monitor their body language when in public places (Goffman 1963). Consistent with this, these women respondents report being aware of their body language and the image it projects when they are in public places. Women consider the amount of eye contact they give strangers, the speed at which they walk, and try to do things like "appear confident." When asked what, if anything, they do to avoid unpleasant sexually suggestive speech from strangers in public places, many women said they avoid making eye contact with strangers, occasionally using props to aid in that endeavor.

> I suspect I avoid eye contact. (40-year-old white woman, interview #12)

> I guess just trying to avoid eye contact. But with sunglasses on, they can't look into your eyes anyway. (26-year-old white woman, unemployed, interview #30)

Women speak in very concrete terms about avoiding eye contact. But, it is not simply avoiding eye contact; this part of the detailed calculus for being in public is related to looking "in control." Consider these women's comments:

> I used to, when I initially started riding the BART I used to be very afraid of, you know, people approaching me? So I guess I would look afraid, so now I try to look in control. You know? (19-year-old East Indian woman, unemployed, interview #71)

> I think I totally would want to avoid talking to anyone, and I would just walk around with my head down ... But if I do feel scared, and that's only like if it's at night or there's no one around, no one else around except for me and whoever, then um, I want him, usually it's a guy—to feel like that I'm confident. You know, because if you're looking down on the floor, then I think, um, they can feel your fear—so I always make it a point to feel—or to appear confident. So no one will attack me or whatever. (21-year-old Asian American woman, student, interview #17)

She believes that proper body language reduces the likelihood that a stranger in a public place will assault her, carefully noting that feeling confident and appearing confident are not necessarily related. Women do not go through the detailed calculus just because they would rather not hear some offensive words; they go through the detailed calculus because of a realistic fear, based on prior experiences, that interactions with men they do not know might lead to violence. Body language is the first signal to the potential speaker that she cannot be bothered with him and that he better not bother her.

Women change their appearance in any number of ways, from deciding what they should or should not wear, to how they style their hair, to whether or not they use makeup. Some women cover their "questionable" outfits with more clothes:

> Well, sometimes maybe I'll wear a jacket over my—whatever I'm wearing.
>   Q: Like if you're wearing a dress or whatever?
>   A: Mm hm. Like I'll wear a jacket over it if it has short sleeves or—you know, and I'm kind of self-conscious about myself sometimes. (34-year-old African American woman, unemployed, interview #77)

Other women change the type of clothing they wear altogether:

> Uh. I would say that I am somewhat sensitive—somewhat self-aware in terms of how I'm dressed, um, and how I appear to, my physical appearance. And I would say that like, I have a tendency, if I'm gonna be at a place that is sort of more, that could be less accepting of sexual orientation stuff, I probably, like, look more straight. Make an effort to look more straight.
>   Q: Mm hm. How do you make an effort to look more straight?
>   A: [laugh] Um. You know—wear makeup. Wear like tight fitting clothes instead of loose fitting clothes, you know. (29-year-old white woman, lawyer, interview #16)
>   Q: Mm hm. Do you ever avoid certain places or attempt to change your appearance to avoid them?
>   A: Um, yeah. Wow. Good question. Yeah, when I first started my job, actually, I wore a lot of skirt suits, and now, I wear pants. So that helps a lot. (23-year-old white woman, marketing manager, interview #59)

> I think I'm conscious of how I dress, I won't wear like a plunging neckline . . . I'm not overly modest, but I also—I think I'm conscious to not wear very sexually suggestive type of clothes. (28-year-old white woman, lawyer, interview #98)

In the minds of many women subjects, appearance and comments were directly correlated.

> I also learned there to present myself in ways that—that um—what's the word? Tended to decrease the numbers of those comments.
>   Q: In what ways would you—
>   A: Actually, I would sometimes avoid construction workers. . . . I don't think I ever had that much of a persistent problem with it just because of

where I've worked and stuff. Um. And I've always tended to dress fairly modestly. There was very few times in my life have I ever consistently dressed in like short skirts or tight clothing. So I think that minimized it too. (54-year-old white woman, project manager/brokerage firm, interview #32)

These women believe that changing their appearance will make it less likely that they will receive such comments. As a corollary, women who would rather not be bothered with sexually suggestive speech but fail to adequately alter their appearance sometimes are blamed for making themselves a target. Women who dress that way are thought to "get what they deserve."

I'm proactive. That's how I handled it. It's a hell of a lot better than walking around clutching your two hundred dollars cash in your purse, wearing pearls and high heels. I mean, *that's the first mistake, never wear high heels or a dress. . . . That's a mistake.* Because you're just spotted for a victim, and if anybody is into physical violence, they'll pick the weak person to pick on. They won't pick somebody that's strong. Plus, I've got this bad ass old man. (51-year-old Hispanic woman, laborer, interview #43, emphasis mine)

A few women recognize that appearance has little to do with whether or not one is harassed. They think that being made a target has more to do with the harasser than with the appearance of his potential targets.

You know, I probably do play down my appearance, because of the area I live in . . . I probably do play down. I 'm not that concerned with what I wear. I don't really try to put on any extra makeup or anything like that because—*yeah, I guess I do try to avoid it. That doesn't really stop them, though. They don't really care*—I don't know, I don't think they really care— (52-year-old African American woman, business professional, interview #90, emphasis mine)

Despite her belief that it would not influence the harasser very much, if at all, this woman still reports altering her appearance in response to this potential threat.

ALTERING ROUTES

Women also change their route or avoid certain locations altogether to avoid being made the target of offensive sexually suggestive speech. Altering one's route can include anything from moving a few steps out of the way to more dramatic alterations. This woman is willing to move a few steps:

I try to keep my distance from people.

Q: You mean your physical space distance?

A: Right, right.

Q: And how do you do that?

A: Um. If I anticipate an interaction like that, I'll try to sort of, um, *I'll try to avoid it by walking a few steps away* from them, or um, you know, if usually some guy looks like he wants to talk to me, I'll try to avoid it, or, you know, use my body language to say that I don't want to deal with him. (22-year-old white woman, journalist, interview #13, emphasis mine)

Depending on the incident and the man involved, other women report more dramatic alterations to their route:

He just said the vilest things, and not necessarily, he's not even a really big guy, so I didn't think he was going to like take me down, but just— and it was in daylight, but it just makes you worry that some night you'll be walking along and he'll come up and target you for some reason.

Q: Mm hm. Do you do anything in your everyday life to avoid these sorts of interactions?

A: Sure. If I see that guy, I always go away. *Sometimes I'll take a different bus route or something, for a little while.* (18-year-old white woman, student, interview #82, emphasis mine)

Sometimes the threat of sexually harassing speech makes women decide not to go to particular places. A few days after a man harassed and followed her, the woman whose quotation appears below encountered him in one of her favorite restaurants.

Yeah, I might try to get up and run to the bathroom real fast—duck down in my seat, or something of that nature. Something so that he doesn't see me period, rather than creating a scene. When I was younger, I would create a scene. Since I've got older, I've tried to just avoid the situation by removing myself from the equation altogether.

Q: Did you stop going to that restaurant?

A: Oh, definitely—that's a really good restaurant, and he [made me stop going there]. (29-year-old African American woman, account representative, interview #79)

After being approached by a man who said, "I hate women, they're all sluts," one woman said:

I just thought—I mean it was . . . disturbing, and I was afraid of the person. You know, if he was going to be violent toward me. [And I thought] I just should probably avoid BART stations late at night from that point on. (24-year-old white woman, student, interview #10)

This woman has no car, so avoiding BART effectively means that she is unable to go out late at night. Other women spoke of avoiding bars and even entire areas of town altogether to avoid such harassment:

> I think just the way I dress, and I don't go out to bars, that kind of thing. I've kind of changed my behavior in that way. I don't need to surround myself with people like that. (23-year-old white woman, marketing manager, interview #59)

> I try and avoid that part of town. Um. I know I don't like to go out at night, um, dressed in such a way that would invite comments like that. . . . Other than that, I can't really think of anything. (24-year-old white woman, student, interview #10)

This young woman student reveals how embedded the detailed calculus really is. She discusses two significant changes in her behavior but at the same time, she is fairly dismissive of the questions. She presented changing what she wears and where she is willing to go as fairly minor inconveniences.

Although the woman quoted in what follows does not report changing her mode of transportation, she takes it into account when making her calculus about being in public:

> And it depends on my transportation. If I'm going to drive and park, then I know I'm fine door to door, but if I'm going to have to take BART or walk a long distance because of parking, then I'm really—I'm concerned about that. (23-year-old white woman, marketing manager, interview #59)

It may not seem as though changing appearance or taking common-sense measures to avoid having strangers address one in a public place amount to much of a burden, but the above examples of women altering travel patterns to avoid such behavior reveals the significant effect that sexist harassment and the concomitant fear of assault have on the everyday lives of women.

ASSESSING THE INTERACTION

Women's detailed calculus for being in public also includes assessing the speaker or the potential speaker.

> Usually there's something about either the way the person's dressed, and the type of things they say. Sometimes it's just the way they look at you, the way they make eye contact. (31-year-old white woman, student, interview #74)

> If they're younger, then I am not afraid because . . . they are out to . . . impress their friends, so they don't have any intention of acting on it. If

they are on foot, I am less threatened, if they're in a car, I'm a hell of a lot more threatened. . . . And also if it is in my immediate neighborhood [I am more threatened] because I feel it is a possibility that they'll find out where I live. Or know where I live. (29-year-old white woman, lawyer, interview #16)

As is evident from this woman's comments, considering the interaction is quite complex. She must take into account the target's body language, her location in relation to the target, his mode of transportation, and his age. The person with whom the subject is traveling also makes a difference:

If I'm alone—I'll often walk on the other side of the street. But if I'm with someone else, especially my husband, then I don't alter my route. (26-year-old white woman, unemployed, interview #30)

The behavior of the harasser also seems important. In addition to the concrete things women report noticing about the speaker, they also are willing to try to make a judgment about more intangible qualities of the interaction. These things that might make an interaction more frightening are difficult even for these women to articulate, but they go into the calculation.

Q: And what would make it more threatening, or scary?
A: Persistence on the whistler's part, or saying as you walked by, like a construction crew or something, they'd say "Hey baby" or things like that. That made me feel more uncomfortable, if you will. (51-year-old white woman, unemployed, interview #26)

Although many women spontaneously mention the race of the speaker, none explicitly claimed to be more or less afraid based on the race of the harasser. Nonetheless, a certain degree of racism surely is inherent in such interactions.

Clearly, the detailed calculus for being in public is complex, but how much mental energy does this detailed calculation really consume? Frequent victims of offensive sexually suggestive speech in public places report that the detailed calculus represents a serious endeavor.

Q: So would you consider the sexually suggestive comments from strangers to be a problem for you?
A: *A huge extreme, big, daily problem* . . . It touches me every day. I have to think about it every day. It changes the way I behave when I'm in a group as well as when I'm alone, but especially when I'm alone. And um, it makes me—it makes me—*it takes away time and energy from productive things that I could be doing.* (27-year-old white woman, student, interview #67, emphasis mine)

Um. I mean, *I think about them every weekend when I'm getting ready to go out. It affects the way I dress, it affects where I want to go.* Um. Yeah. I think about it on Friday night when I'm getting dressed, I think about I'm going out with my girlfriends, where we're going to go, who we're going to see there, what the outcome could be . . . (23-year-old white woman, marketing manager, interview #59, emphasis mine)

How early are women taught that they must make this kind of calculation or risk being a victim? One woman told of learning this lesson as a young child:

When I was really—pretty young—maybe around 10 or 11. I grew up in Oakland—I used to take the bus to school. I would say at about 10 or 11, some friends and I decided—we already had this idea—I remember this one friend said, "Never, never look people in the eye." . . . I mean later on I thought—that's really kind of sad that we got this message by the time. . . . You know, it just makes you more wary than some other people. I can remember my friend saying that. "Don't look at people in the eye" and you know, "Don't look at anybody." And I thought it is so sad that people feel that way. (35-year-old white woman, unemployed/homemaker, interview #34)

Women's detailed calculus for being in public is complex. All the factors mentioned must be considered, and much of that consideration is occurring in a moment of fear—or at least "heightened alert" for the target of such interactions. Offensive and sexually suggestive public speech and the fear it engenders in its targets have a significant effect in the day-to-day lives of average women.

THE DETAILED CALCULUS FOR AVOIDING RACIST SPEECH

Unlike sexually suggestive speech which women (perhaps mistakenly) believe they can do things to avoid, people of color almost unanimously reported that there is little, if anything, targets can do to avoid racist speech from strangers in public places. The prevalence of the practice makes avoiding racist speech nearly impossible.

Q: Is there anything that you do in your everyday life to avoid these sorts of interactions?
A: Um, actually no, because I don't know—What could you do, really? (25-year-old Chinese American man, service worker, interview #28)

The only thing the target can do is respond in such a way as to not escalate the situation:

I can move away from the comments, or I can adjust to it. You know, I don't decide—tend to get into fighting, I don't raise my voice at people. You know, you call me a black bastard, I'm going to say, "Thank you very much," and I'm gonna keep on moving if I can. I'm just going to keep moving. (44-year-old African American man, stockbroker, interview #29)

When the perpetrator was a homeless man who tended to sit in the same place by the target's place of work, one subject reported not wanting to change his route although the interaction was predictably racist and offensive.

Actually, like when I would see him, there were times when I was like, "Oh, here he is." I would think in my mind, "Oh, I should go walk across the street?" But in a way it's like—I don't want things like that to prevent me from going forward—I don't want to play chicken. So at first I was like, "Let's walk away, let's go somewhere else." [But later] I would just go forward. (26-year-old Asian American man, customer service, interview #84)

When a certain degree of familiarity is established, this man becomes confident that these sorts of interactions will not lead to violence, but many targets of offensive, racist speech fear it will. The detailed calculus for avoiding racist speech is complex, and it is difficult to disentangle two separate but important factors that affect day-to-day movements. Targets of racist speech may attempt to avoid it because it may lead to violence; others seek to avoid it because it is offensive. Until these interactions have occurred, it is impossible to know if one is going to be assaulted or "only" offended. It is therefore difficult to know how much of the detailed calculus is to avoid offensive speech and how much of the detailed calculus is to avoid assault.

CONCLUSION

These quantitative results and qualitative accounts document the extent of encounters with offensive public speech, the depth of feelings it generates in targets, and the lengths to which people are willing to go to avoid such harassment. The data reveal that white women and people of color disproportionately suffer these problems. Because racist and sexist assaults are designed to be out of earshot of others, those who are not the intended targets are often unaware that these interactions even occur. While sometimes these insults and epithets are shouted loudly, they are typically one-on-one interactions in which one person is victimized, leaving members of nontarget groups ignorant about such interactions.

Critical race theorists and critical feminist scholars are correct; the depth of the harm is severe and the frequency of the harm is great. Additionally, the phenomenon plays into existing hierarchies of race and gender. But how do these experiences translate into views on legal remediation? Courts typically do not allow for legal regulation, but what do ordinary citizens think about legal intervention? This is the fundamental question in the chapter that follows.

Chapter Four

OFFENSIVE PUBLIC SPEECH AS A PERSONAL PROBLEM, SOCIAL PROBLEM, AND SUBJECT FOR LEGAL INTERVENTION

IN CHAPTER 3, I demonstrated that sexually suggestive public speech is a frequent problem for women in society, which deeply affects how and when they move in public. Similarly, people of color often are the target of race-related offensive public speech which requires them to steel themselves for unpredictable but troubling encounters. I also found some evidence that men and whites do not well understand the frequency and gravity of the harms that sexist and racist speech impose on target groups. Yet to what extent do groups—frequent and infrequent targets—regard offensive speech as a personal and social problem? And, are members of target groups more likely than others to favor legal intervention to curb such speech? In this chapter I examine the links between people's experiences with offensive public speech, whether they consider it a personal or social problem, and whether they believe it should be restricted by law or by some other mechanism.

The results are surprising. Many people consider offensive public speech to be a serious personal and social problem. Those who are more frequently the targets of begging and racist public speech and those who perceive these forms of speech as personal and social problems are more likely to favor their legal regulation. With sexist speech, however, this pattern is *reversed*. Individuals who say that sexually suggestive speech is a serious personal and social problem are slightly *less* likely to favor legal regulation than those who do not. And overall, regardless of their experience and attitudes, most respondents do not think law should intervene. Chapter 5 goes on to explain these findings by analyzing the discourses informants invoke in talking about the relationship between offensive public speech and the law.

This chapter begins by describing the answers of respondents to questions about whether the three types of speech are personal or social problems or both. I then consider five possibilities about attitudes toward restrictions on different kinds of offensive public speech. As elaborated in appendix A, my strategy of inquiry was to remain silent about law until late in the interview. I constructed the interviews to insure that law was mentioned only near the end, so respondents could introduce the subject of legal intervention on their own. After asking about subjects' experiences with the forms of public speech in question, I asked if they believed each type of speech was a personal problem. After they had answered yes or no and discussed their answers, I asked which they considered to be the most serious problem for them personally. I went on to inquire about whether each form of speech poses a social problem, asking: "Do you consider begging between strangers in public places to be a social problem?" "Do you consider sexually suggestive speech between strangers in public places to be a social problem?" and "Do you consider race-related speech between strangers in public places to be a social problem?" I then asked which, if any, they considered the most serious social problem. I introduced questions about the law only after asking these questions. I then asked whether respondents favored legal restrictions on different kinds of offensive public speech, using a variety of questions and formats. The questions included legal sanctions ranging from an infraction, "a ticket with a fine"; civil liability, "meaning you could sue the person who said that to you" ; and criminal sanction, "meaning it would be a crime and the person would face punishment such as probation or jail time." I also posed a series of items that sought to measure respondents' attitudes about the First Amendment and about the use of law as a remedy for social problems. Thus it is possible for me to locate respondents' attitudes about offensive public speech within the context of more general attitudes about speech and law.

Is Offensive Public Speech a Personal Problem?

Begging

Even though relatively few people say that begging is a problem for them personally, experience with begging is very common in my sample. While some 87% of respondents say they are the targets of begging every day or often, only 40% say that begging is a problem for them personally. Begging appears to be perceived similarly by men and women, for there is no significant difference between men and women on this question (40% of both women and men report it as a personal problem). Of those 40%, a number indicate that it is a problem only insofar as it reminds them of poverty. Others feel it is invasive or threatening.

TABLE 4.1
Respondents' Categorization of Offensive Speech by Race and Gender

	Personal Problem (% Yes)	Social Problem (% Yes)	Favor Legal Limits (% Yes)
Sexually Suggestive Speech			
Gender			
Women	55% (32)***	78% (45)	39% (23)
Men	15% (5)***	71% (25)	42% (15)
All	40% (37)	75% (70)	40% (38)
N	93	93	95
Race-Related Speech			
Race			
Whites	20% (9)***	96% (44)**	33% (16)
People of Color	51% (24)***	83% (40)**	40% (19)
All	36% (33)	89% (84)	37% (35)
N	93	94	95

Chi-square significance ** p ≤ .05, *** p ≤ .01

Note: Numbers in parentheses signify number of respondents answering yes to the following questions: "Do you consider race-related speech between strangers in public places to be a problem for you personally?" "Do you consider race-related speech between strangers in public places to be a social problem?" "Do you think that race-related speech between strangers in public places should be limited by law?" "Do you consider sexually suggestive or explicit speech between strangers in public places to be a problem for you personally?" "Do you consider sexually suggestive or explicit speech between strangers in public places to be a social problem?" and "Do you think that sexually suggestive or explicit speech between strangers in public places should be limited by law?"

Well, [begging is] just invasive. It's just invasive ... I'm always being asked, and either I have to ignore or give them money, or—you know.

Q: And both of those are problems?

A: Well yeah. I'd rather do it in a—you know, in a jar and give to everybody. I feel like if I give to one person, I have to give all or— I give to nobody. It's just too complicated for me. So, I feel like it's very invasive....

Q: Okay. Which, if any of these, would you say is the biggest problem for you?

A: Well, it's the panhandling.

Q: Because?

A: Because it's all the time—it's always— it's everywhere. (45-year-old white woman, school counselor, interview #48)

Still others consider begging a personal problem because they do not like beggars' lifestyles.

> Personally, I don't like to be approached by strangers who, let's just say—I've got to qualify this a couple ways. If someone has the body language of looking for the type of help that is, what do you say—noncommittal. You know, directions, or what time it is, I don't have any problem with that. But when somebody wants me to give them something because they're either really or allegedly in some kind of need—I really have a problem with that because I'm personally motivated to improve my condition . . . . I think there's enough going on, particularly in an urban area, that people could do something to improve themselves. And to that end—it bothers me in a sense that I wish they could do something about it that's going to produce something more than you know—a quarter or a buck here and there. . . . I don't feel like they're really helping society. (45-year-old white man, project manager/construction, interview #33)

Finally, the number of subjects who consider the *act* of begging to be a personal problem actually is slightly smaller than 40%. The following subjects' comments about begging were typical of those who say begging is a problem for them personally, not because the act of begging is annoying, but because it brings the problem of poverty to the forefront in a way that makes them uncomfortable:

> Well, like I said, it varies; is it a problem for me? I don't think it's a problem that people are asking me for money. But it makes me aware of a social problem that I don't always want to think about. It's not a problem for me. (28-year-old white woman, lawyer, interview #98)

> There are so—I can't even begin to tell you the number of issues I have. Um. I could start at I think it's a reflection of society right now, and it's really a horrible reflection of what's going on in society. Um. It's—so that would be, from a social standpoint, I find it really horrible. (49-year-old white woman, business owner, interview #49)

> Q: And why is it [begging] a problem for you?
> A: Because I'm—I'm not one to give money. So I feel sort of guilty, and obligated to make up in some fashion for it. (19-year-old East Indian woman, unemployed, interview #71)

Despite fairly extensive personal experience with begging, the majority of respondents do not consider it to be a personal problem.

Sexually Suggestive Speech as a Personal Problem

Sexually suggestive speech is considered a personal problem by 40% of those asked, and here there is a significant difference by gender (see table 4.1). More than one-half (55%) of women say that they consider offensive sexually suggestive comments from strangers in public places to be a personal problem. Only 15% of men have a personal problem with such comments. This pattern is hardly surprising. Men are much less likely to be subjected to these sorts of comments.

The reasons that subjects consider these interactions a personal problem mirror the reactions and responses reported in the previous chapter. Some women find it a problem because it is threatening:

> Q: And why is it a problem for you, or what makes it [sexually suggestive comments from strangers in public places] problematic?
> A: I think because it has that—the offensiveness of it is one thing, but it can also be very dangerous—it seems like the person's next move would be to do something dangerous to you—so it's very um, I don't know, alarming. (35-year-old African American woman, manager, interview #80)

Other women are troubled because the remarks are degrading.

> Well, I mean—because this person doesn't know me—so I'm just an object to them, and it's actually a power trip, is how I feel. It's like they're making me feel uncomfortable because they can do it. Um. And of course it may not be that for them. I can't say for sure, but that's how it seems. (54-year-old white woman, project manager/brokerage firm, interview #32)

> It's another thing you have to you know—it's invasive, and you have to ignore. I have to ignore. I just keep walking, and it makes me feel kind of creepy. You know? (45-year-old white woman, school counselor, interview #48)

> I hate that. . . . Cars slow down when I'm walking down the street, and basically check me out for a while and then drive away and say "gorgeous" and drive away. . . . It's not flattering. It does not feel good. It feels like I'm just on display for them. Like they get some kind of show from me. Ugh. It's yucky. . . . (27-year-old white woman, student, interview #67)

> Because it's something that's not asked for or wanted and um, because of the way it makes you feel—humiliated feeling you get from someone doing that, or—total lack of respect, and someone ought—someone saying something about being able to take no, or not taking you—not responding to them as a way of just saying "Leave that person alone and go to someone who will respond in a positive way to your comments." (37-year-old African American woman, librarian, interview #94)

Men who say it is a personal problem raise similar issues, if less graphically than women. For some men, there is the discomfort experienced by men whose sexuality is called into question.

> See, I'm heterosexual, and . . . if I get a compliment from a gentleman . . . or a sexually explicit compliment from a gentlemen, I find that uncomfortable. (22-year-old white man, security officer, interview #56)

Thus, there is a clear difference between begging as a form of offensive or annoying speech and sexually suggestive remarks. Women are far more likely than men to think of sexually suggestive remarks as personally problematic, and women are far more likely to experience these sorts of comments on a regular basis.

Race-Related Speech as a Personal Problem

Race-related speech is considered a personal problem by 36% of those asked. Again, there are striking differences across target groups (see table 4.1). While 51% of people of color reported that these comments are a problem for them personally, only 20% of white subjects did so. While this difference was expected, it is surprising that only slightly more than half of people of color think of race-related or racist comments from strangers in public places as a personal problem.

Racist comments were very offensive to informants although they could not always articulate why.

> Um. I don't know—they just sort of seem to hit me personally, I guess. I really don't know why—but it's just when something racially comes up, I just take it more like it's sort of my duty to correct it. Or sort of try to deal with it. (25-year-old Chinese American man, service worker, interview #28)

Given that this subject believes he has some sort of "duty" to correct the problem exposed by someone who makes a race-related comment to him, it is not surprising that he finds these comments to be a personal problem. Others also find racist statements inherently hurtful.

> 'Cause. I don't know. I just find [racist comments] more offensive than the others. (18-year-old African American man, gas station attendant, interview #31).

> Because um, it hurts. It [a race-related comment] hurts my feelings, and you don't know if you want to stoop down to their level or just ignore it. There's really nothing you can do about it—I mean, they're ignorant. (18-year-old African-American woman, unemployed, interview #54)

I take them a little more—I take them a little harder. Because I mean, if the guy doesn't know me, and I have friends of—very close friends, of just about every race you could think of. And for him to say something like that to me, and he doesn't know me, it kind of—it doesn't sit well with me. (25-year-old white man, security guard, interview #64)

This subject seems to think that if only the speaker knew him better, it would prevent the speaker from making the racist comments. This man's problem is simply that he is being misjudged. Some subjects connect the problem of racist public speech with broader systems of race hierarchies and stereotypes about people of color.

I don't know—I guess I just—America's the most multidiverse country I've ever been in, and it's just like one of the most, I'm sorry to say this, but ignorant. In that we don't look at each other as people, we look at people as "He's black, he's white, he's Asian, he's Hispanic, he's Persian, whatever." It's like we just see the person's color, and we don't really see who they are as a person. I don't know—I always hear the stereotypical Asians—we're just great in math, you know, we suck in English, we're all uptight perfectionists, and you know, all these stereotypes, and I hear it often. (26-year-old Asian American man, customer service, interview #84)

Mm. It's not a problem if they do it, because that's just their own ignorance that they have to deal with—it's a problem that they haven't been educated enough to know that's not something that you do, and that um—in this day and age there are still people who really, you know, train the kids to respect people of all cultures, and not do—turn it around and say how would you feel if someone did the same thing to you. So in that sense, it's a problem. If someone calls me a name, I try not to let it affect me, because that's their own ignorance, their own—um it has to do with their own—I don't know, I can't think of the word right now. (37-year-old African American woman, librarian, interview #94)

Many of the targets of offensive race-related public speech blame the incident on the ignorance of the speaker. They believe that when an individual makes a race-related or racist comment, it is due to his or her own ignorance. The same claim is not made about those who make sexually suggestive comments to women they do not know in public places, possibly because, as suggested in chapter 3, sexually suggestive comments are thought to be, in part, the fault of the woman target. Targets of race-related speech do not suffer this blame.

Obviously, those who actually experience a particular kind of offensive public speech are more likely to find that kind of speech a personal problem. As table 4.1 shows, people of color are far more likely than whites to consider race-related speech to be a personal problem.

TABLE 4.2
Which Form of Offensive Speech is the Most Serious Problem for You?

	Begging	Sexually Suggestive Speech	Race-Related Speech	All 3
Race***				
Whites	31% (14)	27% (12)	13% (6)	29% (13)
People of Color	26% (11)	21% (9)	47% (20)	7% (3)
Gender***				
Women	29% (16)	35% (19)	18% (10)	18% (10)
Men	27% (9)	6% (2)	49% (16)	18% (6)
Education				
< College	28% (11)	15% (6)	39% (15)	18% (7)
College or More	29% (14)	31% (15)	22% (11)	18% (9)
Total	28% (25)	24% (21)	30% (26)	18% (16)
N	88	88	88	88

Chi-square significance * p ≤ .1, ** p ≤ .05, *** p ≤ .01
Note: Numbers in parentheses signify number of subjects who report that each form of speech is the most serious personal problem. Percentages that do not add up to 100% are due to rounding.

Women are far more likely than men to view sexually suggestive speech as a personal problem.

But which type of offensive public speech is the most serious personal problem for the respondent groups? Because some people reported that all three forms of offensive public speech pose personal problems, it is important to understand which of the forms has the greatest effect on its targets. Laws prohibiting speech are based on calculations about the nature of the harm each type of speech has on its targets, so it is crucial to explore which of these forms of speech poses the most serious personal problem for ordinary people. To discern which form of speech poses the most serious personal problem, I asked respondents which, if any, of the three forms of public speech was the most serious personal problem? Sexually suggestive speech was reported as the most serious personal problem by 35% of women, followed by begging (29%), and then race-related speech (18%) (see table 4.2). Men gave very different answers. Almost half of men (49%) report the most serious personal problem is race-related speech, followed by begging (27%), and all three forms (18%).

The findings about what kinds of speech pose personal problems are straightforward. Although begging is reported as the most serious personal problem by 28% of respondents, there are no differences by social group. Those who experience sexist and racist speech—namely women and people of color—are likely to find them to be a personal problem. A full 47% of people of color report that race-related speech is the most serious personal problem. Table 4.2 illustrates exactly what one might expect—people who are more likely be targets of a particular form of speech also are more likely to consider it a personal problem.

Is Offensive Public Speech a Social Problem?

Having established which forms of speech were personally troubling for subjects, I asked them to discuss whether each form of speech was a problem for society. When I asked about speech to which the subject was frequently a party (that is, when I asked women about sexually suggestive speech or people of color about race-related speech), the answers came quickly. When I asked subjects who had little or no experience with a particular form of public speech to make an assessment, the respondents were more hesitant. Asking a white man whether or not race-related speech between strangers in public is a social problem requires first that he determine whether a particular kind of interaction actually occurs. To make matters more difficult, he has rarely, if ever, been a party to these sorts of interactions. Next, he must estimate how frequently it occurs. In other words, the subject must determine, with little or no firsthand experience, at what point an offensive or annoying social interaction goes from being a fluke or an irritation to a "social problem." The determination of whether these interactions are social problems depends then on how frequently the subject believes these interactions occur. As I showed in chapter 3, men underestimate how frequently women are the targets of offensive sexually suggestive speech. Similarly, whites underestimate how frequently people of color are subjected to comments about their race from strangers in public places.

Nonetheless, subjects generally are in agreement about which of these forms of offensive public speech constitute social problems. Consistent with the previous discussion about people not wanting to label begging a problem because it is stigmatizing to the beggars, begging was least often declared to be a social problem. Some 58% of subjects reported begging as a social problem. A full 75% of those asked reported that sexually suggestive speech between strangers in public places is a social problem (see table 4.1), and 89% of subjects reported that race-related comments between strangers in public places is a social problem (see table 4.1). With each of the three forms of offensive public speech, there are clear differences by race and gender in who views each as social problems.

Begging as a Social Problem

In contrast to racist speech, about which there is near unanimity, only 58% of subjects report begging is a social problem. As with the determination as to whether begging is a *personal* problem, there is no significant difference between men and women or among the races on the subject of begging as a *social* problem. Those subjects who consider begging to be a social problem do so because they feel threatened. Many subjects cannot untangle poverty from begging and want to claim that poverty itself is a social problem.

Still, several find interactions with beggars problematic for society:

Q: Do you consider begging to be a social problem?
A: Mm. Actually, for me, no. But I think for some of my friends, maybe.
Q: Mm hm. And why might it be for them?
A: 'Cause. I think people deal with situations differently, and for them, I think they would just rather not deal with all the different things going on in life. They would rather not have to deal with that. Because they still feel intimidated, or they feel like they might have to give or—something might happen. (25-year-old Chinese American man, service worker, interview #28)

Many people recognized that whether or not something is a social problem is related to the frequency with which it occurs. This woman's comments were typical:

Yeah. It's really—for me personally, it's the gender one, because that's the one I deal with most often. But for the homeless person, it's—it's the poverty, and for the person who more often deals with the race issue, it's race. . . . They all stem from the same thing, which is a misunderstanding of the differences between different groups of people. But I think that probably the poverty one is the most um, it's not just not understanding a different group of people, it's also how do they get to the point where they're in that poverty situation. So I would say that has more underlying it. So maybe that would be the biggest problem. (27-year-old white woman, student, interview #67)

For this woman, the most serious *personal* problem is sexually suggestive speech as it is the one she "deal[s] with most often." Nonetheless, begging is considered to be a more serious *social* problem because of the connection to the larger problem of poverty.

Although begging is considered to be a social problem by a majority of those asked, people in all social groups are affected similarly. Begging affects people no matter what their social location. It is thus unlike gender-based and race-related offensive public speech, which have disproportionate effects on white women and people of color.

Sexually Suggestive Comments as a Social Problem

A total of 75% of those asked reported that they think sexually suggestive comments between strangers in public places constitute a social problem. Although there is a significant difference by gender as to whether sexually suggestive comments are a *personal* problem, and despite the fact that men underestimate the frequency with which women are made the targets of such comments, there is no significant difference between men and women on whether it is a social problem. More than 70% of men and 78% of women reported that sexually suggestive comments constitute a social problem. Women often connect sexually suggestive public speech to broader systems of gender hierarchy in society. They see this kind of speech as an aspect of a larger social problem.

> I think—I mean, our advertising, our television shows, our movies, everything is just filled with it, and I think it makes for a much harder time for women to be respected and taken seriously, because that is still okay to say those kinds of things to women. I mean, it's not okay with us, but it must be okay with somebody because they persist. (33-year-old white woman, teacher, interview #20)

> Well, I think since they're usually directed from men toward women . . . it's a problem with the views that men have of women, and the stereotypes they have of them that they feel that they could say these things, or ask it in way and that it's socially acceptable. It's nothing they should be ashamed of, or afraid of.
> Q: Do you think that they do think it's socially acceptable?
> A: Oh yeah. Totally. I don't think—they think there's no problem with it, and you should just sort of deal with it. That they weren't doing any harm. But of course they are. (22-year-old African-American woman, student, interview #55)

> It reflects society on a whole as in like derogatory terms towards women. And um, it's—although a lot of people you know, say—scientists and researchers "Oh, we've gone so far in elevating women's status and having them as equals" that's so far from . . . it's a lot closer than it was, but it's still nowhere near they say—they want you to think it is. Because it just won't happen, I don't think, in this society. It's just been so long, we've been so entrenched in thinking the woman is the passive sex and the men are aggressive and they can do anything, basically. (19-year-old Chinese woman, lab worker, interview #72)

This woman sees sexist comments as stemming from and perpetuating a system of gender inequality. Subjects of both genders distinguish between "polite" comments about appearance and offensive or sexually suggestive comments.

I feel like the person who wants to say something to me that they think is a compliment, and then they're going to go on about their day, then that's not such a big deal for me. But it does bother me that there's just a general climate where women are prey. And men feel like "I get to say anything I want to you because you're a woman and you're out on the street." And I feel like a lot of men um—feel like because they can do that, that they can do other things to women, too. (26-year-old white woman, unemployed, interview #30)

Still other subjects think that these comments are a social problem because it interferes with women's ability to travel unrestricted through public places.

I think that—especially now, lately, ten years ago, I think you could walk down the street and you wouldn't have that problem, but with things that go on in the world now lately, it's getting worse, and people—just, their attitudes toward other people. They don't have as much respect for each other. (22-year-old Hispanic woman, human resources professional, interview #36)

[Sexually suggestive remarks are the biggest social problem because] for females it's like—they're getting scared to even go out. (26-year-old Asian American man, customer service, interview #84)

A number of men also connect the problem of sexist street speech to broader systems of gender hierarchy:

I mean, especially the way I was brought up, my brother was brought up and my friends—I've never seen any of our parents or any of my friends' parents tell us how to treat a woman, or say "be polite to a woman" or stuff like that. It's always "You're the guy, she's the woman, men are stronger" you know, "Don't let a woman tell you what to do" you know, this machismo attitude. We were just brought up that way, then the bombardment of you know how TV commercials are—*women are just looked at as sexual objects*—so when you interact with women, it's just like—*they're just bodies*, you don't really treat them as a regular person. You're like—that's why a lot of women have to deal with these sexual comments from men. *Because they're just looked at as sexual objects, rather than a regular person.* (26-year-old Asian American man, customer service, interview #84)

These subjects describe the troubling aspects of sexually suggestive speech. It is a problem because it interferes with women's ability to travel through public. It is a problem because it perpetuates women's subordinate status without repercussion. It is a problem because it makes women feel frightened and objectified. Most of all it is a problem because it is a burden not shared by male counterparts. As one male subject put it:

> Well, again, on that sort of interfering from people getting from Point A to Point B, um, it's just not very nice to hear that—that kind of thing as you're just getting from Point A to Point B—you don't go out expecting to get that sort of . . . I'm trying to distinguish between that and the panhandling. The panhandling thing is pretty nonselective. They pretty much—they'll take money from anyone who's got it. Whereas the sexually harassing remarks um, yeah, again, I don't see a justification for it, and I don't think people should—I don't think people should have to be subject to it. (28-year-old white man, student/disk jockey, interview #76)

Women *know* that sexually suggestive comments regularly are made and that they pose a social problem. Men express some disbelief about the occurrence, but agree that when sexually suggestive comments are made, it is a problem. This is true even though men do not fully understand the frequency or nature of these sorts of interactions.

Race-Related Comments as a Social Problem

Racist comments between strangers in public places are viewed as a social problem by a full 89% of those asked (see table 4.1). There is an important difference between whites and people of color on this question, but not in the direction one might expect. Surprisingly, people of color were *less* likely to report that race-related comments between strangers in public places are a social problem than were whites. As table 4.1 shows, only 83% of people of color consider them to be a social problem, while 96% of whites consider race related comments to be a social problem. This pattern may seem curious, but there is still near consensus that racist public speech is a social problem. Respondents offered several reasons why race-related comments between strangers in public places are a social problem. Some think that such comments can lead to other forms of violence:

> Because that [race-related comments] leads to too many other things. And I think [race-related comments are] more prevalent. Usually if someone's insulted, it is because of their race or something that they've done. Sexual comments don't go back and forth that much I don't think. (53-year-old white woman, property manager, interview #21)

TABLE 4.3
Which Form of Offensive Speech is the Most Serious Social Problem?

	Begging	Sexually Suggestive Speech	Race-Related Speech	Race and Sex Speech
Race				
Whites	13% (5)	10% (4)	60% (24)	18% (7)
People of Color	20% (8)	10% (4)	55% (22)	15% (6)
Gender				
Women	20% (10)	12% (6)	50% (25)	18% (9)
Men	10% (3)	7% (2)	70% (21)	13% (4)
Education				
< College	18% (7)	15% (6)	56% (22)	10% (4)
College or More	15% (6)	5% (2)	59% (24)	22% (9)
Total	16% (13)	10% (8)	58% (46)	16% (13)
N	80	80	80	80

Chi-square significance * p ≤ .1, ** p ≤ .05, *** p ≤ .01
Note: Numbers in parentheses signify number of subjects who report that each form of speech is the most serious social problem. Percentages that do not add up to 100% are due to rounding.

Some targets of racist speech consider it problematic because of how it makes them feel personally.

Well, 'cause I've never had a problem sitting down and saying damn, man, you're black or you're white. You know, I don't care about how people's skin color turns out from pigments. Sometimes, it gets on your nerves, you just want to be accepted like everybody else. (34-year-old African American man, laborer, interview #35)

Still others speak of the insidious way that racist comments work. These subjects say racist comments create, reinforce, and perpetuate division between the races and tend to perpetuate the subordinate status of people of color in this country.

That goes all the way back to, I guess—it's all based on the slavery thing, and black people not having an economic base in this country, and most of us being unemployed—especially our male population being imprisoned and unemployed, and this is basically why we have the conflict between the black and the white, because the blacks feel like they don't have proper uh, you know, political standing in this country. . . . So there's always going to be that conflict there. White men feel threatened you know—

Q: So how do you see the racial comments playing into that?

A: It's like it's sort of reminding you that there's a place for you—

Q: Mm hm. And it's not with me.

A: Yes. To keep us separated. (52-year-old African American woman, business professional, interview #90)

Because obviously we don't live in a colorblind society. And we probably never will. But—it only—comments made in public, which do happen, does perpetuate, you know, like differences between the races. It only can like polarize them even more. So I would consider it to be a problem. (20-year-old white woman, student, interview #40)

Yeah, I think I do [consider race-related comments between strangers in public to be a social problem]. I think it's just, sometimes just in everyday life, there's just so much tension, and when you bring in certain race issues, it just creates more tension that people don't really need. (25-year-old Chinese American man, service worker, interview #28)

As these comments suggest, many respondents perceive that these microinteractions have a powerful effect on systems of racial hierarchy in society. Race-related or racist comments between strangers in public places are but one way that division between races is reinforced and maintained. Many subjects mention other forms of racial oppression, such as discrimination in the workplace or in education, in conjunction with racist public comments, demonstrating that they view these events as related.

A number of subjects for whom race-related speech does not rise to the level of a social problem explain that comments alone are not a social problem. Social problems occur only when the words turn to actions. Consider this woman's explanation:

I don't think it's [race-related comments] a problem until people get violent about it. People can say what they want. (45-year-old African American woman, student, interview #88)

Which of these three forms of speech poses the most serious social problem? As with personal problems, race-related speech is considered the most serious social problem by a much larger proportion of respondents than are begging or sexist speech.

As reported in table 4.3, 58% say that racist speech is the most serious social problem. Nearly 16% identify begging as the most serious social problem, and only 10% of these subjects report that sexually suggestive speech is the most serious social problem of the three. Some subjects (16%) were not willing to separate racist and sexist speech and insisted they are equally problematic. Thus, respondents are more than three times as likely to say that racist speech is the most serious social problem than its closest competitor.

These data reveal a clear hierarchy of concern within this sample. Racist speech is the most socially troubling. Whether one experiences such speech personally or not, virtually all agree that racist speech is a social problem. Begging and sexually suggestive speech are considered the most serious social problem for only 16% and 10%, respectively. If those who classify racist and sexist speech as equally problematic are added to those who rank sexually suggestive speech or racist speech as the most serious social problem, only one in four respondents (26%) think sexually suggestive speech is the most serious social problem; but roughly three in four respondents (74%) indicate that racist public speech is the most pressing social concern.

Should Law Limit Offensive Public Speech?

According to most of my subjects, racist and sexist offensive public speech pose serious social problems. But do average citizens think the law should restrict these forms of speech? I first consider the different measures I used to address this question. I then turn to five hypotheses that predict who is likely to favor or oppose legal strictures on offensive public speech.

Like many scholars who study attitudes, I found that attitudes about offensive public speech vary according to how questions are asked. Even in the open-ended questions used in this study, when I present a particularly offensive example of racist public speech and then ask if law should restrict it, I get a different answer than when I pose the question in the abstract. Different formats also generate different answers. Asking "Should this action be allowed?" generates different responses than when the question is, "Should this action be restricted?" even when the action is the same. My data demonstrate similar ambiguity about whether or not people think that there should be laws regulating offensive public speech.

Attitudes toward regulating offensive public speech vary depending on how concretely the question is presented to the subject. In the most general form, almost everyone is opposed to the regulation of offensive public speech. When the question contains more specific types of speech, but without reference to specific examples, people are more willing to accept legal regulation. Finally, when the question provides specific, graphic examples of offensive public speech, the number of subjects who support legal intervention increases greatly. This paradox is predictable, but makes it difficult to determine whether subjects are actually in favor of regulating offensive public speech.

When subjects speak of their own experiences and about "offensive public speech" in general terms, the number of people who favor regulation is low.[1] Only 12% report that they want to see laws enacted that prohibit offensive public speech. As table 4.4 shows, when asked if they would favor laws against offensive public speech with reference to the topics of begging, sexually suggestive speech, and race-related speech, 35% favor laws prohibiting begging, 41% favor laws against sexually suggestive comments, and 37% favor laws against racist comments between strangers in public places.[2]

When the questions were made more specific through the use of hypothetical examples, there was a greater willingness to regulate offensive public speech by law. I presented to my subjects a continuum of hypothetical situations from quite benign forms of public speech to very offensive scenarios and illegal activities.[3] Following each of those hypothetical situations, I asked, "Would you be in favor of a law to prohibit that?" When these hypothetical situations are presented to subjects, more favor using the law to prohibit these forms of offensive public speech. When provided with the most extreme hypothetical situation in the interview regarding begging ("You are walking on a public street when a man, apparently homeless, asks you for money. When you refuse or ignore him, he follows you for about one block, making repeated requests."), the number of subjects who favor legal regulation jumps to 54%. Similarly, the number of people willing to regulate offensive sexually suggestive speech rises to almost 66% when presented with an extreme hypothetical ("A woman is walking on a public street and a man she does not know shouts 'suck my dick' at her.") Finally, those willing to regulate offensive racist speech climbs to over 48% when subjects are asked in the context of an extreme hypothetical situation ("An African American man is walking down a public street and a white man shouts, 'I'm gonna get you, nigger.' ") One additional extreme hypothetical situation about race-related speech that explicitly mirrored key elements of the Supreme Court's opinion in *R.A.V. v. City of St. Paul*, a case protecting cross burning on private property under the First Amendment, garnered even more support for legal intervention. The hypothetical read, "A white man, without trespassing, manages to burn a cross in the front yard of an African American man's front lawn." More than 88% responded that this should be illegal.

Which is the fair measure about limiting public speech? For the purposes of this analysis, I settled on the second set of measures—those which ask specifically about regulating three types of speech but not

TABLE 4.4
Percentage Favoring Restrictions by Type of Speech

	Begging	Sexist Speech	Racist Speech
1. Experience			
Often or more	37% (27)	27% (9)**	32% (7)
Less than often	25% (3)	51% (23)**	39% (23)
Total	35% (30)	41% (32)	37% (30)
N	85	79	81
2. Personal Problem			
Yes	47% (17)*	34% (12)	57% (17)***
No	30% (16)*	45% (25)	29% (17)***
Total	37% (33)	41% (37)	39% (34)
N	90	90	89
3. Social Problem			
Yes	47% (24)**	39% (26)	40% (31)***
No	22% (8)**	50% (11)	30% (3)***
Total	36% (32)	42% (37)	39% (34)
N	88	89	89
4. Occupation			
Professional/Manager	47% (17)**	41% (15)	43% (16)
Other	28% (16)**	40% (23)	33% (19)
Total	35% (33)	40% (38)	37% (35)
N	94	95	95
5. First Amendment Scale			
Low	42% (8)	50% (10)	40% (8)
Medium	38% (13)	37% (13)	39% (13)
High	39% (10)	44% (11)	42% (11)
Total	40% (31)	43% (34)	40% (32)
N	79	80	80
6. Legal Remedy Scale			
Low	35% (7)	30% (6)	16% (3)**
Medium	41% (15)	49% (18)	43% (16)**
High	42% (10)	44% (11)	50% (13)**
Total	40% (32)	43% (35)	39% (32)
N	81	82	82

Chi-square significance * p ≤ .1, ** p ≤ .05, *** p ≤ .01
Note: Numbers in parentheses signify number of respondents in favor of legal restrictions on speech.

those based on an offensive hypothetical. But why choose that form of
the question?

I do not dwell on the results from the most general questions for two
reasons. First, they generate little variation (only 12% favor laws restricting speech). Second, I find that regular people, unlike the courts,
make distinctions about different kinds of speech when they are considering whether or not law should regulate such speech. Thus, it is important to use a question that incorporates a reference to the content of
the speech about which I ask. Using extremely offensive hypothetical
situations, however, is problematic also. Although these data are an illuminating illustration of how question wording affects responses on First
Amendment issues, they do not capture the more general orientation of
citizens to the legal regulation of offensive public speech. They do not
reflect the hesitation that accompanies the desire to outlaw extremely
offensive speech. Additionally, extreme questions are so inflammatory
that they create a situation in the interview where people may simply
be giving the socially desirable answer. Indeed, McCloskey and Brill
(1983) argue that attitudes about civil liberties vary with class in part
because those with higher levels of education learn the socially correct
answer. When you ask a subject if a person should be allowed to shout
"nigger" at an African American man in a public place, I suspect subjects feel that they are being tested about their compassion or their political correctness. The result may be a skewed set of answers.

What explains variation in support for legal restrictions on offensive
public speech? Here, I consider five prominent possibilities. They are:
(1) More frequent targets of offensive public speech are more likely to
favor legal regulation; (2) Those who see these forms of offensive public speech as personal and social problems are more likely to favor their
legal regulation; (3) Those who favor legal intervention to solve social
problems generally will favor legal intervention in the case of offensive
public speech; (4) Attitudes toward regulation will correspond to attitudes about the First Amendment in other contexts; and (5) Support
for civil liberties (and, hence, opposition to legal restrictions on offensive public speech) varies with education and social class.

1. More Frequent Targets of Offensive Public Speech Are More Likely to Favor Legal Regulation.

The implicit hypothesis of many critical race legal scholars is that those
people who are more frequently the targets of offensive public speech
are the most likely to favor its legal regulation. The explicit argument
made by critical race legal theorists is more legally oriented than this,
however. Critical race theorists such as Delgado and Stefancic (1997)

argue that insofar as racist hate speech perpetuates systems of racial domination, allowing such speech interferes with other constitutional principles, most importantly the equality guaranteed by the Fourteenth Amendment. A corollary of their argument is the suggestion that judges and lawmakers are not familiar with the experience of being the target of racist public harassment because they are overwhelmingly white. Yet the data show a weak link between being a target of racist public speech and favoring legal restrictions.

As previously shown, people of color are only slightly more likely to favor legal restrictions on racist speech than are whites (40% v. 33%). Indeed, panel 1 of table 4.4 shows that those who are *more* often targets of racist public speech are *less* likely to favor its legal restrictions (32%) than those who are its targets on a less-frequent basis (39%).[4] I explore the reasons for this in more detail in chapter 5, but this reflects the distrust of authority and cynicism about law generally experienced by many people of color, especially African American men, who disfavor the use of the law to remedy such problems.

Similarly, those who are *more* often the targets of sexually suggestive speech are *less* likely to favor legal regulation of these comments. More than 50% of those who are infrequent targets favor the regulation of sexually suggestive speech, but only 27% who are regular targets support legal intervention (see table 4.4). Men are slightly more likely to favor restrictions on offensive sexually suggestive speech in public than are women, with almost 42% of men in favor of restrictions on sexually suggestive speech and only 39% of women in favor of them.

With begging the relationship is more as one might expect. Those who are more frequently its targets are more likely to favor the legal regulation of begging (37%) than those who are less frequently its targets (25%) (see table 4.4). These data on racist public speech stand in direct opposition to the claims made by critical race legal scholars, because they show that the relationship between experience and attitudes about regulation are more complex than previous speculations about this relationship have anticipated. Thus, hypothesis number 1 is supported in the case of begging: those who are more frequent targets are also more likely to favor its regulation. However, with regard to racist and sexist speech, this relationship is reversed.

2. Those who see these forms of offensive public speech as personal or social problems or both are more likely to favor legal regulation than those who think that these interactions do not pose a personal and/or social problem.

A second, related theory is that those who view these forms of speech as personal and/or social problems would be more likely to favor legal intervention than those who think that these interactions do not pose a personal or social problem. Framing the question this way decouples attitudes about legal intervention from experience with each form of speech. For example, although I am a white female, I may recognize that racist public speech is a social problem and favor regulation despite the fact that I may have never been the target of such speech.

As panel 2 of table 4.4 demonstrates, those who think begging is a problem for them personally are far more likely to favor legal regulation of begging than are those who do not think begging is a personal problem. Seventy percent of those who do not think begging is a problem for them are opposed to laws restricting begging, while 47% of those who think begging is a problem would be willing to restrict it. The same pattern is true for those who think begging is a social problem (panel 3 of table 4.4). Those who do not view begging as a social problem are less likely to favor its legal regulation than those who do think begging is a social problem. Still, a solid majority are unwilling to restrict begging, a finding I turn to in the next chapter. Thus, attitudes about whether begging is a personal problem are related to attitudes about regulating begging.

A similar pattern emerges with race-related speech. Those who regard racist speech as a personal problem are also more likely to favor the regulation of such speech. Almost 57% of those for whom race-related speech is a personal problem favor regulations restricting it, but 29% of those for whom race-related speech is not a personal problem favor such restrictions. Similarly, those who think racist speech poses a social problem are more likely to favor its regulation (40%) than those who think racist speech does not pose a social problem (30%). Thus, although attitudes about restricting racist speech are not related to how frequently one is the target of such speech, they are related to whether or not the person finds them to be a personal or social problem.

Attitudes about regulating sexually suggestive speech between strangers in public places are more difficult to interpret. As table 4.4 demonstrates, the relationship between attitudes about whether sexist speech is a personal and social problem and attitudes about legal regulation are reversed from what we see for begging and racist speech. Those who think that sexually suggestive comments are a personal problem are *less* likely to favor legal regulation of these comments (34%) than those who do not think they are a personal problem (45%). And those who think that sexually suggestive comments pose a social problem are also *less* likely to favor legal intervention (39%) than those who think sexually suggestive speech is not a social problem (50%).

Although these relationships are not statistically significant, it is important to note the direction of this effect.

It may seem counterintuitive that those who think of sexually suggestive speech as a personal and social problem are less likely to favor legal regulation than those who do not, especially when the opposite is true for begging and racist speech. The finding implies that the relationship between the speaker and the target, and the hierarchy of which it is a part, is distinct for sexually suggestive speech. It appears that women internalize the blame for sexually suggestive speech in ways that do not occur among the targets of begging and race-related speech. In chapter 5, I examine the explanations that women offer for this pattern.

3. *Those who favor legal intervention to solve social problems generally will favor legal intervention in the case of offensive public speech.*

Perhaps the disposition to regulate offensive public speech is related to whether or not an individual believes that the law is a good mechanism for dealing with social problems. Obviously, some people think the law is helpful in remedying social problems, while others are less optimistic about law's ability to accomplish social goals. Those who are optimistic about the law in general may be more likely to view the law as an appropriate tool for dealing with this particular social problem.

I constructed an index variable, called the "legal remedy scale," to measure subjects' attitudes toward law and legal regulation, particularly the application of law to race and gender-related social problems. I posed a series of Likert scale items to respondents[5] and the answers were added to create a scale in which subjects with higher values were more likely to favor the law and legal regulation, while those with lower values were less likely to favor law and legal regulation as a remedy for social problems. I converted scale values into a trichotomy of low, medium, and high scores. As table 4.5 shows, women and people of color favor legal intervention to remedy social problems in general in significantly greater numbers than do men and whites, respectively. Thus, it is interesting that in general, women are less likely to favor legal restrictions on all three forms of offensive public speech than are men.

Does the legal remedy scale tell us anything about who wants to regulate offensive public speech? Yes. As panel 6 of table 4.4 shows, those who score "low" on the legal remedy scale are the least likely to favor legal regulation for all three types of speech. The difference is greatest for racist speech. Those who generally favor the law and legal

TABLE 4.5
Demographic Characteristics by First Amendment and Legal Remedy Values

	First Amendment Scale			Legal Remedy Scale		
	Low	Medium	High	Low	Medium	High
Race						
Whites	14% (6)	48% (20)*	38% (16)	30% (13)	47% (20)	23% (10)
People of Color	33% (14)	43% (18)*	24% (10)	19% (8)	42% (18)	40% (17)
Gender	26% (13)	43% (22)	31% (16)	17% (9)	38% (20)***	45% (24)
Women						
Men	21% (7)	49% (16)	30% (10)	37% (12)	55% (18)***	9% (3)
Education						
< College	29% (11)	50% (19)	21% (8)	25% (10)	43% (17)	33% (13)
College or More	20% (9)	41% (19)	40% (18)	24% (11)	46% (21)	30% (14)
Occupation						
Professional/						
Manager	22% (7)	44% (14)	34% (11)	19% (6)	47% (15)	34% (11)
Other	25% (13)	47% (24)	29% (15)	28% (15)	43% (23)	30% (16)
Total	24% (20)	45% (38)	31% (26)	24% (21)	44% (38)	40% (17)
N		84			86	

Chi-square significance * p ≤ .1, ** p ≤ .05, *** p ≤ .01
Note: Numbers in parentheses signify number of respondents who fall into each category.

regulation to solve social problems are significantly more likely to favor regulation of racist public speech.

The desire to regulate begging is not so clearly related to attitudes about law. There are relatively few differences across position on the legal remedy scale, perhaps because respondents saw the legal control of begging as something closer to what the law already does.

The relationship between general attitudes about law as a remedy and support for restrictions on sexist speech are complex. Despite women being more favorable to legal intervention generally and despite the fact that they find sexist speech a personal problem, they do not favor legal restrictions on sexist speech. Respondents with low scores on the legal remedy scale are less likely to favor restrictions on sexist speech, but those with "medium" scores are slightly more supportive of restrictions than those who score "high." The reversal at the upper end of the scale may result from the ambivalent position of women on these issues.

Thus, the third hypothesis—with some qualifications—appears to hold. Those who are more supportive of legal remedies generally are more supportive of using law to restrict offensive public speech. But it also is the case that target groups—white women and people of color—are more likely to support legal remedies. It is difficult to distinguish these effects.

4. Attitudes toward regulation will correspond to attitudes about the First Amendment in other contexts.

This hypothesis is similar to the previous one because it is based on the assumption that people have consistent ideas about law and legal regulation. It postulates that those who tend to support the First Amendment in other, perhaps less extreme situations, will support the First Amendment here. I developed a scale to measure commitment to the First Amendment in more traditional contexts.[6] Questions with Likert-scale responses were tabulated to assign respondents a measure of commitment to the First Amendment. The scale produced meaningful statistical variation. In a similar way that I handled the legal remedy measure, I grouped subjects into three categories: those with a low, medium, or high commitment to the First Amendment.

Table 4.4 indicates that First Amendment values are not related to the desire to regulate any of the three forms of offensive public speech. In fact, 39% of those in the "high" First Amendment category favor laws against begging, 44% favor laws against sexually suggestive speech, and 42% favor laws against racist comments between strangers in public places. These numbers are roughly similar to those with "low" First Amendment values.

How does one explain this apparent contradiction? A possible explanation is that the First Amendment is not the paramount concern when subjects are deciding if they favor or oppose legal regulation of offensive public speech. Although subjects might favor protecting speech in more traditional contexts (such as labeling or censoring books and records), they do not carry this sort of thinking into the realm of micro-level interactions in which the state has no obvious role. In other words, when asked whether "public authorities" should have the power to make decisions about books in the library or music on the shelves of a music store, images of censorship are triggered. But when presented with street-level aggressions between two private citizens and asked if these comments should be allowed to continue with impunity, subjects are more reluctant to adhere to their own First Amendment principles. This finding tells us something important about why people favor or oppose regulation of various kinds of offensive public speech. Unlike the courts, which cannot or do not distinguish between an opinion and a targeted epithet, average citizens can and do make these distinctions. The willingness to make such distinctions may be attributed to muddled, untrained thinking, as many legally and academically trained scholars might suggest. In the alternative, we might attribute the willingness to make such distinctions to the common sense of average people. Additionally, this schism between First Amendment values in one context versus another reflects the contingency of legal consciousness. How one thinks about the law varies according to circumstance.

5. Support for civil liberties (and, hence, opposition to legal restrictions on offensive public speech) varies with education and social class.

So far, I have shown that the desire to restrict offensive public speech is not related to First Amendment values in any predictable way. We also know that attitudes about restricting offensive public speech are not strongly related to race or gender. But what about measures of class? Support for civil liberties, including the freedom of speech, has long been recognized as related to education, income, and political/ legal sophistication (McCloskey and Brill 1983; Stouffer 1992). The more education, income, or political/legal sophistication a person has, the more likely that individual is to support civil liberties in the liberal legal sense. This research would therefore predict that those with higher socioeconomic status are more likely to be supporters of free speech. They may, therefore, be more tolerant of and willing to protect even offensive speech.

The two major indicators of class that I used were education and occupational status. I chose these two because education is the most important factor for explaining attitudes about civil liberties according to McCloskey and Brill (1983); occupational status also is positively correlated with civil liberties scores. Table 4.5 reveals that the college educated tend to score higher on the First Amendment scale, as do managers and professionals compared to other occupational groups. But the differences are not statistically significant. Yet, as table 4.4 shows, the pattern does not carry over to attitudes about restricting offensive public speech.

Indeed, the direction of the effects of education and class are reversed from Stouffer's findings. Education does not have a significant effect on attitudes toward regulating the three forms of offensive public speech studied here. Occupational status is significantly related only to attitudes to restrict begging. And the higher status group is *more* likely to favor legal regulation of begging. Forty-four percent of those with college education favor restrictions on sexually suggestive speech between strangers in public places, as do 36% of those with less than a college degree, a nonsignificant difference. There is virtually no difference across occupational status in these attitudes. Almost 30% of high school graduates favor restrictions on racist public speech, but 43% of the college educated favor laws restricting race-related offensive public speech, again a difference that does not reach statistical significance.

Given that more educated and higher status groups are more likely to favor legal restrictions, it is tempting to say there may be a "political correctness" effect for offensive public speech that distinguishes these findings from the usual "Stouffer effect." There are other significant differences from the kind of speech at issue for Stouffer, McCloskey, and other large-scale survey researchers and the kind of speech I study here. First, all three studies address questions about allowing unpopular ideas to be heard in a political or academic setting. My research examines what some speech scholars call "low-value speech," which has very little or no redeeming value. In contrast to political speech, which may be offensive but has intrinsic value because it furthers political debate, low-value speech such as racial epithets can be constructed as having no redeeming value.

Second, the speech I inquire about involves comments targeted at particular individuals. There is something about being singled out for abusive words that people find more objectionable than a lecture in a classroom or a protest in the street. Finally, in the hypothetical situations explored by these researchers, there is a forum for responding to offensive or problematic comments. The street does not offer such a forum.

ANALYSIS

The findings in this chapter begin to illuminate some of the complexities of the relationship between offensive public speech; the hierarchies of class, gender, and race to which offensive speech is linked; and legal consciousness. Although offensive public speech is widely perceived to be a personal and social problem, most respondents are opposed to legal restrictions on such speech. The reasons vary by type of speech and by social group. Here I review the variations by type of speech and consider some of the implications for theories of race, gender, and class. Chapter 5 probes more deeply into the legal consciousness of my respondents.

Given that begging is the least likely to be a personal and social problem for the sample, it is not surprising that almost two-thirds of respondents do not favor legal restrictions on it. It is interesting that the opposition to restricting begging is not related to First Amendment values or to a general disposition against using law as a remedy. Rather many respondents think that beggars should have the ability (or even a "right") to do what they need to do to survive. Subjects do not want to criminalize what may be a last-ditch effort for survival.

> I don't think it's right to punish homeless people or people who are—who feel that they don't have any other access to livelihood besides asking other people for money. I don't think it's right to punish them for that. And I would be more in favor of some other kind of social program that would help them get what they need in life. (31-year-old white woman, student, interview #74)

Still others recognize that being reduced to begging for a living is most likely not a choice for the beggar:

> I think somewhat it is that they're trying to survive, and kind of—don't know. I wouldn't say it's all their choice. They're kind of—they've been pushed to it in a sense. I mean, I wouldn't—like try to criminalize begging. You know what I'm saying? I don't think it is a problem in that sense. And I handle it pretty well, I think. I'm not like offended by it or feel threatened by it. (20-year-old white woman, student, interview #40)

Finally, some respondents indicated that they have had to beg for money on occasion. Although two respondents said they had begged for a living, more common were stories by people who found themselves momentarily without cash, such as this one:

> I've been a position where I was in college, I ran out of gas, I didn't have my Versateller card, it was like 2:30 in the morning in Los Banos, you know, we had to ask somebody for a couple bucks, and that's sort of an innocent, "Oh god, we're stupid," so yeah—people are stupid, and they need money every once and a while. (30-year-old white man, student, interview #53)

These data show compassion for beggars and a general perception that begging is not a very serious personal or social problem.

Race-related or racist speech presents a different, but relatively straightforward, pattern. Those who are its targets think of it as a personal problem with which the law should deal. Those who are not its targets are in agreement that it poses a social problem, but are modestly less likely to favor legal intervention than those who actually suffer the attacks. Unlike begging, there is no articulated justification for allowing racist speech, other than general concerns about whether the government can or should intervene.

Sexually suggestive speech poses the most complex pattern. We know why many people oppose the regulation of begging—they do not view begging as a problem and do not think it should be restricted. Similarly, a number of people, both men and women, oppose the regulation of sexually suggestive or offensive speech between strangers in public places because they see value in it. Sexual banter may lead to amorous relationships between people who meet on the streets.

> I know there's laws against sexual harassment, but I—I don't consider one comment in the street, one comment, as being sexual harassment. I just don't think so. Then you will limit interactions between men and women, then there would be no—no relationships. Somehow you want to tell a lady that she's beautiful, to flatter her . . . (32-year-old African American man, engineer, interview #86)

> Like with the Monica Lewinsky case—sexual, although you know—whatever. But there's such a fine line between sexual harassment and just banter. . . . (19-year-old Chinese woman, lab worker, interview #72).

Some people think that it should not be limited because they find compliments and even sexually suggestive comments, pleasant and flattering:

> If it's meant in a nice way—I mean, everybody is attracted—you know, I'm very much attracted to women and if a very beautiful woman I say looks nice today—
>
> Q: Mm hm. So that wouldn't be social problem?
>
> A: Yeah, you're looking nice . . . but if it goes too far—where you go around slapping women on the butt and all—that's way out of the range. But I don't think it's going to hurt anything. If it's between male and female and it's respectful—I'm all for it. You know what I'm saying? I have nothing against that. I love women, and I love when women tell me how good I'm looking. (34-year-old African American man, laborer, interview #35)
>
> Q: Okay. A woman is walking on a public street and a man whistles, cat calls, and shouts, "looking good." Should this be legal?
>
> A: Uh. Yeah. It's okay. I mean that's not too far—some people may say, "Hey, she's pretty—maybe she doesn't have a boyfriend." Some women are—you know, East Coast women, they don't have a problem with that too much. (23-year-old African American man, office manager, interview #37)
>
> Q: Okay. A woman is walking on a public street and a man whistles, cat calls, and shouts, "looking good." Should this be legal?

A: I have two friends who would welcome that. (30-year-old Asian American woman, executive, interview #46)

Finally, some subjects explicitly mention the difference between begging and sexually suggestive speech.

That's a difficult issue [restricting sexually suggestive speech] because what is a sexually explicit remark to one person may not necessarily be the case to another. It's not as clear-cut as saying, "Do you have a spare quarter?" A person making some kind of comment that I think is inoffensive and someone could consider very offensive.

Q: Right.

A: And so—that's the differences in interpretation between individuals, comes into play. (28-year-old Latino man, sales associate, interview #68)

Sexual access to women differentiates the case of sexually suggestive speech from that of racist public speech and begging. Both men and women want to allow men to "pick up" women. Sexually suggestive speech between strangers in public places may be one way that this occurs. Additionally, according to respondents, there is a near-universal understanding that race-related speech between strangers is never permissible. The ambiguity of the interaction and the difficulties associated with interpretations provide many men and some women with powerful justifications for opposing the legal regulation of sexually suggestive speech, despite personal opinions that the phenomenon poses a personal and social problem. Finally, as I elaborate in the following chapter, a number of women deny the victim status associated with the invocation of law to solve such a problem.

Stories people tell about begging and race-related speech have a consistent character: where people see a social problem, they are likely to believe the law should address it in the absence of a compelling reason. With begging, opposition to regulation is rooted in compassion. With race-related speech, there is recognition that there is little or no value to this form of speech. Those with firsthand experience as targets are willing to consider regulation.

There is no such consistent story about sexually suggestive public speech. Even white men recognize that racist hate speech is a problem, but everyone sees a reason to allow some sorts of sexist harassment. This subject explains it very well:

You can probably assume that people don't want to get comments about their race, but you have the problem with men and women trying to meet. So some borderline sexual comments might be a feeble attempt [to get a date]. (31-year-old Arabic man, student, interview #97)

Why do so many people who perceive race- and gender-based public harassment to be a social and personal problem disfavor the legal regulation of such speech? While I have begun to develop an explanation by examining who favors regulation of such speech, it is necessary to investigate the ideologies that underlie these attitudes. I turn to these ideologies in chapter 5.

Conclusion

Although respondents are in substantial agreement that racist and sexist speech poses a serious problem, the strong majority view is that offensive public speech should not be regulated except in its most extreme forms.[7] When asked generally about the regulation of offensive public speech, only 12% of respondents favored legal regulation. Even when presented with specific examples of the types of speech, only 35% of respondents favor the legal regulation of begging (not shown in tables), 40% favor the legal regulation of sexually suggestive speech between strangers in public, and 37% favor the legal regulation of race-related speech between strangers in public places.

This surface-level agreement masks the diverse underlying reasons subjects gave for opposing the legal regulation of offensive public speech. One possible interpretation of these findings is that most people generally resist the intrusion of law into their lives. They prefer to handle problems, even problems they regard as fairly serious, on their own. Another interpretation of these data is that they vindicate conventional First Amendment theories. Even the "victims" of offensive speech are unwilling (or at least reluctant) to limit public speech because they recognize the value associated with allowing speech. A more critical analysis is that the dominant cultural ideology regarding the First Amendment has a powerful hegemonic effect resulting in strong opposition to the regulation of speech. Because none of these theories is drawn out in the quantitative data, we must look to the discourses respondents use to talk about their opposition to the legal regulation of offensive public speech. In the section that follows, I describe what the respondents say.

Chapter Five

ORDINARY CITIZENS' VIEWS ON THE LEGAL

REGULATION OF STREET SPEECH

IN THIS CHAPTER I explore more deeply the fundamental reasons why subjects often oppose the legal regulation of offensive public speech. In chapter 3, I demonstrated how often street harassment occurs and the profound harm felt by those who are targets. In chapter 4, I showed that subjects frequently report that offensive public speech about race and sex poses a personal and social problem. Indeed many who are *not* frequent targets consider offensive public speech a serious social problem. Despite the fact that people generally view the law as an effective tool for resolving issues of race and gender discrimination, most are not in favor of legal regulation of offensive public speech, even racist and sexually suggestive comments. Moreover, women are slightly *less* likely than men to favor the regulation of sexually suggestive speech between strangers, and people of color are not significantly different from whites in their attitudes about regulating offensive racist speech in public places. This chapter attempts to explain why. I seek an explanation for these apparent contradictions in the patterns of legal consciousness among ordinary citizens.

In this chapter I analyze the legal consciousness of ordinary citizens by examining how experiences with and legal attitudes toward offensive public speech vary by race, gender, and class. Subjects offer a variety of reasons to justify their opposition to the legal regulation of such speech. Members of different racial and gender groups articulate distinctive discourses about offensive public speech and the law that invoke various and competing schemas regarding law. These understandings reflect their prior experiences with the law and their attitudes about the prospects for social change through law. This variation suggests that an explicit comparison of particular legal phenomenon across categories of race, gender, and class provides a more nuanced understanding of legal consciousness. Members of different race and gender groups tend to use different discourses. These differences also suggest that the legal consciousness of ordinary citizens is not a unitary phenomenon, but must be situated in relation to particular types of laws, particular social hierarchies, and the experiences of different groups with the law.

The subjects' own words suggest that there are four relatively distinct paradigms that express grounds for opposing the legal regulation of offensive public speech: First Amendment, autonomy, impracticality, and distrust of authority. The paradigms are not mutually exclusive. Respondents often spoke of many reasons for opposing the legal regulation of offensive public speech. Here I categorize attitudes according to the primary reason respondent gave for opposing the legal regulation of offensive public speech. Almost all of the subjects referred in some way to freedom of speech or to the First Amendment, although it was not always the primary reason for disfavoring the legal regulation of offensive public speech.

I first discuss another important typology of legal consciousness, that was developed by Ewick and Silbey (1998). Then, I discuss the four paradigms I found in the discourses of my respondents. I will discuss each paradigm in turn, after a brief discussion of which groups invoke these paradigms.

Typologies of Legal Consciousness: Ewick and Silbey's, *Common Place of Law*

Legal consciousness research examines the role of law (broadly conceived) and its role in constructing understandings, affecting actions, and shaping various aspects of social life. It centers on the study of individuals' experiences with law and legal norms, decisions about legal compliance, and a detailed exploration of the subtle ways in which law affects the everyday lives of individuals to articulate the various understandings of law/legality that people have and use to construct their understanding of their world.

Legal consciousness also is how people do *not* think about the law. That is to say, it is the body of assumptions people have about the law that are simply taken for granted. These assumptions may be so much a part of an individual's worldview that they are difficult to articulate. Thus, legal consciousness can be present even when law is seemingly absent from an understanding or construction of life events. Because studies of legal consciousness focus on ordinary people and how they view law and its efficacy, this line of research has broad implications for justice, legitimacy, and ultimately social change.[1]

Ewick and Silbey's recent book (1998) represents an important attempt to develop an empirically based theory of legal consciousness. They asked respondents general questions about their lives and the problems they face in their schools, workplaces, and communities, allowing respondents to elaborate whether and how they thought of law's role in these spheres. They thereby allowed the subjects to articulate their understanding of the law and the role that the law might possibly play in various disputes, rather than introduced the concept of law into the interview or limited their interviews to people who already had mobilized the law in one capacity or another. Thus, they explored legal consciousness "organically"—as it came up for the subjects rather than as the researcher defined it. Ewick and Silbey found that there are three general orientations toward law; subjects can be "before the law," awed by its majesty and convinced of its legitimacy. Alternatively, subjects can be "with the law," utilizing it instrumentally when it favors them and generally understanding law to be like a game. Finally, subjects can be "against the law," cynical about its authority and distrustful of its implementation.

Ewick and Silbey's typology is instructive but is not meant to be a discrete set of options to describe the legal consciousness of particular individuals at particular times. Rather, in mapping the terrain of legal consciousness, Ewick and Silbey explain these prototypes as culturally available schema to be referenced and employed in different ways and at different times. And, even as "law" is invoked, not invoked, ignored, and resisted, law is assigned a role in people's everyday lives. These processes of creating "legality" mean that legal consciousness is contingent and changing.

Ewick and Silbey's effort provides important insights into legal consciousness, but leaves some crucial unanswered questions. For example, they hypothesize that orientations toward law will correlate with social status: members of disenfranchised or subordinated groups will be more likely to be "against the law" and to employ methods of resistance to law (1998 p. 235). Yet, as some commentators note, they do not systematically analyze the consciousness of informants by social status (McCann 1999). How does experience with law translate into attitudes and opinions about other areas of law that are not so commonly encountered? Do the three orientations or prototypes of legal consciousness hold true for individuals across problems and contexts? How do established cultural schemas about the law, such as those surrounding the First Amendment, affect legal consciousness, if at all?

While Ewick and Silbey sought to provide an overview of legal consciousness, my project is somewhat different. I constructed an analytic framework to explore variation in legal consciousness according to race, gender, and class. To do so, I thought it necessary to narrow the focus of inquiry and to hold constant certain variables. I inquire about a specific kind of problem, with a particular set of relevant legal categories (although I let the subjects define them), and I ask only about what happens in a particular location. Thus, my study of legal consciousness is situated doctrinally (the First Amendment), with reference to a particular social phenomenon (offensive public speech), and within a particular location (the public sphere).

Ewick and Silbey make a general argument about which types of individuals may be more likely than others to invoke the orientations they describe. I sought to examine this distribution more systematically. The research provides a format to examine the orientations toward law elaborated by Ewick and Silbey's subjects, thereby "testing" the scope of their theory[2] and demonstrating how legal consciousness takes shape with reference to a particular event and across groups.

Because legal consciousness is contingent, it may change according to the area of social life about which the researcher asks, with the social location of the subject, and knowledge about the law and legal norms. Indeed, I suggest that studies of legal consciousness should attempt to describe such contingency—to situate consciousness along these axes rather than treat it as a static set of opinions and attitudes. I designed a sample that allowed me to explore group differences in legal consciousness.

FINDINGS

The data that follow explain the rationales used by respondents as they discuss whether they favor or oppose the legal regulation of offensive public speech. Respondents largely oppose the legal regulation of speech for one of the four reasons described above. However, a relatively small proportion of respondents favored legal regulation of speech. This section explores the rationales of each group beginning with those who favor legal intervention.

Those Who Have No Opinion or Affirmatively Favor the Legal Regulation of Offensive Public Speech

The majority of this chapter is dedicated to exploring the reasons that the vast majority of respondents say they disfavor the legal regulation of offensive public speech. However, as I made clear in chapter four in the discussion of which measure I used, there are respondents who either have no opinion or who affirmatively favor the legal regulation of offensive public speech. Using the midlevel measure, eighteen subjects either express no opinion or favor legal regulation. Who are the eighteen people who fall into none of these paradigms?

Six respondents simply are undecided about whether or not they favor laws to prohibit offensive public speech. These six consist of two white women, one African American woman, and three Asian men. Two of the three Asian men may fall into this category due to language barriers. These two Asian men subjects spoke enough English to answer questions, but not enough to explain the complicated ideas associated with the paradigms.

In addition to the six subjects who were unclear or undecided, twelve people affirmatively favor laws prohibiting offensive public speech, even in its fairly mild forms. These twelve people consist of: one white man, two white women, three African American men, three African American women, one Hispanic woman, one Asian man, and one Asian woman. Although people of both genders and various races are represented in the twelve advocates of laws to regulate offensive public speech, they are concentrated among the African Americans, especially considering the numbers on the sample. Nonetheless, those who favor legal regulation span race and gender categories, which is consistent with the findings in chapter 4 that neither race nor gender alone predict attitudes about the regulation of offensive public speech.

The twelve respondents who favor legal regulation do so for interesting, law-based reasons. These subjects' rationales can be reduced to four themes. The first reason that these respondents favor restricting speech is that they believe they have a "right" to be left alone. Second, some favor the symbolic effect such laws would afford. A third reason for favoring legal intervention in public speech encounters is that subjects believe these remarks often are precursors to violence. Finally, some respondents favor proscriptive laws due to the sheer offensiveness of offensive public speech. Although these respondents are in the minority, their rationales deserve some attention.

RIGHT TO BE LEFT ALONE

The "right to be left alone" is a theme that arose often in the interviews, even for those who do not favor legal intervention. Of course, there is no formal legal "right" to be left alone, but many individuals think there is or should be. They therefore favor laws protecting their personal space—both physical and mental.

> Like, I'm sitting here, all I want to do is get home, and relax, take a nap, maybe, and there's this guy making me pay attention and be alert. (29-year-old white man, student, interview #3)

> That's infringing on my space. [They should] just get a fine for that. That's [a fine] not too dramatic. (51-year-old white woman, unemployed, interview #26)

I just think it's (sexually suggestive or explicit comments) very disrespectful. And it's very uncomfortable. Especially when it's coming from somebody you don't know, and you just feel very uncomfortable. And especially in a public place you feel like you should be protected somehow and somebody's kind of violating [my] privacy . . . [my] ability to go out in a public place—you have that right, and *it's kind of like an infringement of your right, to hear something like that.* (22-year-old Hispanic woman, human resources professional, interview #36, emphasis mine)

[Y]ou have a right to go out and—-*not be . . . uncomfortable.* Because some people feel insulted when they talk to you in that way. I mean, I do. . . . And you feel like you can't do anything about it. (22-year-old Hispanic woman, human resources professional, interview #36, emphasis mine)

These subjects use very legalistic terms in describing their "right." One says that she has a "right" to go out in a public place and another has a "right" not to be spoken to in an offensive tone of voice. Of course, these are not legal rights, but these subjects think of them as politeness norms. These respondents believe they have or should have a legal entitlement to their physical and mental space.

SYMBOLIC EFFECT

Another reason that some individuals favor the use of the law to combat the problem of street harassment is for the symbolic effect these laws would have. For example, after discussing how difficult it would be to prove that an individual had made an offensive remark to them, the following subjects said:

I think even—even just knowing there is a law, I think it would prevent people from—you know, having second thoughts about calling someone a name, a racial name or something, because you never know who's listening. Someone could say this person heard it, this guy called me a racial name. (25-year-old white man, security guard, interview #64)

Um. I don't really think it [a law against offensive public speech] could be enforced, but . . . Just, I mean, idealistically, it should be in there . . . Just kind of like, you know your one vote is not going to count, but you should still do it just because. (19-year-old Asian American man, part-time sales, interview #92)

For these subjects, offensive public speech merits legal attention even though enforcement of such laws would be difficult at best and most likely impossible. The law represents a way to codify social norms and to make the statement that such behavior is socially unacceptable. In addition to symbolic effect, these respondents also think that even the remote possibility of sanctions might deter some potential speakers.

PREVENTING VIOLENCE

Some individuals favor laws prohibiting offensive public speech because they believe offensive speech directly leads to violence. These individuals blur the line between the violence of speech and the violence that could result from such speech.

> I think that [sexually explicit speech] should be limited to people in close contact or something, not a stranger. Because that can lead to other complications, you know—violence and all that—you never know.
>
> Q: Right. You don't know what's going to happen. And do you think there should be legal limitations on race-related speech between strangers in public places?
>
> A: Yeah. For the same reason. You know, it can lead to violence—a violent act or something. (32-year-old African American woman, word processor, interview #81)
>
> A: Yes, there should be [some kind of limitation on race-related speech between strangers]. Right. Because um, if you have something to say, say it behind closed doors, not in public really. What you do behind your closed doors is your business as long as it ain't hurting nobody else. You know, I don't hear it, the whole world don't hear it—it's only between him and God, right?
>
> Q: Mm hm. But in public places, you'd—
>
> A: Yeah, I think they need to chill on that crap, because they could get a whole race war started and it ain't even worth it. (34-year-old African American man, interview #35)

This last respondent views these comments as leading to a very dire situation—a race war. These people are making rational calculations based on their assumptions about what may happen if such speech is allowed to go unpunished.

OFFENSIVENESS

The fourth and final reason that people cite for being in favor of limiting offensive public speech is that they simply find it offensive. Here, it is not the respondents' right to be "left alone" that leads them to favor legal intervention. Rather, it is the right to be free from offense.

> Q: Do you think that there should be any kind of legal limitations on sexually explicit speech between strangers in public places?
>
> A: . . . yes.
>
> Q: And what kinds of restrictions would you be in favor of?
>
> A: Um. Vulgar comments. Um. Vulgar. Vulgar and obscene comments.
>
> Q: Okay. Do you think that there should be legal limitations on race-related speech between strangers in public places?

A: If it's offensive, yes. (43-year-old African-American woman, project manager, interview #45)

Yeah. I definitely think racial slurs should be—there should be a law against racial slurs.

. . . I know under the First Amendment we have the freedom of speech, so that would be a problem. Already people say that would be a problem because the First Amendment gives you freedom of speech, but then there are laws already, like in schools, where you can't use slanderous language, a teacher's not permitted to use slanderous language against a pupil. And pupils, students, can't use it—they can be expelled. So I guess basically, the major law can do the same thing. But then, I don't know, because there's so many people in the world, how could you prove it?

Q: Mm. Hm. If it's from a stranger in a public place.

A: A stranger, right. You'd have to have a witness. Uh huh. But I think even—even just knowing there is a law, I think it would prevent people from—you know, having second thoughts about calling someone a name, a racial name or something, because you never know who's listening. Someone could say this person heard it, this guy called me a racial name. (52-year-old African American woman, professional, interview #90)

All of the subjects who favor legal intervention to prevent racist and sexist speech have strong feelings that they should not be subjected to it. While the reasons these informants offer for regulating offensive public speech appear reasonable in light of the reported scope of the magnitude of harm caused by such speech, theirs is a minority view.

Discourses on Opposing Legal Regulation: Four Paradigms

The unstructured portions of the interviews reveal that respondents offer four "paradigms" for opposing the legal regulation of offensive public speech. The four paradigms, which I document, using the subjects' words, are: the freedom of speech paradigm, the autonomy paradigm, the impracticality paradigm, and the distrust of authority paradigm. Each represents a well-thought-out rationale for disfavoring the legal regulation of speech. Those who make a First Amendment argument say that they disfavor the regulation of any speech due to their allegiance to the principles they think the First Amendment embodies. Those who espouse the autonomy paradigm say that they disfavor the legal regulation of offensive public speech because those are interactions best dealt with by the individual target. Those in the impracticality paradigm say that offensive public speech cannot feasibly be regulated because of resource constraints in every phase of the legal system from law enforcement to the judiciary. Finally, some subjects oppose

TABLE 5.1
Respondents' Primary Reason for Opposing the Legal Regulation of
Offensive Public Speech, by Race and Gender

	First Amendment	Autonomy	Impracticality	Distrust of Authority	Total (N)
Race*					
Whites	46%	22%	28%	4%	100% (46)
People of Color	33%	17%	22%	28%	100% (36)
Gender*					
Women	32%	28%	30%	9%	100% (53)
Men	55%	3%	17%	24%	100% (29)
Race/Gender					
White Men	80%	—	13%	7%	100% (15)
White Women	29%	32%	36%	3%	100% (31)
African American Men	22%	—	22%	56%	100% (9)
African American Women	46%	36%	—	18%	100% (11)
Other Men of Color	40%	20%	20%	20%	100% (5)
Other Women of Color	27%	9%	46%	18%	100% (11)
All	40% (33)	20% (16)	26% (21)	15% (12)	100% (82)

Chi-square significance ** p ≤ .05, *** p ≤ .01
Note: Row totals may not equal 100% due to rounding.

the legal regulation of offensive public speech because they do not believe that such laws would be enacted or enforced fairly by legal officials, reflecting a general distrust of authority.

Paradigms vary by social group. As table 5.1 demonstrates, whites are more likely to say that the First Amendment was their primary reason for opposing the legal regulation of offensive public speech (46%) than are people of color (33%). People of color are far more likely to cite the distrust of authority paradigm (28%) than were whites (4%). Nearly one-third of women cite autonomy as their primary reason for opposing the legal regulation of offensive public speech, whereas only 3% of men do so. Women are more likely than men (30% v. 17%) to say they think such regulation is impractical.

Like Ewick and Silbey, I do not mean to suggest that these categories are static. Indeed, a number of subjects demonstrate the polyvocality highlighted by Ewick and Silbey (1998 p. 52), moving freely from one discourse to another as they justify their opposition to the regulation of offensive public speech. However, because this research is situated with regard to a particular social phenomenon and within particular legal doctrine, these paradigms, or orientations, may be more stable than the categories of legal consciousness Ewick and Silbey elaborate (1998 p. 50). The paradigms capture how these groups of citizens depict the problems associated with the legal regulation of offensive public speech in the current milieu.

FREEDOM OF SPEECH PARADIGM

While many respondents at least mention First Amendment concerns about the legal regulation of offensive speech in public places, only some cited the First Amendment as their primary motive for opposing legal regulation. The most common argument put forth by respondents who fall into the free speech paradigm is what lawyers call the "slippery slope" argument. The reasoning is that if one form of speech is restricted, other, presumably more valuable, speech will ultimately be restricted as well because there is no way to make a principled distinction in content of speech for purposes of regulation. This subject's comments were typical of those who make the layperson's version of the slippery slope argument:

> I don't know, I think it's hard. I think once you start restricting one thing, it can get carried away and you can restrict other things. I guess generally I think that people should just have a little more respect for each other and their own space and stuff. (30-year-old white man, interview #01)

The previous quotation demonstrates recognition of the problem of the slippery slope and offers a nonlegal solution (more respect for each other). The solution is to forget about law and move toward a more "civil" society in which we allow each other space. Consider this example of the slippery slope argument:

> I think there should [be legal limitations on sexually explicit speech in public places], but if they can illegalize that, what else can they?
> Q: So . . . you would be in favor of very limited type legal restrictions, or no legal restrictions?
> A: Probably none. Because once you restrict one, you can restrict others. (18-year-old African American woman, interview #54)

This woman's concerns regarding the First Amendment trump her opinion that there ought (in some ideal world) to be restrictions on sexually suggestive speech between strangers in public places. This subject said that offensive, sexually suggestive speech is a routine and serious problem for her, but one that she thinks should not be addressed by law. Another respondent offers similar analysis:

I think it [sexually suggestive speech between strangers in public places] shouldn't be done. . . . I think it would be best if people didn't do it, and I really wish people wouldn't do it, but I can't say I think it should be illegal because that's a violation of free speech. . . . Part of free speech is taking the good with the bad that comes from it, and I think it is really hard to separate the good from the bad. . . . Because laws like that could be abused [and used to] keep other things silenced. . . . So I think although it is bad, I think it is better to teach people to have more tolerance. . . . rather than take away certain freedoms. . . . Because I like think that *the freedom of speech is the most important thing in this case.* (21-year-old white man, interview #15, emphasis mine)

Both of these subjects appreciate the problems of offensive speech in public places and yet their beliefs about the First Amendment are the primary concern. Although the last subject is clearly troubled by the problem of offensive and even threatening sexually suggestive speech between strangers in public places, his analysis favors allowing this concrete harm rather than risking another, more serious harm.

Many people echo similar concerns about encroaching on free speech, but use more dramatic language to express their fears regarding limiting any form of speech—offensive or otherwise. These people argue that they are not in favor of "censorship" or "thought police." Subjects refer to these concerns and invoke this language even though all of the examples of restrictions proposed in the interview were fairly specific and narrowly tailored. Nonetheless, the way that people immediately conjure ideas about "thought police" demonstrates the absolutist First Amendment philosophy that lives in the minds of some people.

But I really do not like the idea of, huh— *thought police.* (40-year-old white woman, interview #12)

This kind of comment is evidence of the particular veneration afforded the First Amendment in American society. Even narrowly tailored restrictions on some forms of speech are equated with the "thought police." Consider these three subjects' discussion of censorship:

You know—at first if a person doesn't like the comments, they can feel free to walk away. That's a way to get out of that situation, but you can't stop someone from saying something.
Q: Why?
A: Because it's our First Amendment right?
Q: Hm. You mention the First Amendment—for freedom of speech. What do you mean by that? What principle is that supposed to protect, in your opinion?

A: Well, if you were to stop—if you were to stop someone from saying one type of comment because people find it offensive, then the doors open for—to start *censoring* people's speech. (27-year-old white woman, interview #18)

Q: Okay. Do you think there should be any kind of legal limitations on sexually explicit or offensive speech in public places?

A: Speech—no . . . I don't think so. It would spill into other things, I think.

Q: Uh huh. Like what?

A: Well, you've got your freedom of speech, and you don't want to ever encroach upon that I don't think. So preventing someone from saying something they felt they had to get out, and is of a sexual nature, seems it would be, I don't know—*censoring*. (35-year-old African American woman, interview #80)

I'm just afraid that there would be some kind of—that there would be too much *censorship*. That's what I don't want to see, you know. Maybe getting people more educated about other races, but making laws to limit speeches about other races, I don't think that would be good. (32-year-old African American man, interview #86)

All of these comments refer to "censoring" or "censorship" as though any restriction on speech amounts to censorship. In reality, there are any number of examples of speech that are prohibited as a matter of law. It should not be overlooked that many of the subjects who possess more insidious views about censorship are people of color. Indeed, table 5.1 shows that the leading reason people of color reject legal intervention is the First Amendment, followed closely by the reasons elaborated in the "distrust of authority" paradigm—a paradigm invoked by very few white subjects.

Other subjects make rather simplistic, but heartfelt, assertions of rights and freedoms. Their arguments amount to little more than "This is America!" Underlying this argument is the idea that in America, people should enjoy certain freedoms not enjoyed by citizens of other countries in the world.

Well, I know the City of Berkeley does have limitations [on asking strangers for money in public places]. I guess I would like to see some means where they didn't have to ask, but I also legally, I mean, *this is America*, you are supposed to have freedoms. So no, I don't think there should be. (58-year-old white woman, interview #23)

One African American man vigorously defended free speech, even after a lengthy conversation about the extreme forms of offensive public speech he had experienced personally. In order to cross the line to illegal acts, this subject believed that an individual would have to physically threaten or harm another individual or property. According to him, "just" speech or even "just" burning a cross should not be criminal because of the First Amendment.

> Oh. As much as I hate it [extreme forms of racist public speech], I mean, I don't see how that could be illegal. . . .
> Q: Mm hm. And why not?
> A: If . . . he just went and burned a cross in my yard—I don't see how that could be illegal.
> Q: Uh huh. Because of the First Amendment concern?
> A: Right. Exactly. (23-year-old African American man, interview #93)

This subject brings up an important question—at what point does "speech" become an "action" that can be legally restricted? A number of subjects struggled with this question throughout the interview. The law also struggles with this question because it recognizes that many actions, such as burning a draft card, a flag, or even a cross on the front lawn of an African American's home, are acts with sufficient communicative intent to be protected as free speech. There is no easy way to distinguish between speech and action, and any distinction will necessarily be arbitrary and thus problematic. However, a number of subjects tried to make this distinction for purposes of expressing when they thought sexually suggestive or racist speech should be legally curtailed. For these people, restrictions on speech are problematic. But, if these people could restrict actions only, they would be in favor of laws.

> Q: Okay. Now I'd like to ask your views on whether or not these comments should be legal or illegal. Do you think there should be any kind of legal limitation on asking strangers for money in public places?
> A: Uh. No . . . No, I understand the whole free speech thing, and. . . . I really do think, you know, believe in free speech and all that.
> Q: So what would push it over that legal line for you? What type of speech? Or would there have to be an action?
> A: *I think it would have to be an action more than speech.* (27-year-old white woman, interview #62)
> Q: Okay. Do you think that it is legal to make sexually suggestive remarks to strangers in public places?
> A: I think that would depend on if the person is offended by it.
> Q: Okay.
> A: *Or if it's likely to start a fight or something.*
> Q: Right, right. Okay. But short of that—
> A: Short of that they have their right to their opinion and freedom of speech.

Q: Okay. And do you think that it is legal to make race related comments to strangers in public places?

A: Same rules apply, I guess. They have their right to their opinion and freedom of speech. (25-year-old white man, interview #64, emphasis mine)

When words incite actions—that is, when words may cause people to do something—perhaps there should be legal intervention according to this subject. This layperson has intuitively stumbled onto the standard articulated by courts in the clear and present danger test. Of course, this test has its difficulties, but it also has merits for drawing a distinguishing line. In accordance with this distinction, many people (88%) say that they think burning a cross in the front yard of an African American's home should be illegal. The reason? Burning a cross is considered action, not speech, by ordinary people—and action can be legally restricted.

This distinction between speech and action troubles members of the general public as much as it does the courts. Individuals who fall into the First Amendment paradigm acknowledge the price that some people pay for the First Amendment. They expressly acknowledge the harms posed by allowing offensive public speech among these individuals. Some people within the First Amendment paradigm even say that they are personally bothered by such speech, but they nonetheless hold fast to the notion that it would be a worse problem to live in a society with some form of speech restriction.

I—as long as the person who's receiving it is not offended by it—I think, I mean, there are some comments that are good—I mean, it depends on the person who takes it. It depends on the person who's receiving it. If the person feels offended, then there's an issue. But um . . . I think because of a First Amendment issue—freedom of speech allows you to say whatever you want. . . . I think that there shouldn't be a law against that. If they feel they need to express themselves, as long as they don't offend the other — as long as they don't start to cause—*I'm sure it will probably hurt he person's feelings, but as long as they don't cause physical harm, then it's okay.* (23-year-old Asian man, interview #78, emphasis mine)

The crux of this argument is based on a comparison of the harms they contemplate would come from living in a society that has some form of speech restriction with the actual lived harms associated with being the target of offensive racist or sexually suggestive public speech. Those who fall into the First Amendment paradigm weigh these harms and consistently come up with a preference for accepting the harms associated with living in a society with unfettered speech.

On the theory that Americans construct many problems in terms of rights, one might expect the freedom of speech paradigm to cross social groups. Despite the assertion that rights are substantively vacuous (Tushnet 1984), some scholars claim that Americans increasingly talk about and frame disputes in terms of rights (Glendon 1991). Others claim that members of traditionally disadvantaged groups may have a greater stake than relatively privileged people in the use and preservation of rights as a strategic tool in the struggle for equality (see Williams, 1991, p. 233).

My data suggest that none is exactly the case. While it is true that rights-based reasoning underlies much of the opposition to the legal regulation of offensive public speech, this is largely true only for a particular subset of respondents—white males. For others, rights-based reasoning about the First Amendment is not the *primary* reason they disfavor the regulation of offensive public speech. People of color, especially African American men, were far less likely to cite the First Amendment as their primary reason for the opposition to legal regulation of offensive public speech.

How many people make the First Amendment argument and who are they? Thirty-three of the hundred people interviewed stated that free speech was the main reason they oppose the regulation of offensive public speech. Of those thirty-three, more than a majority, twenty-one (64%) are whites. Among whites, the First Amendment was the most common reason given for opposing the legal regulation of offensive public speech. It was given by almost 46% of whites. The First Amendment paradigm was not, however, exclusive to whites. A total of twelve people of color (33%) also reported reluctance to regulate offensive public speech due to their concerns about the First Amendment.

Not only is the First Amendment paradigm largely espoused by whites, it is largely espoused by men rather than women. As table 5.1 shows, only 32% of women claim that the First Amendment is the main reason that they oppose the legal regulation of offensive public speech, while over 55% of men give the First Amendment as their primary reason.

This finding may be due to a number of factors. First, white men are the least likely of all the groups to be the targets of offensive public speech. They may, therefore, bring a more "rational," legally oriented perspective to the issue. Second, when they are the targets of offensive speech, it tends to be begging, the least personally invasive of the forms of speech. Third, white men may not as readily perceive offensive speech as connected to violence as are other members of society. Being removed from the violent and potentially violent aspects of such speech may make white men less likely to recognize its extreme consequences.

THE AUTONOMY PARADIGM

About one-fifth of subjects oppose the legal regulation of offensive public speech due to their feelings about autonomy. As table 5.1 shows, the
autonomy paradigm is almost exclusively espoused by women; of the
sixteen subjects who spoke of autonomy, only one was a man. The autonomy paradigm is based on women's understanding of the phenomenon of street harassment, on their understanding of how best to remedy
the problems of gender inequality, and their views of the proper role of
law in that endeavor. Even women who report being the target of frequent, offensive speech from strangers in public places tend to downplay the seriousness of such interactions when the idea of law was introduced as a possibility for dealing with the problem. These subjects have
a sense that women can control being made the target of offensive public speech. They also say that women do not need lawyers or courts to
fight what should be considered "personal battles."

As chapters 3 and 4 demonstrate, women respondents spend significant time explaining how and why these comments are problematic, classifying them as personal and social problems, and detailing
the complicated actions they take to avoid being made the target of
sexually suggestive speech. Nevertheless, when asked about the possibility for legal intervention, these women respond by explaining strategies used to reduce the impact of unsolicited sexually suggestive comments. In other words, instead of embracing the law to remedy or to
prevent the problems that accompany sexually suggestive street
speech, women prefer to control the situation by reinterpreting the situations as relatively harmless; some women deny that street speech
affects them in any way.

One way that women downplay the significance of sexually suggestive remarks from strangers in public places is by arguing that it is
not as bad as it seems. Some argue that the problem of public sexual
harassment is not as bad in the United States as it is elsewhere in the
world.

> I don't know if it [sexually suggestive or explicit comments between
> strangers in public places] is so much a social problem—because I don't
> think they have to be stopped. I guess I would compare it to—well, one
> time I went to Mexico, and it seemed like there it was a lot more prevalent,
> and in Italy, too—there a lot more. They seem much more open that way,
> with that sort of stuff. So I would guess it is more of an individual prob-
> lem. (35-year-old white woman, interview #34)

This attitude is not evidenced prior to introducing the idea of law
as a legal remedy. When asked only about the interactions, these

women say they are deeply troubled and affected by such comments. In addition to arguing that the law should not intervene because the problem is really not severe, women in the autonomy paradigm disfavor legal intervention because they think that women can avoid being made the target of such speech and can control the situation when they are nonetheless targeted.[3]

The autonomy paradigm is a location in which two powerful normative systems about appropriate gender roles conflict. One role that women must play to conform to social norms about appropriate female behavior is that of the "good girl" (Madriz 1997). The good girl does not invite sexually explicit comments by dressing or acting provocatively or by traveling to inappropriate areas of town (Madriz 1997). The opposing pressure is that of individualism or non-victimization. According to this theory women should be autonomous and self-sufficient and should not tolerate harassing behavior. Self-sufficiency implies taking care of problems on one's own rather than looking to others (men) or to institutions (the legal system) to solve problems of gender inequity. Several women referred to the tension between these two roles, but one subject put it very well:

> I don't think it would be sensible in some ways to make it illegal because . . . if we always try to crack down . . . when are people ever going to . . . defend themselves and speak up for themselves? And I think women really need to do that. And we're definitely not taught to. In fact, we're taught the opposite . . . [in a sing-song tone of voice] "always be nice, and be polite, and respond appropriately," even when the initial comment is inappropriate. And it should be the other way around, where we should feel free to ask for information when we need it and also say, you know, "I think that's an inappropriate comment," and hopefully leave. But there's not always that option of changing your environment. (27-year-old white woman, interview #02)

This woman argues that women should just "leave," but only after telling the speaker exactly what they think of the comments. Note the tension and the appearance of the detailed calculus again. She has two goals: preserve her safety and achieve social change (in that order of priority). Thus, she must make a calculation about whether or not the speaker is truly dangerous (in which case she would simply leave) or if he could safely be reeducated (in which case she responds, "That's an inappropriate comment"). She also struggles with her knowledge that this method of social change will ultimately be ineffective because women are taught to accept obnoxious behavior without comment. She concedes that it is not always possible to change one's environment but when it is possible, it is the woman's responsibility to leave in order to diffuse the situation. It is preferable, in this woman's mind, for the woman to have the burden to diffuse such a situation instead of asking the law to provide some remedy. The following quotation is from a woman who makes similar arguments for "just leaving" when subjected to sexually suggestive comments from strangers in public places:

> I think if you walk away and don't give anybody a chance to even take notice of you for any longer period of time, I don't think there's all that much to be afraid of.
>
> Q: So it sort of depends on the circumstances; being in public helps because you feel like there are other people around.
>
> A: Mm hmm. I feel like if you stay, and take notice, and respond in some way, it might be even more dangerous. (40-year-old white woman, interview #12)

By controlling the situation both ex ante (not letting anyone take notice of her) and ex post (denying to respond), this subject is confident that she can preserve her own personal safety, and she goes on to conclude that therefore the law need not intervene. There is no discussion of the fact that perhaps not all women are able to control their situation as well as she is or any recognition that this burden is one that she need not necessarily shoulder. Another woman expresses similar sentiments:

> Um. I would rather see efforts be put into social programs to get them off the street, and educating the public as to why they're doing that . . . . Besides, I think many of these things can be averted by walking away or dealing with it immediately. (45-year-old white woman, interview #47)

Again, the fact that the woman feels she can control the situation *ex post* by simply walking away contributes to her opinion that the law need not bother with remedying the problem of street harassment. In her mind, money would be better spent educating the targets.

These women articulate the tension between behaving in a way that is socially appropriate (be nice and polite), standing up for oneself (saying "that's an inappropriate comment"), and preserving one's own safety (leaving the situation if possible). A number of women say that they do not want the law to intervene because it would weaken their response and undermine their self-sufficiency.

The fundamental principle that underlies the autonomy paradigm is that women can and should be able to handle these situations on their own. Women who invoke the autonomy paradigm do not even reach the normative question of whether they should have to handle these situations. The fact that these interactions will occur is taken for granted. In this view, the most important thing is that women should not rely on anyone else. Some women were blunt when placing the responsibility for these situations on women:

> A woman . . . can take care of herself. If she doesn't like what a man is saying to her, I think she can turn around and tell him. I think she can stop it if she wants to. (59-year-old white woman, interview #60)

The autonomy paradigm presumes that many problems of gender inequality cannot be resolved effectively by the use of law. In this view, by invoking the law, rather than by dealing with the problem at the individual level, women make themselves appear helpless or as "victims." This posture ultimately would undermine the status of women further.

> We have that right—free speech—so people are going to say what they want to say, you just shouldn't let it bother you. If it doesn't offend you, just keep going on.
> Q: Uh huh. And if it does?
> A: Yeah. Yeah. Just say what you have to say back to him and just go on about your business. (34-year-old African American woman, interview #77)

All of the foregoing quotations demonstrate the idea that women can control these situations by making a retaliatory comment of some fashion. Women have to "come on with attitude" or "turn around and tell him" she does not like what he is saying, or "say what you have to say back to him." Like the subjects who say that the woman should simply leave the situation, the subjects who think the woman should say something and then leave also place the responsibility on the woman to rectify the situation in a way that satisfies her. These subjects feel the law is not there for them, that it cannot help. They also seem to suggest that by answering or walking away, the damage is minimized or disappears altogether. The ability to answer or to walk away allows these women a chance at triumph and vindication, feelings they would be unable to retain if they allow themselves to become "victims" before the law. The irony is that the feelings of triumph and vindication in the moment are followed by fear and anxiety when women consider another outing that may subject them to this sort of speech.

The idea that women should handle these comments on their own is also in sharp contrast to what a number of women said about the perception of danger in these situations.

> I guess being a guy—in this case, being an Asian, I . . . leave it up to the person [the target of offensive comments about race] to deal with it.
> Q: Uh huh. So sort of deal with it on a personal level rather than—

A: Yeah. On a personal level, as opposed to a law level. (23-year-old Asian American man, interview #78)

Q: Mm hm. Do you consider sexually suggestive or explicit comments, or the race related comments to be a social problem?

A: Well, once again I look at it as an individual problem for that person. (29-year-old African American woman, account representative, interview #79)

You know—at first if a person doesn't like the comments, they can feel free to walk away. That's a way to get out of that situation, but you can't stop someone from saying something. (27-year-old white woman, interview #18)

The burden is on women to control the situation ex post (by walking away) because the law cannot stop someone from saying something. Ultimately, the woman must make a calculation about the level of danger in the situation. In addition to maintaining their safety, the "walking away" strategy fosters silence. When it is unsafe to retort, women have no capacity for counterspeech. According to the traditional First Amendment model, counterspeech is the accepted means by which people are supposed to respond to speech they dislike. In the case of offensive sexually suggestive speech, the threat often embedded in the comment fosters just the opposite.

These statements about women being responsible for controlling the situation and downplaying the harm stand in direct contrast to previous statements about how seriously offensive public speech affects their lives and the fear that stems from these interactions. As soon as the idea of law as a potential remedy is introduced, women discount the harm that they have just explained. It is a refusal to admit the problems that they have already detailed. This is what might be called an "antivictimization feminism" in which power or feminism is derived from or requires that one not define oneself as a victim.

Prior studies of legal consciousness also have found that the invocation of antidiscrimination law is equated with labeling oneself a victim. The concern about being labeled a victim serves as one of the most serious barriers to mobilizing the law in the context of civil rights (Bumiller 1988). Bumiller's subjects had (or at least arguably had) a legal claim. In the context of offensive public speech, on the other hand, we see that the same thinking is present even where subjects lack a legal remedy that would aid them. Indeed, it prevents individuals from being able to conceive of having a legal remedy. Here, the desire to appear strong and not to be labeled a victim justifies the absence of a legal remedy.

Some men share the view that women would be hindered, rather than helped, by laws to prevent sexually suggestive speech between strangers in public places, some men made derogatory comments about women who would be in favor of such laws. Comparing the case of public sexual harassment to workplace sexual harassment, one man said:

[E]very time something happens, especially with sexual harassment—they [women] run to "big daddy court," and "big daddy court" helps us out. I feel like, in a situation like this, with a man or a woman, whoever's making the comment, put them aside . . . in a safe place where we could talk about it, where we could address the issue. Not just go directly to the employer, or go to the lawyer and say, "I want to sue this person because he . . . said something derogatory." (26-year-old Asian man, interview #84)

These men agree that running to "big daddy court" only makes women appear weak; handling the situation in the moment is the best way to proceed if one is interested in achieving gender equality.

Women who invoke the autonomy discourse make rational arguments against legal intervention in the area of public speech and in gender relations more generally. They make this judgment based on their assessment of the magnitude of the harms posed by street harassment. When they compare the harms of street harassment to what they consider to be the more serious problems of gender equality such as equal pay or sexual harassment in the workplace, offensive public speech is relatively unimportant. Additionally, these women believe, perhaps correctly if the statements of some of the men are to be believed, that utilizing the law to enforce equality claims makes them appear weaker in the eyes of men and other women.

The thinking that underlies the autonomy paradigm ignores the broader social apparatus of gender subordination and chooses to view street incidents as isolated from the social institution of sexism. The autonomy paradigm reflects competing expectations for women's behavior. Women must choose between being a "good girl" and being autonomous. These women choose autonomy, adhering to traditionally masculine norms about self-sufficiency despite life experiences with street speech that differ significantly from that of men. These women claim significant harms when reporting stories of street harassment, and yet as "equal" members of society, they have and want no legal recourse for this harm. The price of citizenship, according to women in the autonomy paradigm, is that one must stand up for oneself, rather than rely on state intervention in the face of these affronts to dignity.

It is difficult to determine if these women would view the problem of street harassment differently if it were recognized as a legally action-able harm; the absence of a legal remedy may partly account for their reluctance to construct one. Until recently, workplace sexual harass-ment was a common problem considered by many simply to be part of the employment landscape for women. And, many people resisted the imposition of laws designed to correct this abuse because they thought women should be able to handle it on their own and that there would be a backlash that would ultimately disserve the interests of women in the workplace.

The autonomy paradigm thus represents a "boundary of law." Of-fensive sexually suggestive speech between strangers in public places represents the point at which many women are willing to say the law should not intervene. This may be due, in part, to the seeming legiti-macy of the status quo. In other words, because there is currently no law, women within the autonomy paradigm think there ought be no law. The law not only defines what *is*, but it also constructs what these women think *is possible*, at least in part. Nonetheless, women in the autonomy paradigm articulate rational reasons for the construction of such a boundary.

The women in the autonomy paradigm acknowledge the harms as-sociated with offensive public speech. But, in their experience, laws intending to protect women actually work in the reverse. Thus, women within the autonomy paradigm are quite instrumental about the use of law. If they thought it would work and would not create the unin-tended "backlash" effect, they might be in favor of such laws. Or, they might favor such laws if they felt the harms of lewd speech were greater. But, their experiences with law attempting to mediate gender issues do not make them think it would work in this case.

IMPRACTICALITY

The third rationale subjects invoked to oppose the legal regulation of offensive public speech is the sheer impracticality of catching, trying, and punishing individuals who would violate such laws. In general, people within the impracticality paradigm express concerns about en-forcement in the streets and enforcement in the courts.

Enforcement in the Street. Those concerned with enforcement in the street think that it would be difficult to find police officers to apprehend viola-tors of proposed anti–hate speech regulations. One woman said:

> I just can't imagine that [arresting or otherwise punishing people for mak-ing race-related remarks]. It would just tie up too much time for the police. No. (53-year-old white woman, interview #21)

Others within the impracticality paradigm report that the nature of the comments—the fact that the comments are made quickly and quietly by strangers—makes it difficult even to identify the person who made the comment, thereby making apprehension (and later proof) very difficult. Consider this woman's story:

> I was walking to work, or, my bus stop a couple of weeks ago, and there was an older Caucasian man—he's a homeless man—*he came up really close, in fact, he was right up against my side, and um, he kind of made eye contact. I was startled because I turned right around into his face*, and he said, "You're a very pretty girl, very pretty girl." . . . There were a lot of people around so . . . I didn't feel immediately threatened by it, but it was definitely intrusive. (24-year-old Asian American woman, interview #100, emphasis mine)

This woman's story is not uncommon, and it illustrates the difficulty of apprehending violators reported by respondents. Offensive speech often is accomplished in very private ways despite the broader public contexts in which these interactions occur. The ways some speakers create a small, private environment in which they have the freedom to say such things makes the targets, familiar with these techniques, skeptical about enforcing laws against such speech. The private and hidden nature of the act and the concurrent problems with proof are notorious in the area of date rape and workplace sexual harassment. Perhaps experience with these areas of law partly explains the reason that these subjects are reluctant to impose laws preventing such behavior.

Even if arrests and identifications could be made, some respondents within the impracticality paradigm are concerned that enforcement of a law prohibiting offensive public speech would burden the courts. These subjects base their opinion on the pervasiveness of the problem and the relatively minor harm they associate with offensive public speech. They question whether it is worth it to impose on an already overburdened legal system.

> [I]t probably wouldn't do much, kind of like a jaywalking law, and it would tie up . . . precious court time and our taxpayer money essentially, so we wouldn't win anyway. (23-year-old African American man, interview #23)

Despite enforcement difficulty and cost, many laws on the books routinely are enforced. For example, think of almost any crime committed in private places. How do the police monitor what occurs in private spaces? Nevertheless, the laws exist and are enforced because the regulated behaviors (spousal assault and drug dealing to name just two) are considered to be troubling for society. In addition, laws often are passed for symbolic and deterrent effects. Simply having a law on the books (whether or not it is enforced) may discourage some behaviors and conveys a message of societal disapproval for certain conduct. Nonetheless, those within the impracticality paradigm are not in favor of laws they think would be impossible to enforce.

The impracticality paradigm is interesting, in part, because many subjects make the argument that there *ought* to be laws prohibiting such remarks, but concerns about the inability to enforce such a law overwhelm this normative belief. Consider this woman's comments:

> I don't know how you would do that [enforce laws prohibiting offensive public speech]. Because you can't have a policeman on every corner—*I think you should be arrested for that. . . . But like I say, that's impossible. Because we can't have a policeman everywhere in the city.* (51-year-old white woman, interview #26, emphasis mine)

This woman firmly believes that making racist comments to strangers in public places should be a criminal offense. She does not think that the First Amendment provides a barrier to the criminalization of it. Her reservation about a legal remedy is based on her opinion that the police would be unable to enforce such a law.

Another facet of the impracticality argument addresses the reality of a society in which perpetrators of very serious offenses are not always apprehended. Despite a belief that these sorts of comments should be illegal, some subjects think that police attention should not be diverted from more serious matters:

> [G]ranted, it's a problem, it's a burden, it's an annoyance to the general public, but to lock someone up for that kind of offense . . . when there are people committing like murders or assault. I mean, I would rather see those people put behind bars. (28-year-old Latino man, interview #68)

These comments represent an implicit ordering of criminal wrongdoing. This subject has made a calculation about what crimes or actions he would prefer to see the police, courts, and corrections system focus on. As long as there are more serious offenses occurring that demand official attention, offensive public speech will have to wait.

Enforcement in the Court. Even if arrests and identifications could be achieved, some respondents are concerned that enforcing a law prohibiting offensive public speech would burden the court system. These subjects are also making informed judgments based on the pervasiveness of the problem and the relatively minor harm they associate with the phenomenon of offensive public speech. They question whether an additional burden on the court system is worth it.

[I]t probably wouldn't do much, kind of like a jaywalking law, and it would tie up—when it did work it would be a waste of time tying up precious court time and our taxpayer money essentially, so we wouldn't win anyway. This way, we can say, "No, I'm not giving you any change." But if there was a law passed to that effect, then we would be paying out of our tax dollars for more court cases, more court time—a waste of money. (23-year-old African American man, electronics salesman, interview #93)

This man equates the harms associated with street harassment of the begging variety to the harms associated with jaywalking and says that it would amount to a waste of money to pursue such cases. His argument is also predicated on a belief that the harms associated with offensive public speech are relatively incidental. As another informant suggested:

Q: . . . Do you think there should be any kind of limitation on asking strangers for money in public places?
A: Um . . . it doesn't help. . . . I mean, what's the use of throwing them into jail? I mean, it's really a burden on the society, I don't think—it's not very cost effective at all.
Q: Right. Do you think there should be any kind of legal limitation on sexually explicit speech between strangers in public places?
A: Um. I think it's very hard to draw a line. I mean, if there's going to be a law, it's very hard to enforce, so I mean, it's not very feasible. (30-year-old Asian woman, lawyer, interview #83)

The last part of the comment is very important. She says, "It's very hard to enforce, so it's not very feasible." She makes the leap from the view that the law would be difficult to implement to, therefore, we should not have the law. This may or may not be true. There are many laws on the books that are more difficult to enforce. For example, think of crimes committed in private places. How do the police monitor what occurs in private homes? Nevertheless, we have these laws because the behaviors regulated (spousal assault, drug dealing) are considered to be so troubling for society. Additionally, we occasionally pass laws for their symbolic and deterrent effects. Simply having a law on the books may discourage some behaviors or ensure that a strong societal message of disapproval is relayed to citizens concerning certain actions.

Still others believe that law is not a practical way to solve the problem of offensive public speech because the problem is not with the interaction itself, but the social hierarchy the interaction manifests. These subjects fundamentally believe that the law cannot change the way that people think (or change the beliefs of a racist or sexist individual). In their view, law is not a viable solution.

> I don't think it's an issue of free speech. No. . . . But it just seems kind of ludicrous, because I don't see how you'd ever enforce it; I think it would clog the courts with tons of people.
>
> Q: Mm hm. Okay. Do you think there should be any kind of legal limitation on race related speech between strangers in public places?
>
> A: Well. I think racism should—well, I guess—see—
>
> Q: It's a tough issue.
>
> A: Um. I think in general, I'm not in favor of—I don't think that having laws against things is the way to solve them. I think these are all—well, let's see—at least the race issue, is a social issue that's a larger problem in society, and I don't think having laws prohibiting people to do things is a way to address that issue. (21-year-old white woman, student, interview #74)

Regarding the racist attitudes of some members of society, others believe that censoring such speech will impede social change rather than aid it. In other words, they see the racist or sexist comments made at them by strangers as opportunities to teach the bigoted individuals about that speech. By restricting these remarks, the law would actually foreclose opportunities to combat racism.

> Because if people keep their feelings in then they will never learn. Like if they can't express their feelings—like for instance if someone comes up to me and says something [racist], and I come back at them with knowledge, and give them maybe a little bit of understanding and compassion, then that helps them. But if they keep it bottled up, you know, then they're not going to go anywhere. I'd have to say it's okay to do that. I'd rather someone told me that—you know how many times I wish I could tell someone is looking at me funny and I wish they'd just tell me so I could talk to them, you know—
>
> Q: Because there's no way to respond—
>
> A: There's no way—if they don't say anything—there's no way to state my position or—you know, expand their mind or horizon at all when they keep it bottled up. So I would say no [to laws that restrict offensive racist speech]. (23-year-old African American man, electronics salesman, interview #93)

From the street to the courthouse, these subjects do not think law will work because it simply cannot. Over 27% of whites in this sample fall into the impracticality paradigm, whereas only about 8% of African Americans and 22% of all people of color do so. Similarly, among these respondents, women are far more likely to cite impracticality as their primary reason for opposing offensive public speech than are men, with almost 30% of women citing impracticality while 17% of men do so. Practicality is an important consideration for white women. White men may not express practicality concerns because they adopt the First Amendment model, while African American men do not reach practicality concerns because they tend to adopt the distrust of authority model.

DISTRUST OF AUTHORITY/CYNICISM ABOUT LAW

The final reasons respondents give for opposing the legal regulation of offensive public speech stem from a general distrust of authority and cynicism about law. The distrust of authority paradigm connects past experiences with law and legal actors to the issue at hand—regulating offensive public speech. These responses are predicated on the belief that the law cannot really help or actually will be used against those it was intended to protect. As table 5.1 shows, the distrust of authority paradigm is widely held among African American men in this sample. Although some African American women echoed this concern, the idea that eventually the law would be used against those it was designed to protect is largely absent from the discourses of white respondents.

The cynicism and pragmatism paradigms are similar. In both, subjects believe the law cannot affect changes in the behavior of others or in a broad social sense. What distinguishes those who primarily engage in a discourse of cynicism from those in the impracticality paradigm is that those who are cynical base their opinions on past bad experiences with the law or legal actors. These respondents believe they were treated unfairly or dismissed completely in past interactions, and this serves as the basis for their opinions about the law.

For example, despite frequent instances in which she was the target of offensive sexually suggestive speech in public places, one subject was skeptical of laws prohibiting such behavior, not because of her commitment to the First Amendment, but because of her cynicism about law's ability to alter behavior. Her cavalier attitude toward the First Amendment was typical of many white women and people of color. Consider this woman's comments about the efficacy of laws prohibiting sexual harassment in the workplace and how her experiences there affect her thinking about the prospect of restricting street speech:

> Well, yeah, the First Amendment and all that. . . . But, you know, even if it were illegal, it wouldn't do anything. I mean this kind of thing has been going on forever. I mean, sexual harassment in the workplace, I mean, *I have been harassed at every job I have ever had and it's illegal*, but it doesn't do any good. (19-year-old Latina woman, interview #06, emphasis mine)

Clearly, she has little hope for the law to change behavior, much less affect broad-based social change. She bases her opinion on her experiences with another form of sexual harassment—that which occurs in the workplace. Laws intended to protect her in that setting have not worked to her benefit and the mere existence of these laws has not made her work life any more tolerable.

Others in the cynicism paradigm simply do not believe that any action the government could take would translate into altered behavior on the part of those who engage in offensive public speech:

I don't see how . . . a total stranger coming up to you and saying something totally derogatory, sexually or racially, and he gets fined for how many dollars or thrown in jail or whatever. I don't see how that would actually make him learn or make him understand that it's not the right thing to do. (26-year-old Asian man, interview #84)

This man believes that if the law cannot make the individual understand that sexual comments or sexual harassment in public places are not the "right thing to do," then the law should not be employed to control such behavior. He thinks the ultimate goal is to teach tolerance and understanding and that the law is not the effective mechanism for doing so.

Others have a more insidious view, believing not just that the legal system would be ineffective, but that "the system" itself is corrupt and would therefore not work to achieve the goal of eliminating racist and sexist speech.

Well, the dilemma I'm in is that I think the whole [legal and political] system is so bad and so rotten that uh—making it larger doesn't make a lot of sense. I think the whole thing needs to be—I think we need to scrap this one and start over. (59-year-old African American woman, interview #85)

African American men tell sadly familiar tales of unjust police actions that lead them to question the implementation of any law designed to protect them from racially harassing speech. Others within the distrust of authority paradigm discuss legal and political institutions and their view that they are corrupt and unhelpful. One African American man said, "They're never going to enforce laws like that anyway. Look at affirmative action—it's all going away anyhow." (32-year-old African American man, business professional, interview #89)

Even if such a law could be passed, he is skeptical about enforcement. After all, affirmative action was designed to help people like him, and in California, where these subjects were recruited, affirmative action had recently been eliminated by the electorate in a ballot initiative. Uncertainty about remedy makes this subject and the others who fall into this paradigm skeptical about the future of laws designed to protect the disadvantaged from certain classes of harms.

The deeply engrained social status hierarchy leads to a different sort of legal consciousness—one in which victims are so accustomed to being victimized, rather than aided, by law that they view a remedy by law as untenable. This problem takes many different forms. First, the recipients of the harassment feel their cause will go unheard. Second, these subjects fear some sort of harm befalling them if they report the situation. Third, they cannot believe any help will truly come to such a degree that reporting is seen as a ridiculous waste of time. Fourth, these mostly African American men harbor such a resentment and distrust of police that they must first overcome that consciousness before they could begin to see the law as an ameliorative tool.

Subjects also mentioned a final twist on the cynicism paradigm: the law cannot and does not change society. A number of subjects spoke about the inefficacy of courts and legal actors to force social change. There is also a cynicism about society as it is reflected in the law:

> Yeah. I think that they should all be legal because I don't think that the comments themselves are the problem. I think that they're symptoms of a greater problem that is sort of lies behind them. And I feel like it would actually be more dangerous to silence the symptoms of deeper problems, and not have that evidence that a problem exists. Then just to make the symptom go away. . . . I mean, it is like taking Tylenol for a broken leg instead of just setting the leg. Or like—and then if you keep taking Tylenol or morphine, or whatever your drug of choice is, you're never going to know that your leg is broken. You're never going to get to the problem. And I mean, that's, I feel like, [laugh] I feel like begging is a symptom of poverty, and you know, racist, sexist and homophobic speech are symptoms of racism, sexism and homophobia, and you know, if somebody calls me a "white bitch" who's black, it is probably because they've been the recipient of those kinds of comments or violence themselves. And like, I just don't think it is a good idea to silence that stuff. (29-year-old white woman, interview #16)

This quotation demonstrates how some subjects are cynical about the law not because the law is necessarily powerless and ineffective but because the social institutions of racism and sexism that these laws would be attempting to rectify are so omnipotent and powerful that they are unable to imagine that laws will have any effect on changing them.

The cynicism paradigm, like the autonomy paradigm, is based on rational beliefs. In some ways, it is more rational than the First Amendment paradigm. Those who invoke the First Amendment paradigm have little or no empirical evidence that restricting speech is actually harmful. In fact, in several European countries, speech protections are not nearly as stringent as in the United States, and freedom of speech is still upheld and respected in those countries. Those who fall into the cynicism paradigm recount past experiences that demonstrate, in these subjects' opinions, the futility of laws designed to protect their interests—or worse, that the behavior of legal officials often hurts their interests.

These individuals point out the obvious yet important fact that law does not create and enforce itself. People create laws, police enforce laws, and courts impose punishment for the violation of these laws. Those within the cynicism paradigm have experience at all three points in the administration of laws. These experiences inform their assessment about the possible efficacy of laws designed to prevent racist street harassment.

Toward a Theory of Situated Legal Consciousness

Both attitudes about and experiences with offensive public speech are complex. There are significant differences across groups in experience with offensive public speech. White women and people of color are far more likely to experience racist and sexist speech from strangers in public than are white men. Members of traditionally disadvantaged groups are more likely to view these interactions as personal problems. However, whether offensive public speech is viewed as a social problem does not vary by group—there is near unanimity that racist and sexist speech pose serious social problems, while relatively few subjects think begging does. Moreover, there appears to be a near consensus that law should *not* regulate offensive public speech.

This near-unified opposition to the regulation of offensive public speech masks the variation in citizens' reasoning about the problem and the role of law in dealing with it. Accordingly, analysis of offensive public speech that does not probe beyond opinion research would be somewhat misleading. Although it is possible to explore opinions about legal intervention and street harassment (or any other social problem, for that matter) and to find patterns (in this case, that people generally disfavor the use of the law to remedy this social problem), such research does not provide the insight that a more nuanced study of legal consciousness provides. This surface consensus opposing the regulation of speech obfuscates the underlying differences that tell an important story about the law, legality, the role of these in people's lives, and how their experiences in one area may sometimes provide the basis for general attitudes toward law, legal institutions, and legal actors.

It is only through an examination of ordinary citizens' discourses that a fuller picture of legal consciousness as it relates to offensive public speech emerges. There is *not* unanimity across social groups as to why people disfavor the legal regulation of offensive public speech. The white males in this sample are most likely to disfavor legal intervention because of traditional First Amendment values. African American male subjects are more likely to disfavor legal regulation due to distrust of authority and cynicism about law generally. Among these respondents, women were far more likely than men to argue that offensive public speech should not be legally regulated because to do so would present them as victims and further undermine their social status or because it is "impractical." The fact that subjects are not randomly distributed across these reasons for opposing the legal regulation of offensive public speech suggests that the social location of subjects plays an important role in shaping their attitudes on this topic specifically and perhaps on legal consciousness more generally.

My purpose is to explore situated legal consciousness and map variation across social groups, and as such, these data do not provide a basis for a competing system to Ewick and Silbey's model of legal consciousness (1998). Rather, these findings emphasize the value of studies of legal consciousness that hold constant legal doctrine and social phenomenon to better understand variations in legal consciousness. Each of the paradigms reported bears some relationship to Ewick and Silbey's general orientations. Those within the First Amendment paradigm are not unlike Ewick and Silbey's subjects who are classified as "before the law" (1998, p. 79), privileging law above even their own life experiences. Women within the autonomy paradigm espouse a legal consciousness similar to Ewick and Silbey's subjects who are "with the law," treating law instrumentally to serve their purposes when it can be made to do so. In their analysis, offensive public speech is not one such arena. Those within the distrust of authority paradigm are not dissimilar to those within Ewick and Silbey's "against the law" model. Ewick and Silbey's subjects recount frustrations dealing with the law on a variety of topical matters from welfare and social security to the criminal law, and complain that the law and legal actors downplay or ignore the needs of some people. These data demonstrate the lived truth of this orientation toward law.

Studies of legal consciousness that elaborate typologies of legal consciousness demonstrate variation in it (Ewick and Silbey 1998), but how do we account for this variation? These data go beyond describing general orientations toward the law to trace the factors that influence how people arrive at their general position vis--vis the law, demonstrating that people make connections from their past experiences—good or bad—which arise in part from the social position which they occupy, and how these experiences shape their understanding of law. The social location of subjects and experiences that arise from those locations are a vital part of our understanding of legal consciousness. From these data, we learn that being a member of a traditionally disadvantaged group has a significant effect on how an individual is likely to be oriented toward the law.

These data also clearly demonstrate that one factor that affects legal consciousness is past experiences with law and legal actors. And, we know that past experiences with law and legal actors are closely related to social location. Life experiences are different for members of different social groups. Obviously, experiences in which one is the target of offensive public speech increase if one is a member of a traditionally disadvantaged group. Many women report a "backlash" effect when they invoke the law to solve "gender" problems; many African Americans, especially men, report indifference, corruption, and blatant racism in their brushes with law. These experiences both with life and with law affect their legal consciousness, and these data demonstrate how subjects relate such experiences to offensive public speech and the First Amendment.

Because the data demonstrate that many people disfavor legal intervention to solve the problem of offensive public speech, one reading is that the law is nowhere in these interactions. I argue exactly the opposite. Although most subjects denounce the idea of introducing the law to solve what they perceive to be a serious social problem, their reasoning nonetheless was based upon their understanding of "law" in the broadest terms. Legal consciousness affects not only how people think about invoking the law or the general utility of law, but also how people interpret events in their everyday lives. The law shapes what remedies respondents believe are possible and plausible, as well as respondents' understanding of these common everyday events, as a troubling yet unavoidable and unremediable part of social life.

By asking about offensive public speech, rather than law, as the interviews began, I was able to explore the phenomenon of street harassment, to understand how people make sense of such interactions, and to observe that the law was prominent in this understanding for most subjects even before I introduced law as a topic in the interviews. Most subjects believed (probably correctly) that speech—even offensive public speech—is legally protected. The legality of speech is the primary mechanism through which subjects transform what they describe as a significantly troubling experiences into something that simply should be tolerated. Some say this speech must be tolerated as the price of a free society; others say the police could not or would not enforce these laws anyway. Still others propose tolerating such events because making speech illegal transforms targets into "victims" and thereby reinforces their subordinate status in society. Even without inquiring about the law, it is obvious that law affects what ordinary people think is possible as a remedy for this social problem.

Even as law was specifically denounced or ignored as a possible solution for the problems associated with offensive public speech, and as individuals explained that they thought there ought be no laws prohibiting it, these beliefs were couched in and explained with reference to subjects' understandings of law. None of these subjects could or did understand offensive public speech outside their understanding of the law, even though conceptions about the influence of law varied dramatically.

The different discourses and the complex reasoning that underlies each demonstrate that respondents understand law and their position within it, perhaps better than either absolutists or critical theorists. Attention to differences in social location and careful consideration of the life experiences of members of different social groups leads to a clearer understanding of the role of law in the everyday lives of ordinary citizens.

FALSE CONSCIOUSNESS AND LEGAL CONSCIOUSNESS

The autonomy paradigm could be read as a version of a "false consciousness" argument. As Catharine MacKinnon argues, "when you are part of a subordinated group, your own determination of your injuries is powerfully shaped by your assessment of whether you could get anyone to do anything about it, including anything official" (1987 p. 105). This argument holds that sexism is so deeply ingrained in society that women are essentially unaware of the ways in which they are sexually subordinated and are thus unable to make rational judgments about their best interests regarding how to overcome such discrimination. Proponents of the theory of false consciousness would argue that although most women disfavor the legal regulation of offensive public speech, this judgment is clouded; laws should be enacted to combat sexually suggestive speech between strangers in public places because without powerful institutional support to combat the social structures that reinforce sexism, no change is likely to result. Critics of this view make the autonomy argument, saying that women are the best judges of whether laws are effective in such matters.

Women who think of themselves as autonomous do not think the law will do anything about the problem, so they downplay the harms associated with such speech and unrealistically overemphasize their ability to handle it on their own. What women might think is in their best interests reinforces the status quo. The misperception of women about their own social status results from basic social structures and institutions that obscure options for women.

Whether or not targets of offensive public speech suffer "false consciousness" is important but, ultimately, very difficult to know and impossible to empirically test. It is clear, however, that the false consciousness perspective fails to accept or to account for the lived experiences of women. Both learned feminist scholars and ordinary women who contemplate the status of women in American society have opinions about the best way to achieve social change and improve gender relations. The opinion that the law is not the appropriate mechanism for remedying social ills is shared by formal equality feminists. These scholars believe that providing any remedy specific to gender ultimately disserves women because it tends to reify differences between the sexes and thus ultimately serves to reinforce women's subordinated social position. Rather than attempt to determine if targets suffer a form of "false consciousness," I seek to explore their legal consciousness, which I believe results from their attempt to resolve competing notions of appropriate social roles.

Part of better understanding the offensive public speech, legal consciousness, and false consciousness requires an analysis of people's self-help mechanisms. In other words, if targets do not look to law because they prefer instead to handle offensive public speech on their own, we must understand what responses and reactions targets have, what motivates their reactions and responses, and how they feel about them when the interactions have ended.

Conclusion: Solving Problems on the Street

These data demonstrate that respondents share a belief that the law should have little role in solving problems associated with offensive public speech, but for very different reasons. Underlying all of these rationales, and quite explicit in the autonomy and First Amendment paradigms, is the idea that targets should be able to handle the problem of offensive speech on their own in the moment. In the next chapter, I look to how often these sorts of "solutions" are employed in public places, detailing the reactions and responses respondents report when they are made targets of offensive public speech.

Chapter Six

POWER IN PUBLIC

REACTIONS, RESPONSES, AND RESISTANCE TO

OFFENSIVE PUBLIC SPEECH

As OTHER RESEARCHERS have demonstrated and as I elaborate in chapters 2 and 3 of this book, white women and people of color regularly encounter offensive racist and sexually suggestive speech (Davis 1994; Duneier 1999; Feagin 1991; Gardner 1995; Nielsen 2000). Moreover, there is both empirical evidence and commentary that suggests that such speech is harmful to its targets (Delgado 1993; Feagin 1991; Landrine and Klonoff 1996). Chapters 3 and 4 show that the vast majority of subjects say that offensive sexually suggestive or racist speech in public places poses a personal and social problem.

Nonetheless, both the formal law and individuals claim that it is not proper for law to intervene in offensive public speech encounters, at least those that revolve around racist and sexist speech. In fact, chapter 5 shows that most people disfavor the use of law for redressing the harms associated with being the target of offensive public speech (Nielsen 2000). Individuals have competing stories as to why they do not think the law should intervene to prohibit offensive public speech, but most respondents indicate that racism and sexism, when manifested this way, can and should be handled by its targets. White men are most likely to disfavor legal intervention because of traditional First Amendment values. African American men are more likely to disfavor legal regulation due to distrust of authority and cynicism about law generally. Among these respondents, women were far more likely than men to argue that offensive public speech should not be legally regulated because to do so would present them as victims and further undermine their social status or because it is "impractical."

If racist and sexist speech encounters are problematic, it is important to understand how targets react to such speech. The narratives about the refusal to involve law seem to indicate that targets are willing to handle these problems on their own. This chapter asks: How do targets react to racist and sexist speech? Does this differ from how targets deal with begging? Do targets have standard responses that reflect their resistance to racism and sexism? The empirical data show that targets of racist and sexist hate speech do little to resist the systems of domination employed and invoked in such encounters. The reinscription of hierarchies of race and gender goes on in public places largely unchallenged by targets. Some targets actively resist by engaging the speaker physically or verbally, but the vast majority, and almost all the women, do not. Moreover, when targets do something to indicate their distaste for such comments and their rejection of the racist and/or sexist worldview, the mechanisms of resistance are difficult to analyze.

Begging provides a unique comparison case. It is not only individuals who are the target of begging who respond and resist but also municipalities, merchant organizations, and the police. Resistance to begging (unlike resistance to racist and sexist street speech) comes backed by the force of the state. Merchants mobilize their economic power to urge municipalities to pass laws to protect business and tourism, and the police enforce the laws against beggars.

The data that make up this chapter focus on reactions and responses to problematic public speech of all three varieties. I demonstrate that when the interactions are directed at people who are more privileged, both formal and informal options for resistance and prohibition are available. I theorize the reactions and responses in the resistance literature with an emphasis on the power relationships of the involved parties.

Law's Recipe for Resistance

The law's story as to why legal intervention in such interactions is improper centers on allowing speakers' freedom; the remedy for the offended target, according to conventional First Amendment theory/doctrine, is "more speech" in the face of racist or sexist remarks from strangers. In a famous dissenting opinion, Justice Oliver Wendell Holmes first elaborated the "free trade in ideas" (*Abrams v. U.S.* 1919). Holmes said, "the best test of truth is the power of the thought to get itself accepted in the competition of the market." Relying on the metaphor of the free marketplace, the jurisprudential answer to offensive speech is more speech.

Although there are notable exceptions (Delgado and Stefanic 1994; MacKinnon 1993; Matsuda, Lawrence, Delgado, and Crenshaw 1993; Meiklejohn 1948), many legal scholars advocate unfettered free speech, claiming that individuals who are offended or harmed by speech can (and should) counter these bad effects with various kinds of "more speech" (Abel 1998; Chevigny 1988; Post 1990). But what kind of more speech? What speech effectively counters the "truth" of a racial epithet or sexual slur? And how realistic is it to expect the target to engage the speaker? In some contexts, more speech may be just what is called for. Organized counterspeech is documented and advocated as a remedy in the face of organized racist hate speech, as when the Nazis march through Skokie (Abel 1998; Downs 1985). In this organized, policed environment, counterspeech may be effective and safe. But what of the victim of individual, targeted hate speech in public?

The "more speech" solution to problems associated with racist speech has been criticized by a number of scholars on various grounds. First, the original speech is said to be "silencing," meaning that the target/ potential responder is overwhelmed so that she cannot engage in effective counterspeech (MacKinnon 1993; Matsuda, Lawrence, Delgado, and Crenshaw 1993). The "more speech" solution also is criticized because it places on members of traditionally disadvantaged groups the burden of rectifying a socially undesirable set of thoughts or actions— a burden we carry with us every time we step out of our homes (Lederer and Delgado 1995a). Finally, the "more speech" solution is criticized as impractical; the threat of violence makes it unlikely that anyone—even the bravest—will confront a racist with conviction so deeply held that s/he is willing to violate all social norms and address a stranger in public (Goffman 1971), using a racial epithet. In what follows, I empirically examine the possibility of "more speech" in the context of these interactions—face-to-face encounters in public places involving racist or sexist hate speech. These empirical data are a starting point for understanding whether the theoretical debates in which legal scholars engage accurately reflect what happens in everyday interactions.

Theories of Resistance

Some of the reactions and responses to offensive public speech reported by subjects constitute resistance. The law's suggestion that those offended by racist and sexist speech should engage in counterspeech amounts to an idealized version of resistance. Resistance is a nuanced and contested subject for study (Engel and Yngvesson 1984; Rubin 1996). Classic studies of the domination-resistance dyad typically examine domination in the form of state power, be it legitimate or illegitimate, and resistant acts designed to thwart the system of domination in which the individual is embedded. Scott defines resistance as an

> act by members of a subordinate class that is or are intended either to
> mitigate or deny claims (for example, rents, taxes, prestige) made on that

class by superordinate classes (for example, landlords, large farmers, the state) or to advance its own claims (for example work, land, charity, respect) vis-a-vis those superordinate classes (Scott 1990).

Scholars of resistance have studied colonizing governments (Comaroff and Comaroff 1990) the welfare bureaucracy (Sarat 1990; White 1990), employment (McCann 1994), and the criminal justice system (Ewick and Silbey 1992), to name just a few. Great acts of resistance might include a coup or the development of a political action group designed to change the law or the government in some way (McCann and March 1996). Smaller acts of resistance include work slowdowns or simply refusing the categories the law requires (Merry 1990).

One way that this study differs from other studies of domination and resistance is that the systems of domination at work in racist and sexist speech are not systems of legitimate authority. The systems of domination at work in the interactions I study are the social systems of race, sex, and class rather than overt forms of state power. In these interactions, as in society generally, white women and people of color are the subordinate groups. That said, I do not mean to essentialize the individuals in these interactions to their race or gender. All people lie at different axes of privilege and subordination at different times and in different places. Hierarchies are not static, and people are simultaneously privileged and burdened by complex and competing hierarchies. For example, in her privileged racial status, a white woman may make a racist comment to a man of color. Similarly, invoking his privileged status as a man, a man of color may make a sexually suggestive comment to a white woman. Finally, with begging, the power in the interactions is embedded in the classes of the parties involved. Unlike racist or sexist speech, begging is a request made by the more disadvantaged to the more privileged.

Although this project does not study state power directly, the state-sanctioned exercise of power is heavily implicated in these interactions. The speaker is the person who seeks to dominate or abuse in racist and sexist street harassment. But it is important to examine the way that the state power works to normalize and justify such interactions. By studying individuals who are not state actors, but who are, nonetheless, exercising dominance (in the forms of racism and sexism) over others, this project expands the scope of the traditional domination-resistance dyad. By moving the study of power from structural notions to a more nuanced one, other socio-legal scholars also have begun to enrich the domination-resistance dichotomy (Darian-Smith 1999). I examine racism and sexism as forms of power, and how they relate to formal state power. State power is implicated here, not only as the actions of legislatures, courts, and police, but also as the hegemony of legal and rights discourse. In simple terms, it is not just important that people make racist and sexist comments; it also is important that they have the tacit approval (or at least indifference) of the state when engaging in this behavior. Law, as an institution and as official ideology, treats offensive public speech as a problem with which its targets must live.

In contrast to racist and sexist street speech, begging is a form of speech in which the state's role is obvious. Despite objections from legal scholars and homeless advocates, local governments often attempt to regulate begging. The state, in the form of city ordinances, police actions, and district attorney prosecutions, intervenes on behalf of targets regularly. Unlike sexist and racist street speech, the law is heavily implicated, and there are a variety of formal and informal legal and extralegal mechanisms designed to reduce the amount of begging in public places.

One of the difficulties associated with the study of resistance is operationalizing the term. Scholars of resistance debate the level to which an act of resistance must rise in order to "count" as resistance. When a resistant act does not amount to a strategy or tactic for accomplishing change, is it really an act of resistance? For example, is it resistance when Millie Simpson, an African American woman wrongly convicted of a traffic violation, thwarts the court's intended punishment by performing her community service at a church where she regularly performs such service? (Ewick and Silbey 1992). This act may be terribly significant for Millie Simpson, who knows she has been wrongly convicted based on her personal characteristics and circumstances, but her act of resistance ultimately does not translate into social change. Indeed, the sentencing court will never discover it. Scholars debate the interpretation of various acts as "resistant," and although Ewick and Silbey determine that Mrs. Simpson's act amounts to resistance, some scholars reject this notion precisely because there is no manifestation of resistance to the superordinate class (McCann and March 1996).

Further complicating the study of resistance is that it may be overt or hidden. "Hidden transcripts" are the

> discourse [and actions] that take place "offstage," beyond direct observation by powerholders. The hidden transcript is thus derivative in the sense that it consists of those offstage speeches, gestures, and practices that confirm, contradict, or inflect what appears in the public transcript (Scott 1990).

The study of reactions and responses to offensive public speech yields a number of coping mechanisms that might be considered versions of hidden resistance. For example, there are elaborate hidden mechanisms by which targets resist being victimized by racist and sexist speech in the form of complex internal processes that defy the interactions, the hierarchies the comments represent, and the label imposed by the speaker on the target. These internal processes are important for individual targets because they provide a mechanism whereby the harms are externalized and individualized, although such mechanisms neither communicate resistance to the speaker nor anyone within earshot.

This chapter examines *all* of the ways in which individuals reported dealing with offensive public speech. Many of the ways of dealing with such speech involve actively or passively resisting the systems of domination that are embodied in such interactions, but only *some* of the actions convey a message of resistance to those invoking the hierarchies of race and gender in such interactions. Sally Engle Merry says that resistance can be "to, by means of, and through the law" (1995). At the outset I might have predicted, based on the research of many critical race legal scholars, support for "resistance through law." If members of subordinated groups sought to resist racist and sexist street harassment, they might have advocated making such acts illegal. Instead, targets largely disfavor the use of the law to prohibit these practices which serve to bolster race and gender domination in the public sphere, saying that they have an adequate way of dealing with such interactions. This chapter analyzes reported and observed reactions to offensive public speech and the ways that members of subordinate groups respond to racism and sexism in public places, with an emphasis on how these mechanisms do or do not convey resistance to racism and sexism. Further, I examine resistance to begging in both formal and informal forms.

In what follows, I report the reactions, responses, and resistance described by targets. I describe the reactions and responses, including the decision *not* to respond, categorizing them as overt or hidden. Overt responses are those that are observable, either by the speaker, other passersby, or other individuals at a later time. Hidden reactions occur when targets reject the speaker's message but do nothing to communicate their feelings. Finally, I report the decision not to respond.

POWER IN PUBLIC I: REACTIONS TO RACIST HATE SPEECH IN PUBLIC PLACES

Unlike sexually suggestive speech, which some may argue serves the quasi-legitimate purpose of allowing men and women to approach one another for courtship purposes, there is far less ambiguity about the redeeming social value of racist or race-related speech between strangers in public places. The vast majority of subjects agree that it is never socially appropriate for a stranger to comment on another person's race. The clarity of this norm makes the target of racist comments able to assess the situation more quickly. Despite this, subjects reported mixed feelings and difficult decisions in determining how to deal with racist comments. This woman's response was typical of targets of racist speech.

I was at a gas station where we came to a point where two cars were trying to get into the same pump, and we had made a U-turn to get the pump, and he wanted to pull in, and my friend pulled in really fast and got it. And the guy jumps out and he's like, "Well, that's my pump, and you guys better move." And we're like "No" and he's like "You fucking people need to go back where you came from. I'm sick of this, you guys come over here, think you can take everything away from us. . ." So I've had several situations like that. I've had in school, where people wrote in the books and they would spray paint on the wall, "nigger exterminator" and things of that nature.

Q: Uh huh. And how did you respond to the guy at the gas station, or people—how do you typically respond to an incident like that?

A: Now, I try to calm myself and just ignore them because whatever their problem, it's *their* problem, and it's not going to go away until *they* fix it regardless of what I do. But [sometimes I'd like to] . . . act as ignorant as they would and scream back and holler back, you know, "What are you going to do about it?"

Q: Uh huh. And was that guy at the gas station white?

A: Yeah.

Q: And is that something that makes you afraid, or more just mad?

A: Mad that people could still be that ignorant.

Q: Uh huh. And when something like that happens, do you think about it afterward or tell anyone else about it?

A: Um. Sometimes. Sometimes I would think about it later on; sometimes I would probably just forget about it. .

Q: Right. Okay. Do you do anything to avoid those sorts of interactions? Or you're saying you've kind of changed a little bit in that you don't escalate them.

A: Yeah. I just try not to escalate them. Whatever. However they feel they feel, and there's nothing I can do about it, so I just pretty much try and ignore it and let it go. (29-year-old African American woman, account representative, interview #79)

This woman's account touches on many of the themes that respondents focus on in their responses to racist speech: anger, fear, self-protection, a desire to ignore it, a sense of helplessness to control it, and

sadness. She first tries to "calm herself" and to "just ignore" such comments. That she must calm herself belies her first reaction to the comment—it makes her upset. She denies her first desire to act "as ignorant
as they are" and engage in a screaming match. In the same breath, she
explains the mechanism by which she is able to calm herself and ignore
comments that are obviously provocative to her. Like other targets of
racist speech, she externalizes the problem. She says, "Whatever their
problem is, it's *their* problem. . . ." By saying the speaker (and not the
target) has the problem, she attempts to distance herself from the interaction, making it easier to deny that such interactions affect her at all.

According to this respondent, not only is the problem the speaker's,
it is one that she is powerless to fix. She says the problem is "not going
to go away until *they* fix it regardless of what *I* do." This target also
speaks of her ability to change the speaker's thinking. She wants to
change things, bemoans the fact that there are people "still so ignorant," but decides she cannot be the one to educate them. This thinking
allows her to externalize the problems of the interaction as well as the
underlying racism that fuels them. It is his problem and she has no
power to fix it, but she is the victim of targeted racist hate speech—the
comment is directed to her, delivered forcefully, and is about the color
of her skin, as well as stereotypes and assumptions about African
American women.

Externalizing the problem and deciding she is helpless to remedy it
creates a contradiction between the targeted nature of a racist comment
and her attribution of the problem to the speaker. Racist comments are
about targets' inherent characteristics, but this target eschews the personal nature of the comment and externalizes its impact. This target
and others like her have elaborate mechanisms of resistance, although
they are invisible to everyone around her. She reconstructs this encounter and others like it as a story about the speaker, even though the
comment is directed toward and about her.

This quotation illustrates many of the tensions faced by people of
color when subjected to racist comments from strangers in public
places. As with sexually suggestive comments, targets refuse to accept
speakers' characterizations of them and must engage in complicated
internal processes to resuscitate one's identity as more than the mere
stereotypes associated with race.

Overt Acts of Resistance to Racist Speech

Overt acts of resistance to racist speech included saying something to
the perpetrator, fighting, speaking another language, and telling others. Most targets of racist speech in public places are loath to respond

for fear of escalating the situation to one of violence, but there are some exceptions. One African American man said the word *nigger* should be legal but that he should be able to use it "in court as evidence . . . because when I hit that guy who called me nigger, I want to be able to use it as evidence that he provoked me." (32-year-old African American man, business professional, interview #89)

Despite this subject's reactions, very few respondents in this study could tell of times when a racist comment actually resulted in a physical altercation. Only sixteen respondents indicated that they had, at one time or another, responded verbally to a racist comment. Of these, two were white men, meaning that slightly more than a quarter of people of color (28%) ever had directly responded to a racist comment, despite the fact that 92% of people of color have experienced such comments. Although people who respond verbally are more likely to be men, one woman told how she "corrects" people who make racist or race-insensitive remarks.

> I don't like hearing racist remarks. You know, and I don't tolerate them. If I hear them, I say something. . . . You know, I'm just not a liberal in the sense that I'm gonna let shit slide, excuse my French. . . . I feel strongly, you know, that if people stop tolerating racist remarks, people would stop making them. Now, I think I'm a perfect example, because those van drivers, for example, got to know me, they don't do it anymore in front of me. . . . They know better. They know that if they say—start—if they say "chink" I'm going to call them on it, if they even say, "Oriental," I'm going to educate them. I'll say, "excuse—" I'll do it very diplomatically. . .— "Chinamen," for example, I'll say, "You shouldn't do that, it's just [like] . . . somebody black being called a nigger. Don't do that. It's offensive. Maybe you don't know that," or I'll say something like that. Or I'll say "You shouldn't call Asians oriental—there are oriental rugs and vases, but not people." You know? And people will usually accept it. They'll say, "Oh, oh, I didn't know that" or something like that. But if you call people on their racism and stuff, usually they'll respond positively. They'll feel chagrined about it, if you call them on it. You know? And I think more people ought to do it, not just letting it slide. (59-year-old African American woman, volunteer worker, interview #85)

Other people responded less politely:

> . . . [T]hree friends and I were all walking, and then this guy said, "Oh, one more of you and you're a gang" or something like that. Or whatever.
> Q: And how did you respond to that?
> A: I—I really—I didn't really care. I—but my friends . . . responded with some vulgar language. (18-year-old African American man, gas station attendant, interview #31)

One subject, perhaps the most adamant about not allowing racist remarks to go by unfettered, was a white man. When people responded to him, making note of his whiteness, he was quite offended and said he would always respond, trying to "educate" the speaker (always a man of color) about his own racism. He said:

> I was in a BART station in San Leandro, and uh—this dude asked me for a cigarette and [when I gave him one], he said, "Thanks whitey, I appreciate that." and I said, "You know, man, I do have a name . . ." I'm pretty comfortable around people enough to the point where I take that stuff and turn it into a conversation and try to gear them away from doing that in the future, but . . . he probably just was—you know. It's a learned response I think. You know, I don't think you're born with that, I think it's definitely learned. (22-year-old white man, security officer, interview #56)

Another white man recounted similar stories, including this one:

> Okay. The other day, again walking on Telegraph, further on Telegraph, um, I had a letter in my hand that I was looking to mail all day, and there was a little mail truck there with the mail guy in it. . . . I handed him the letter and I said "Hey man, do you mind posting this for me?" He said "No, not at all" he takes them and puts them in his little box. And he's talking to two guys standing around the truck, and the mailman in the truck was a black guy, and the two guys on the street . . . I gathered from his accent that he was Persian or Greek or something like that—he says to the mailman "Why you want to help the white man out?" So—I turned around, and got an eyeful of him, and kind of wandered back over and [said], "Probably because he's a decent chap and because I put my thirty-two-cent stamp on it. (28-year-old white man, student/disk jockey, interview #76)

Since men are less likely to be physically vulnerable, it may not be surprising that they are more likely to be willing to engage in a conversation that could potentially escalate into something more threatening. It is interesting, though, that white men were among the most willing to respond.

Yet, perhaps it is predictable that members of a privileged group are most troubled by comments about their race. The entitlement and privilege that accompanies one's status as a white man often is invisible to them (Cain 1989). Because they think they have no race, white men may resent being reminded that others, for whom race is always a salient characteristic, racially categorize them. Comments about whiteness serve as a reminder that race is an important, rather than invisible, characteristic. The power of the myth of meritocracy is in its invisibility; by making race/whiteness visible, these speakers threaten to undermine the legitimacy of the power white men hold.

Similarly, a number of people of color said they felt an obligation to say something in the face of racist speech. It was simply something that they could not ignore.

> Um. I don't know—they [race-related comments] just sort of seem to hit me personally, I guess. I really don't know why—but it's just when something racially comes up, I just take it more like it's sort of my duty to correct it. Or sort of try to deal with it. (25-year-old Chinese American man, service industry, interview #28)

Another subject spoke of this "obligation" to respond to individual acts of racism. As a light-skinned Hispanic mother, this respondent often is questioned about her relationship to her darker-skinned son. She told me,

> There's a repeated pattern that I've already mentioned related to my third world child. And people don't realize that—like there's a wide range of . . . multicultural people . . . my son and I are good examples. We're both biracial; we're both of mixed ancestry, I'm way on one end, and he's way on the other [in terms of looks]. . . . But both are present. And therefore, the most common comment that we received when he was a young, young child in arms, was—or when he was a little toddler, was "Who's your mommy?" or "How come you're black and she's white?". . . They see such a difference in our races that they can't conceive on first glance that I'm his mother. And I got it so much, I got pretty used to fielding it from all races. . . . [One time], the remark was made like "How come you're black and she's white?" And he said—he turned around and in his little bell-like three-year-old voice—he said "It's because of my DNA."
> Q: You have really educated him.
> A: Yeah, because when he asked me, "How come daddy's black and you're white and I'm brown?" I explained the DNA theory—because that's technically why. And I said, "A lot of people are going to have a lot of social prejudice about the situation. Because there's such a wide range in color, but technically [name of child], it's about the DNA, because that's why you have black dogs and white dogs and spotted dogs and brown rabbits and gray rabbits and you know, blue eyes and green eyes, the DNA controls all those characteristics, from the cellular level. Because I had a major in Biology, and so he listened and I explained it, and then not three days later, somebody asked the question. And it was like a drunk black guy. A drunk homeless black guy in the back of the bus . . . [and] the guy asked the question loudly and in a derogatory manner. And the

child . . . said, "It's because of my DNA" and he said it without shame. (51-year-old multiracial woman, laborer, interview #43)

She went on to explain her philosophy about why she responds when people question her or her son about race.

So, what I do is I educate people. You know. Both white and black. Hey— you may not know who you're talking to—is what I use with white peo- ple, and with black people I say "Is that how your mother or grandmother taught you to deal with this issue?" and "What kind of family are you from? Didn't you have a grandmother that taught you the right way to talk to folks?". . . And then with Christians you use "Everybody's blood is red." and with politicians you go "You don't know who you're talking to—it might be a voter that's on your side." There's a lot of ways to re- spond, and the best way is to get—to get past the personal point of being offended and educate people because if they're even discussing it, they are dealing with these racial issues, and they're seeking some kind of reso- lution. You know—people [who] really are prejudice[d] will get up and not sit next to you and stuff like that. Or they're angry and crazy on a different level. You know—they're handling it differently. But at least if people are talking about it—you can use it as a soap box to educate who- ever's in hearing distance. Because the ones that aren't asking are lis- tening. And based on how I respond, that's how I can do good or damage. (51-year-old multiracial woman, laborer, interview #43)

Overt responses are more likely to be made by male targets of racist speech, but overall, very few people respond verbally. And, when you exclude white males, who have different motivation for resisting racist speech targeted at whiteness (privilege), the number of overt respond- ers is even lower. Some of those who do respond do so rudely while others attempt to use such interactions as an opportunity for educating others about the complexities of race and race relations. The nature of the overt response depends on the nature of the comment, the place where the comment is made, as well as a determination about the vio- lent tendencies of the speaker, among other things. The main point is that well under a third of those who have been targets of it ever have overtly responded to racist speech.

Hidden Reactions to Racist Public Speech

My subjects reported several hidden reactions to racist speech. Hidden reactions are those that are not visible to the speaker or to anyone viewing the incident and may be part of the phenomenon of "silenc- ing" described by the critical race theorists as a response to racist speech (Delgado 1993). Targets of racist speech who do not accept the speaker's characterization of them but were unable to communicate that message often had internal or hidden reactions to the speech. The decision not to have an overt response belies the complicated processes that individuals go through when they are targets.

Subjects who had hidden reactions said,

> It [racist comments] would only be a problem if it's really aggressive and—because you know—I never take a big offense to it [race-related comments]. I just think the person has a problem. But it only becomes a problem when they're like—like really disrespecting me and coming at me. (23-year-old African American man, unemployed/artist, interview #37)

> Racial slurs, I mean, it . . . makes me feel like there's something wrong with this guy, but it's not my problem. (28-year-old African American man, student/sales, interview #92).

These hidden responses—reinterpreting the event as external to the target—amount to internal coping mechanisms. They might be said to be versions of resistance because they are internal processes, invisible to the power holder in the situation, that represent the targets' rejection of the worldview invoked by the speaker. The target has a competing narrative that locates the source of the problem in the speaker. Thus, targets that have hidden reactions to racist speech do something to resist the speaker's portrayal of the world as one in which whites are superior to people of color.

The significance of these reactions should not be underestimated for the individuals involved. The decisions not to overtly react and to engage in hidden reaction are made because targets believe they cannot safely engage in more speech. However, to the outside world, there is no difference between hidden resistance and a complete lack of resistance.

No Resistance at All—The Decision to Ignore

The most common response to racist speech between strangers in public is to ignore it. Twenty-one respondents said they typically, "do nothing," "laugh it off," "ignore it," or, "ignore it and leave" when they are targeted. This woman's story about being called a "white bitch" was common; she was subjected to a race-related comment and ignored it.

> And there was a strike somewhere . . . and we had taken a boat ride, and when we got off, the strikers . . . didn't accost us physically, but verbally. And they hollered at us about all being white rich bitches who were supported by their husbands who never worked a day in their lives.

Q: And how did you respond to that?

A: . . . I didn't respond. . . . You know.

Q: Just keep walking.

A: I just keep walking and acting like I'm deaf [laugh]. (54-year-old white woman, homemaker, interview #05)

Again, the reasons for ignoring such speech vary widely. A number of subjects ignore such speech because they say the speaker is stupid or ignorant. The idea seems to be that a response would be useful only if it could change the person's behavior, but the speaker is too stupid to be changed, so why bother?

It [being the target of a racist comment] hurts my feelings, and you don't know if you want to stoop down to their level or just ignore it. There's really nothing you can do about it—I mean, they're ignorant (18-year-old African American woman, interview #54)

It's not a problem if they do it [make racial comments], because that's just their own ignorance that they have to deal with—it's a problem that they haven't been educated enough to know that's not something that you do. . . . If someone calls me a name, I try not to let it affect me, because that's their own ignorance. . . . [I]n terms of the race—that would only be a problem if it was people that feel that so strongly, they would try to harm me physically, then it would be a problem. I have such great self-esteem that whatever people say is because of their shortcoming, their ignorance, their—you know, it's no reflection on me. (37-year-old African American woman, interview #94)

Some people ignore out of fear, as this respondent suggests:

And I was at a gas station, and a guy came out, didn't talk to me directly, but I knew he was talking about me. I was seated in the car, and the driver who was beside me was white, and the guy just said, kind of in the air, "I can see the driver's the only human being around here." Implying I was not a human being.

Q: Uh huh. And did you respond to that in any way?

A: No, I didn't, because I was afraid. (21-year-old Filipino woman, student, interview #75)

Um. I would say, I would say race. Because in terms of sexually explicit [comments], I mean, either—I don't think—it just doesn't really wound you—at least me—you can think "that guy's crazy, or he's an idiot." But with rac[ist comments], I think it combines more things, you feel threatened, you think people are solely judging you on your appearance. That is unfair, and it's you know, based on no knowledge of you—who you are. (24-year-old white woman, child advocate, interview #51)

One subject noted that he does not have the option of responding (negatively) to racist speech due to fear. He said,

> I can move away from the race-related comments, or I can adjust to it. You know, I don't decide—tend to get into fighting, I don't raise my voice at people. You know, you call me a black bastard, I'm going to say, "Thank you very much" and I'm gonna keep on moving if I can. I'm just going to keep moving. (44-year-old African American man, stockbroker, interview #29)

His response is interesting because his acquiescence to the offensive comment betrays his true feeling about it. It is not that he agrees that he is a "black bastard." Rather, he knows he must either adjust to it or move away from it. Like hidden acts of resistance, those who do not resist risk allowing the speaker's characterization of them to appear uncontested.

Conclusions about Reactions to Racist Speech

To look for ways that targets of racist speech resist the racism is not to say that people of color have an affirmative obligation to respond to such speech. Indeed, these subjects demonstrate clearly that there are circumstances in which it would be unwise to respond. Rather, it is to show that the reactions to being made the target of racist speech are complex. Targets who reject racism have various reasons for failing to engage in overt resistance. Obviously, physical safety is a primary concern. The decision to engage in more speech or the phenomenon of being "silenced" is not adequately captured in conventional First Amendment analysis or by the critical race theorists. Targets of racist speech are reasonable people forced to make difficult decisions about whether and how to respond.

POWER IN PUBLIC II: REACTIONS TO SEXIST HATE SPEECH IN PUBLIC PLACES

Women repeatedly make the point that offensive sexually suggestive speech is a problem that they are capable of dealing with on their own, but how do women handle it? Do they follow the recommendation of legal scholars about combating offensive sexually suggestive speech with more speech?

Women had a number of reactions to offensive sexually suggestive speech. Despite the detailed calculus for avoiding such speech elaborated in chapter 3, women often are targeted for sexually suggestive speech and the most common response involves no resistance at all, much less assertive speech in the face of such comments. In what follows, I describe how women react and respond to offensive sexually suggestive speech. Because these interactions are, by definition, unwanted, many women resist them in some way. Overt acts of resistance include verbal response, nonverbal response, and talking to others. Hidden acts of resistance to offensive sexually suggestive speech include ignoring the speech, deciding that it is the speaker's problem, individualizing, and denial. Responses to sexually suggestive speech vary depending on the nature of the comment. Women respond differently to different types of comments.

Overt Acts of Resistance to Sexually Suggestive Speech

Although all sixty-three women interviewed claimed to have been the target of offensive, sexually suggestive speech by a stranger in a public place, well under half (42%) of them reported that they had ever verbally responded to sexually suggestive speech. Of the twenty-four women who talked back, only nine women reported assertive responses about how the speech was offensive. Thus, only 14% of women ever engaged the speaker and complained about being made a target in this way.

Other verbal responses included saying that one has a boyfriend or husband (reported by eight women), saying something ambiguous (reported by five women), being generally rude (reported by three women), and telling a lie (reported by two women). Other overt acts of resistance included telling others about such incidents (reported by eleven women), glaring at the man (reported by three women), making an obscene gesture (reported by three women), and one woman even slapped her perpetrator.

Only nine women reported that they ever had responded assertively to sexually suggestive speech with more speech. The most unusual case came from a woman who seemed afraid of nothing. Although her story is the aberration, it exemplifies the kind of speech that seems to be imagined by scholars who advocate "more speech."

> I was walking down this street toward my house, and this drunk Mexican drove up and asked me to turn a trick, and I had just gotten off work . . . and like I weigh 250 pounds, and I'm fifty years old, and I had like this orange striped reflective vest on and everything. And blue jeans and work boots and glasses, and my hair was all—and I was dirty, and . . . I raised so much hell about it—not because he asked me for a trick, [but] because he was too drunk to tell I wasn't a hooker. I'm a grandmother—a fat old

working grandmother, and he's asking me to turn a trick. "Man," I said, "what is wrong with you—you are drunk—you better take a good look at who I am!". . . So anyway, I'm liable to go off on them. It's just—it depends on what's appropriate. You get a sense for—if you've been in the streets a long time yourself, you know when to just shine somebody on, or when to talk to them like you're one of them. (51-year-old multiracial woman, laborer, interview #43)

This woman's bravado in this particular situation belies the fact that she too seeks to avoid such situations and recognizes that there are some times when a response is not a good idea. She responds assertively, but it does not mean that "more speech" is always the solution. Although she is willing to engage in counterspeech, she has a recipe for avoiding being made a target, just like everyone else. She went on to say:

I mean, if you look gorgeous, you better wear big old loose clothes and big jackets. Don't walk around with no clothes on. That's stupid . . . lots better to protect yourself than to be a target. And if you don't want people to say stuff to you—don't give them anything to talk about. Or you know, carry a bodyguard. Get some big old bad guy, or obviously a boyfriend or a husband, wear a wedding ring. Walk in a certain kind of protective camouflage. You know. It's easy enough to get a big ole, puffy coat or loose wrapping stuff that hangs down to your ankles, and wear it. . . . People out there are crazy and they're messed up and they're deranged, and they're all loose. Police can't protect you—the courts aren't on your side. You know—you better learn how to handle your shit. That's just the way it is. And if you don't want people to make suggestive comments, look them right in the eye, and just dare them to. *And then talk about their Mama. And who raised them.* (51-year-old multiracial woman, laborer, interview #43, emphasis mine)

Her response is designed to embarrass the speaker, calling his family into question ("talk about their Mama"), to point out that such remarks are not socially acceptable. It is an appeal to a set of social norms that the speaker has, at least for the moment, disregarded.

When asked how they respond to sexually suggestive speech from strangers in public places, the vast majority do not respond and those who do typically do not respond as colorfully as the woman quoted above. The most common type of counterspeech response was more ambivalent, such as the woman who says her response is "usually to walk away, or say 'leave me alone' and walk away" (40-year old white woman, interview #12).

Responding with assertive speech is not always a good idea, according to the women.

> Um. Just kind of like sort of come-ons, like comments about my appearance, like "Hey baby you look real good" or "Ooh, come back here and talk to me" or you know. "Let's go somewhere and be alone" that kind of stuff.
>
> Q: And how do you typically respond to this type of comment?
>
> A: It depends. *If I don't feel threatened, then I usually say something* like, you know "Does your mother know you're here—talking to women this way?" or "How would you feel if someone talked to your girlfriend this way?" or something like that. *If I feel threatened, I just pretend like I didn't hear it and I keep going.* (29-year-old white woman, interview #16, emphasis mine)

Again, she makes a calculation as to her personal safety, and then a reference to the women in the speakers' life. The reference to women close to the speaker is an attempt to combat the objectification inherent in sexually suggestive comments. This woman, and some like her, want to engage in counterspeech because to leave the comment uncontested is to concede that she is nothing more than an object of sexual desire, that women in public places are available for sexual derision, or even simply that she was not bothered by the comment.

Some women respond to offensive sexually suggestive speech without speech, but with a communicative message—an obscene gesture. Three women reported making a gesture and one of the three indicated that this response escalated the situation.

> I was taking a walk with a friend, it was when I lived in the beach flat, and I was walking along that street where like all the cars go out, and it was just a bunch of white teenage boys, and they—and we were just really wanting to be—we were like having an intense talk, and we didn't want to deal with a bunch of asshole guys shouting out "hey—blah blah blah" you know—like stupid shit. And so um, and so—I don't even remember what they first said, but I flipped them off, and then they shouted out that I had a fat ass. (26-year-old white woman, unemployed, interview #30)

> I was walking to work one day, when I was in L.A., and there [was] . . . some kind of heavy machine was driving down the street in Westwood and it honked the horn. . . . I'll show you—like that [respondent gestures with both hands palms out chest level and squeezing motion]—like two hands grabbing boobs. And that was really upsetting to me.
>
> Q: There were two guys?

A: There were two guys, yes in the heavy machinery—and

Q: How did you respond to that?

A: I flipped them off. (28-year-old white woman, lawyer, interview #98)

Less obvious, but still overt tactics of resistance came from women who glared or "acted rudely" to those who targeted them. It may require a perceptive speaker to notice, but these women attempted to communicate their message to those who made them targets.

I guess I was just walking down the street—in San Francisco again.

Q: Mm hm. And what did that person say to you?

A: Um. Like, "nice ass."

Q: Mm hm. And how did you respond to that?

A: I just turned around and gave him a dirty look. (22-year-old Hispanic woman, human resources professional, interview #36)

Oh, I was coming from my brother-in-law's office in downtown Oakland. Um, walking—actually, I was walking back to his office in downtown Oakland, and some person got directly into my face and said something totally out of place as far as wanting to . . . screw me.

Q: Mm hm. And is that the word he used

A: Uh . . . "[I] want some of that ass."

Q: Mm hm. And how did you respond to that?

A: I looked at him like he was crazy and kept walking. (43-year-old African American woman, office administrator, interview #63)

It is impossible to know if the speakers received the message intended by the glare. Nonetheless, these women are doing something to communicate that they resist this characterization of them.

Women are more likely to respond to men who make benign or friendly conversation, only to have the conversation take a turn for the offensive. These perpetrators start seemingly polite conversations with women in public places, counting on the woman to respond as is socially appropriate. When the woman indicates that she is uninterested in the man, the situation degenerates. For example, when being approached as though for a date, eight women reported being rude or mentioning their boyfriend or husband when they are unwillingly made the target of amorous attention. Sometimes mentioning the boyfriend is sufficient to make the men go away.

Oh yeah, one time I was at the mall, and I was walking to my car in the parking lot, and I was with my friends, and this guy just came up to me and was asking me if I had a boyfriend or something. And like, um, I didn't really want him to do that or anything, and I was kind of scared.

Q: Mmmm Hmmm. And did you respond to him at all?

A: Yeah, I told him, 'cuz he was asking me like where I'm going and like, do I have a boyfriend, and I said yeah, and then he left. (16-year-old Filipino woman, student, interview #08)

Other times, appealing to one's attached social status does not dissuade the speaker, as these women reported:

Yeah, actually, I was buying some flowers on the cart out at Market Street, and had a gentleman come up and say, "You know, I'd really like to take you out." It was really interesting, he didn't introduce himself or say anything else; he just started with that one statement. So I chuckled kind of at first, and said, "No thank you, I have a boyfriend." And then he continued to hang around, and then one of the last comments, and again I was wearing a skirt, which is interesting, but he said, "Wow, your legs go from your ass to the ground." (23-year-old white woman, marketing manager, interview #59)

Sometimes . . . guys have asked me for a phone number or name, and I'll say "Well, I'm married" and they'll say stuff like "Well, that doesn't make any difference." And I get bothered by that. (52-year-old African American woman, professional, interview #90)

Some women acknowledged that they lied about boyfriends and husbands in order to discourage unwanted amorous attention.

It was a man, and he complimented me on my smile.
Q: Mm hm. And how did you respond to that?
A: I smiled and said, "Thank you."
Q: Mm hm. And how did you feel when he said that?
A: Well, I was a little bit uneasy. You know, I was flattered, but . . . was kind of expecting him to take it further, and he did. You know.
Q: Uh huh. And what did he say after that?
A: Well, he asked me out for coffee. Well, he started a conversation, and then later on he asked me out. And I told him I was engaged.
Q: Uh huh. And is that true?
A: No. That's a lie. (19-year-old East Indian woman, student, interview #71)

Referring to a boyfriend or husband to thwart unwanted sexual attention is a tactic about which feminists may be ambivalent. Although effective in some circumstances, it does not communicate any of the messages that women said they would like to convey—that men do not have unfettered access to them simply because they are in a public place. Nor does it convey the message that it is legitimate for the woman to resist such attention simply because she does not want it. For example, the woman whose legs go from her ass to the ground went on to say, "It made me angry. I was like, 'Who are you to speak to me that way?' You know, I didn't invite this conversation whatsoever." But her response to him did little or nothing to convey that message. The underlying message when she refers to her male partner is that such comments might be welcome if she were unattached, despite most women's claim that there is virtually no chance they would make plans with a stranger they met in a public place. Rebuffing unwanted sexual attention by mentioning a husband or boyfriend conveys a false message to the man. And it plays to the idea that unattached women are somehow open prey for men at all times.

Another form of active resistance is talking to others about the incident. "Consciousness raising" has a long tradition in the feminist movement and encourages women to share experiences with one another. By talking to others about common experiences, consciousness raising seeks to move women's issues from the realm of the individual/private to the realm of the social/public. When women realize the problems they face as individuals are, in fact, problems shared with many women, there is a greater recognition of the problem as a social, rather than individual one. Consciousness raising can be and has been an effective form of resistance when it has overtly political implications. Talking about such problematic interactions could lead to organizing to combat the problem. Although telling a friend or significant other may not rise to the level of political activity, it renders a largely invisible problem visible and has the potential to serve as a catalyst for change. And, eleven women reported that they told a friend, a spouse, and in one case, even a boss, about such interactions.

Far from the idealized model in which shared experience leads to "consciousness raising," women who reported telling others about incidents of offensive public speech were met with everything from practical advice to skepticism and blame. Sometimes telling a friend results in receiving practical advice about the detailed calculus, as in this woman's experience:

> Q: And did you tell anybody else about it [a homeless man who came up to me and said "I hate women, they're all sluts"]?
> A: Um. Yeah, I told a friend of mine.
> Q: And what was their reaction?
> A: Um, let me see—I think it was just basically, "Oh, yeah that was a disturbing thing that happened and you should really try to avoid BART Stations late at night. (24-year-old white woman, student, interview #10)

Another woman told some of her friends and relatives of a particularly disturbing, repeated encounter she had with a man from the neighborhood, only to be told that she must have misunderstood his comments and actions.

> And there were several people that felt that there was really something wrong with *me* for being afraid of this man that was following me. Because they thought, "Oh, that is so cute." You know, it was really insulting. But, [they would say], "Oh, he is such a good looking man, how could you be afraid of him?"
>
> Q: So who might say that? Like you would tell friends?
>
> A: Relatives.
>
> Q: Relatives?
>
> A: Yeah. [And] a couple friends of Audrey's . . . [and] the people that the police talked to—um, a couple neighbors said "Oh, he is such a wonderful man, he is so good looking, he is so nice. He would never do anything like that. She's got to be mistaken." But you know, we had documented it all. (53-year-old white woman, property manager, interview #21)

Consistent with the view that women can take a variety of preventive actions to avoid being made the target of offensive sexually suggestive speech, some women received blame when they sought a sympathetic ear.

> Um, at BART at MacArthur and I was standing on the platform and this guy came up and said "Hey baby, what's going on" and "Do you have a boyfriend" and I was like "Um, yes" and he's like "Okay, that's cool, . . . have a nice day. . . . "
>
> Q: Uh huh. Did you think about it after it occurred, or tell anyone else about it?
>
> A: Yeah, I told my boyfriend. . . [and] he was like, "You better be careful around there, Hillary. Don't talk to people like that." (20-year-old white woman, manager, interview #58)

Others received understanding.

> Q: Mm hm. Did you tell anyone else about the incident [being followed and called a whore and a bitch for about two hundred yards]?
>
> A: Um. Uh huh [affirmative]
>
> Q: Whom did you tell and what was their reaction?
>
> A: I told—I had a bunch of things like that happen to me when I was in Spain, and I told my friend Antoinette about it, and she had lived in Spain for a while, and she told me that really similar things happened to . . . her. Sort of like as opposed to other people she was hanging out with. And that she wasn't really sure why she was singled out for it—but she definitely was. So she could relate. (26-year-old white woman, unemployed, interview #30)

One woman told how her reporting of the story resulted in tangible benefits:

> A: It really upset me. I felt really invaded, and you know, I had a feeling that we should be able to walk down the street, on the way to . . . work, and not have people do things that like to you.
>
> Q: Mm hm. Did you think about it afterward, or tell anyone else about it?
>
> A: Yeah. I thought about it. And I remember strolling into work and saying "these goddamn men, blah blah blah" or something like this. My boss felt so bad about it—[laughing] there's men who feel responsible . . . for all the bad men in the world, and he said he would start paying for me to park so I could drive to work.
>
> Q: Really?
>
> A: Yeah, less than a mile away.
>
> Q: Did you take him up on it?
>
> A: I did.
>
> (28-year-old white woman, lawyer, interview #98)

Although these women told their stories to others, only one of them resulted in some sort of tangible benefit for the target. And the tangible benefit she received allows her to avoid such interactions by providing a mechanism through which she cedes control of public space. Although it improves her individual situation, this solution does nothing to affect the social problem. The women described engage in overt resistance but it is difficult to gauge how these mechanisms of resistance lead to social change, if at all.

Overt acts of resistance to sexually suggestive speech in public places are infrequent and when women do something in the face of sexually suggestive speech, their responses often are ambiguous. This is not to say that women have an obligation to be more forthcoming and jeopardize their safety for the sake of combating sexism. Instead, the purpose of illustrating women's reactions, responses, and resistance is to demonstrate that the seemingly simple solution to combat offensive speech (more speech) advocated both by First Amendment scholars and most of these respondents is not so simple. Targets have a difficult time "handling it."

Hidden Reactions to Sexually Suggestive Speech

Just because few women indicated they engaged in active resistance does not mean that the majority of women simply accepted the offensive characterization of their bodies and selves. Women explained a number of hidden actions taken when they are made the target of offensive sexually suggestive speech. Although the hidden responses are more passive forms and are not obvious to anyone around her, these mechanisms are extremely important to the women who describe them.

These women reported hidden acts including leaving the situation (reported by twelve women), deciding the speaker is stupid (reported by two women), "laughing it off" (reported by four women), externalizing (deciding the speaker has the problem, reported by two women), and "denial" (reported by two women). None of these actions conveys a communicative message to the men making the comments; they are akin to simply ignoring such comments.

Some women externalize the problem. Instead of claiming that such interactions are problematic, these women simply decided that the speaker had the problem.

> [I]n terms of sexually explicit [speech] . . . it just doesn't really wound you—at least me—you can think "that guy's crazy," or, "he's an idiot." (24-year-old white woman, child advocate, interview #51)

Deciding that it is the speaker who has the problem not only externalizes the problem to someone outside herself, but it individualizes it as well. It allows the woman/target to think of this man as the aberration from the norm. It is not all men who think of women/me in this way, it is this one particular man (who has a problem).

Some women deny the interactions altogether because they would rather believe such interactions simply did not occur or were not directed at them.

> [O]ne time I was walking down Telegraph, talking to a friend of mine, we were going off to have some lunch. And a man sort of walked—I think I was talking to her about certain issues having to do with my partner, who is a woman, and he sort of like, like as he was walking by me screamed "fucking lesbians" and kept going. Or "fucking dyke" I can't—probably "fucking dyke" I can't remember which one, but . . .
> Q: Mm hm. And how did you respond to that?
> A: I think I turned to my friend and I said, "I don't think he was talking to me." So denial, basically is how I responded. (29-year-old white female, professional, interview #16)

Hidden reactions to sexually suggestive speech are complex. They are invisible to the speaker, but important for the target because they allow targets to reject the idea that she could be the target of hate on the basis of her sexual orientation. Blaming the speaker, denial, and the other psychological coping strategies engaged in by speakers are important because they are the way that targets continue to be able to travel in public spaces by resisting the hierarchical worldview repre-

sented by the comments of the speaker. While they are important for
the target, they do little or nothing to communicate the message to the
speaker or to produce social change.

No Resistance at All to Sexually Suggestive Speech—The Decision to Ignore

The most common response to sexually suggestive speech from strangers in public places is to simply ignore it. Twenty-seven of sixty-three
women interviewed (42%) said that ignoring offensive sexually suggestive speech was their primary response, although there were many
reasons given for ignoring the speech. Ignoring offensive speech does
nothing to combat the hierarchy that such comments represent. Occasionally, however, women's decision to ignore comments is a form of
hidden resistance, or at least defiance. For example, some women ignore these comments because they think that the man seeks a response.
By ignoring such speech, these women are doing what they believe is
the most effective thing to thwart the speaker's true desire.

> But that actually happens to me a lot when I'm running. Actually, I run at
> Fort Point, I live on the Peninsula, and when I go there by myself, some-
> one always approaches me and talks to me—a man.
>   Q: Mm hm. And how do you typically respond?
>   A: Again, it sort of depends on the situation. Sometimes I ignore peo-
> ple. I rarely . . . give back any response, because that's what they're look-
> ing for, so I usually just ignore them. (21-year-old Filipino-American
> woman, student, interview #74)

Some women ignore such speech because they fear the consequences
of any other response.

> I know just last week, I was in the BART Station at Montgomery and there
> was, um, I think a homeless man who came up to me and said "I hate
> women, they're all sluts.". . . That probably sticks in my mind the most . . .
>   Q: Um, what did you say to the guy who um, informed you that all
> women are sluts?
>   A: Um, I just turned around; I didn't say anything. I was pretty scared
> of him. (24-year-old white woman, student, interview #10)

Some women cannot even recall particular instances of sexually suggestive speech because they have become so accustomed to them, like
this woman:

> Q: And can you tell me about that [a time someone said something to
> you either about your appearance, or something you considered to be sex-
> ually explicit]?

A: Oh boy. I should have thought about this before we started this interview . . . Because I have a hard time remembering anything in particular. . . . Usually there's a comment, and then I walk away. That's why. (40-year-old white woman, interview #12)

Women say that they think there is no other option than to ignore such comments. When asked if a man should face legal action when he says "nice tits" to a stranger on the street, this woman responded, "Jail. [laugh]. No. I mean, you know, we just gotta say nothing and keep on walking" (53-year-old white woman, property manager, interview #21). Another woman mirrored this sentiment saying she *is compelled* to ignore such comments:

It's [sexually suggestive or explicit comments from strangers in public] another thing you have to you know—it's invasive, and you have to ignore. I have to ignore. I just keep walking, and it makes me feel kind of creepy. You know? (45-year-old white woman, school counselor, interview #48)

The severity of the comment also bears little relation to the response. Both aggressive, offensive comments and subtle pervasive comments are ignored, though for different reasons. Women often ignore the offensive, aggressive comments because they fear escalating the situation. They ignore the subtler and pervasive comments because to deal with all of them would be too time consuming.

Um. One time I was in Spain, and it was about two years ago, and I was walking down the street with a loose shirt and no makeup on. Trying to look, as blending-inable as possible. And um, from like, 100 feet down the street, this man starting shouting in Spanish that I was a bitch and a whore—shouting it over and over. And following me down the street.
Q: How far did he follow you?
A: Probably about—I don't know—another 200 feet. . . .
Q: . . . And how did you respond?
A: I ignored him. (26-year-old white woman, unemployed, interview #30)

For others, these comments simply are expected and therefore do not merit any attention or response.

A: Yeah. Usually it happens when I go back to the Midwest, because I'm from Chicago, I was just recently back there, um about two weeks ago, for a conference in Chicago, and also to spend time with my family. It never fails that when I get off the plane at the airport, I usually fly into O'Hare, there will usually be people making comments, either about my ear piercing, or just the way I dress, you know, that has reference to a lifestyle.

Q: Mm hm. And what might they say?

A: Oh, "she looks like a dyke" or "she dresses very butch," those types of things.

Q: And how do you typically respond to that?

A: I usually ignore it. 'Cuz, given where I am—usually in the Midwest, I just consider that pretty typical. (37-year-old white woman, social worker, interview #66)

Women's internal responses to such comments vary widely—some women try to shrug them off, denying that the comment affected her at all, and others are deeply offended and affected, but neither group is more likely to respond.

They [two men I didn't know] were walking by, and then just made a snide comment like "Hello baby." you know. . . .

Q: And how did you respond to that?

A: I was just like whatever.

Q: And how did you feel when he said that to you?

A: I was really upset—like insulted like—I was a piece of meat—like, you know? (22-year-old Hispanic woman, human resources professional, interview #36)

Women ignore because they are ashamed. When a man shouted loudly that this woman had nice legs, she "just kept on walking. I acted like I didn't hear it. I was embarrassed" (43-year-old African American woman, project manager, interview #45). Women are ashamed because they feel they should be able to control being the target of offensive public speech by altering the way they dress, talk, and interact (Nielsen 1999).

It may not be surprising that targets of sexually suggestive speech or racist speech fail to complain, and instead ignore such speech. Studies of victims of discrimination have found that even when victims think they have suffered a legally actionable form of workplace discrimination, they are unlikely to contact a lawyer (Curran 1977; Ewick and Silbey 1998). One reason, perhaps shared by these respondents, is that victims of discrimination do not want to identify as victims, preferring instead to construct an alternative version of the incident (Bumiller 1988) that makes them feel less like victims and more in control of their situation.

As these respondents suggest, by far the most common response to sexually suggestive speech from strangers in public places is to simply ignore it, although the impetus for the response is based on a variety of different, even conflicting, reasons. Many women revert to the narrative of personal safety explored in chapter 3, but others have a calculus about the intentions of the speaker or base their decision to ignore on what is best for their own mental health.

Conclusions about Women's Resistance to Sexually Suggestive Speech

Women resist unwanted sexual attention from strangers in public places in overt and hidden ways. A minority of women report actively responding in an assertive way and telling the speaker what they think about his comment. Far more women either tacitly participate in the interaction, begging off because they are attached or ignoring the speech.

Hidden reactions are complex. By externalizing and individualizing the events, some women are able to deny the interactions altogether, while others engage in an internal mental process meant to thrust the problematic nature of the interactions from the target back to the speaker (that's his problem). Reinterpreting and denying are resistance because women engage in this mental work to reject the speakers' worldview and his view of the woman-target. They are important for the women who utilize them, but they are hidden because there is no outward expression to the speaker or any surrounding passersby that the interaction is unacceptable.

Although no resistance amounts to tacit permission for such speech, the decision to ignore such speech is a measured one. Being in public carries with it fear of violence for women (Madriz 1997). But these are the same women who espouse the autonomy paradigm, rejecting legal intervention for offensive public speech and its accompanying problems.

POWER IN PUBLIC III: BEGGING

In contrast to the other types of problematic public speech, targets of begging are not reluctant to respond to panhandlers. When the initial speech is appropriate according to targets, targets often respond by saying something benign such as "No, thank you" or "Not today." When the initial speech is inappropriate, targets are more likely to respond verbally than are targets of the other forms of speech. Of course, the same considerations for personal safety are present in targets' calculus, but responses to begging are more frequent. One reason for the willingness to respond to begging may be the numerous formal mechanisms of resistance (both legal and nonlegal) to begging.

Informal/On the Street Reactions and Responses

Respondents do not report as many complicated, calculated ways of dealing with begging as they do with the other forms of offensive public speech, and far more subjects simply respond to begging, indicating that this type of problematic speech is less intimidating than most other forms of street speech.

Like the other forms of speech, a very common reaction to begging is to ignore the request for money, but the most common response to begging is actually to respond to the person speaking to resist the idea that the target should give money to the speaker. For example, one man says:

> At the BART station ... there's this gentlemen, you know, I don't know him, but he keeps coming up to me ... and I ain't never seen him before, and he puts on this little friendly act like you know him and stuff, but you don't know him. .... It's really very uncomfortable for me. .... Basically I will tell him "No, I don't have any [money]." He says, "Aw, come on, come on brother." I say, "Brother, I don't have any. I'm trying to go to work and get it myself." And he'll just go about his business. (34-year-old African American man, laborer, interview #35)

> The panhandlers are just working a scam. They don't scare me, because I don't have any money, and I don't feel guilty. Well, hey—I tell a mean old black panhandler—"Hey—I don't give a man my money—my old man would kick my ass." You know, "My old man gets all my money first, and you're SOL." Or I say, "What are you doing asking me for money? You ought to give me what you got." (51-year-old multiracial woman, laborer, interview #43)

> Most of the time, I just don't say anything, I keep going, and then if they get persistent, then I just really tell them ... "just go elsewhere." You know, one time I was in San Francisco and a young boy came up, a young man, dressed really well, and he said he didn't have any money, and gave me this big story, and I said "Well, there's places you can go eat if you're hungry, I don't have any money on me." (59-year-old white woman, buyer, interview #60)

But many people are not as assertive; they just politely say they are unable to give money. The polite response that beggars receive is indicative of the fact that targets do not take offense at begging in the same way they do for racist or sexist speech. Targets think that beggars deserve a respectful response. This is not the case with the other forms of speech.

I always try to be respectful [of beggars]. I will, if somebody addresses me or asks me a question or something, you know, I'll answer; I won't ignore them. And if they ask me for money, I'll say no, and I usually say I'm sorry whether I'm sorry or not. (29-year-old white man, student, interview #3)

If a homeless person walks up to me and talks to me and I don't have any money for them, then I just say, "I'm really sorry but I'm fresh out today." (29-year-old white woman, lawyer, interview #16)

Some targets even respond to panhandlers by saying that they also are poor. This kind of self-identification with the speaker is not reported with the other forms of speech."I just tell them, 'I'm a college student; I'm poor." (18-year-old African American woman, unemployed, interview #54)

Yeah, like I say when I go over to San Francisco, it happens. Even around here in this area, someone will come up and ask you for money. You know, 'cuz I work at the Hospital, and people will come up to you outside and ask you for money, and I'll say, "I don't have any" (59-year-old white woman, buyer, interview #60).

There is certain nonchalance when targets discuss begging. Although they report occasionally being afraid of a panhandler, these interactions mostly are described as trivial and nonthreatening. This comports with the data presented in chapter 3 that shows that respondents view begging as the least serious personal and social problem of these forms of speech.

Formal Mechanisms of Resistance

In addition to the fact that with begging the target is being identified for his or her more powerful position in the interaction, targets of panhandlers may feel less threatened by begging because there are a number of formal mechanisms to eliminate or reduce it in public places. Unlike racist and sexist speech, which encounter no mechanisms of formal resistance, there are many processes by which begging in public places is discouraged. The incentives for cities to try to make their streets free of begging are easy to understand; shoppers and taxpayers should not be inconvenienced or, worse still, threatened as they walk about the public streets. To that end, most large cities in the United States employ a variety of mechanisms to combat begging.

One type of formal resistance to begging is legal resistance. In its 1996 report on "antihomeless" laws, litigation and alternatives, the National Law Center on Homelessness and Poverty documents that of the fifty largest cities in the United States, at least 36 (75%) had city ordinances of one variety or another prohibiting begging (data unavailable for two cities) (Poverty 1996, pp. 8–9). More specifically, ten cities have citywide bans on begging, twenty cities prohibit begging in particular public locations, while twenty cities have ordinances prohibiting "aggressive panhandling" (Poverty 1996, pp. 8–9). In a 1999 update of this study, the National Law Center on Homelessness and Poverty documents that forty-three (86%) of the nation's fifty largest cities had laws against begging (data unavailable for one city) (Poverty 1999, p. ii).

In some of the nation's largest cities, at least, these ordinances and others designed to prevent homeless people from annoying more upstanding citizens are enforced with vigor and with regularity. In addition to an increase in the number of cities that have ordinances preventing panhandling in one form or another, the National Law Center reports that over a third of these cities instituted "crackdowns" on panhandling in the year studied (Poverty 1999). Indeed, mayoral campaigns are won and lost on campaigns to reduce or eliminate panhandling in public (Epstein 1995, 1998; Frankel and Puente 1994; Neuman 1994).

In addition to formal legal mechanisms designed to combat begging, informal mechanisms to resist begging also exist. These programs fall into three categories: voucher, competition, and education. Voucher programs enable potential givers to purchase vouchers in very small increments to hand to panhandlers in lieu of change.

In the summer of 1991, a partnership between the University of California, Berkeley, local businesses, homeless service agencies, and the City of Berkeley was formed to establish the "Berkeley Cares" voucher program. Approximately 100,000 25-cent vouchers are sold from some one hundred businesses annually. Over 95% of the vouchers sold are redeemed at over two hundred businesses (Fagan 1994; Wells 2002). Berkeley's voucher program served as a model for more than a dozen other voucher programs in the United States including ones in Santa Cruz, New Haven, New York City, and Seattle (Wells 2002).

Some cities also employ "competition" programs that are designed to collect the donations of generous pedestrians in coin boxes rather than allowing them to go to panhandlers. Some cities employing this type of program include Buffalo, New York; Santa Monica, California; and Durham, North Carolina (Herz 1994). The money collected is then used for homeless programs and support. Cities erect colorful and compelling containers such as mock parking meters or dolphin-shaped banks (Herz 1994) to attract and educate pedestrians. In some cities, local merchants or merchant associations who display signs encouraging potential donors to refrain from giving cash to the homeless match the funds collected.

Finally, another formal, extralegal mechanism designed to resist begging in public places are awareness and education programs. These programs provide referrals to homeless people in the form of pamphlets listing locations of soup kitchens, homeless shelters, as well as city, county, state, and federal aid agencies. Similar pamphlets are distributed to potential donors that educate them about the options available for charitable donation including nonprofit and religious groups that help the homeless. For example, in New York City, part of the anti-panhandling movement was to convince targets that by giving cash to panhandlers, they would be preventing the person from getting help.

Begging, the form of speech most likely to trouble people with power in our society, is resisted by a number of formal legal mechanisms, formal social mechanisms, and informal individual mechanisms. As such, individuals resisting begging do not have to perform the complex calculations performed by those who resist racist and sexist speech. This is due to a number of reasons. The speech itself, while sometimes offensive, rarely is threatening and is, for the most part, acceptable. Even in its more extreme forms, begging is less offensive than racism or sexism. But the power of legitimate authority of the state to combat begging should not be ignored.

Conclusions: Law and Power in Sidewalk Social Encounters

Reactions and responses to racist and sexist street speech are the product of a complicated calculus made by the target of such speech. Some reactions are overt forms of resistance and convey a message to the speaker and everyone else who witnesses such interactions. Far more common, however, is for targets to have a hidden response or to ignore the speech altogether. One interpretation is that targets of racist and sexist speech effectively and consistently respond with authority to those making the comments. Some First Amendment scholars whose model for combating racist and sexist speech with "more speech" may take heart in these results, claiming that they are evidence that simply allowing more speech is effective. Those who really are bothered by such speech will respond.

This interpretation, however, ignores the silencing that such speech engenders in many of its targets. All targets, whether they reported responding to such speech or not, said that they weighed their options very carefully when deciding how to respond, and the most important factor that determined their response was their own safety in the situation. Just as some critical race scholars claim, these comments engender fear for physical safety (Delgado 1993). Since women are more likely to fear for their physical safety when they are made targets of sexually suggestive speech than are men when they are targets, "more speech" disproportionately burdens women by requiring that they place their safety in jeopardy more often than men. This is in addition to the burden placed by the "more speech" idea in the first instance.

A second interpretation of these data is that there is very little resistance on the part of the targets. With some exceptions, targets mainly allow such comments to stand uncontested and leave the situation without engaging in counterspeech. By failing to contradict such comments, the targets of offensive public speech might be accused of tacitly participating in their own subordination. This interpretation belies the complicated processes that underlie targets' decisions about protesting such comments. These data show that targets are inclined to respond but often are precluded from doing so because they fear for their safety. Targets' options are limited.

Racist and sexist speech are interesting sites for the study of power relations because they represent apparent and blatant invocation of power by one individual over another. The power of racism and sexism, while firmly socially entrenched, is contested in various ways, however. All power relationships involve contests between the subordinate group and the powerful, but racism and sexism are unique in that there is growing recognition that racism and sexism are illegitimate axes of subordination, even by some members of the privileged group. Racist and sexist speech between strangers in public places violates social norms. This translates into permission to challenge racist and sexist speech in public places, but this can be done only when it is safe to do so. And, it is more common to challenge racist remarks than to challenge sexist remarks. This may be due to women's physical vulnerability, but it also may be due to the ambivalence about sexually suggestive speech. Some people consider at least mild forms of sexually suggestive speech acceptable. These also are interesting moments in which to examine power relations because the relationships are transitory. But the hierarchies the interactions reinforce are not.

Those who engage in active forms of resistance may be doing something serious to combat racism and sexism by managing to "redefine positively their general social position relative to the dominant group" (McCann and March 1996, p. 221). Active resistance occurs by making such interactions known—making people who are members of privileged classes know that they happen and happen with some regularity—by talking back in the moment (loud enough for others to overhear) or by talking about them publicly as great injustices. But these acts of resistance are rare. Only certain (i.e., more often whites and more often men) members of the dominated group have the luxury of engaging in overt mechanisms of resistance. Even they are more likely to choose not to do so.

We are left with a phenomenon that occurs often. In its racist and sexist form, it is a phenomenon that most people regard as a serious social problem. It is a problem most people think the law should not attempt to correct. Many people, including targets, think it should be dealt with through self-help. Yet when we investigate what actually happens in response to offensive public speech, targets tell us they usually do nothing. While begging is controlled through the deployment of official and informal mechanisms, sexist and racist public speech goes largely unchecked by formal or informal means.

Chapter Seven

LICENSE TO HARASS

THIS INQUIRY began with the legal and academic debate about the legal status of offensive public speech and moved to an empirical analysis of how ordinary citizens experienced offensive public speech and thought about it with respect to law. By conducting this research at two levels—the official and the everyday—we have learned much about the relationship between law, legal consciousness, and social hierarchy in the contemporary United States. We have learned from a closer scrutiny of judicial opinion that the official treatment of offensive public speech does not seriously consider the costs and benefits of attempting to regulate sexist and racist comments uttered in public. Nor do the courts treat all offensive speech the same: they are more tolerant of efforts to regulate begging than efforts to regulate racist and sexist speech. This inconsistency suggests that the law of free speech contains a bias against the poor, if not against white women and people of color. When this doctrine is placed in the context of what actually happens on the street, including the many ways in which begging is indirectly controlled by merchants, city planners, and the police, the inconsistency in the treatment of different kinds of offensive public speech becomes more glaring.

We also have learned that neither the academic nor the judicial analysis captures how ordinary citizens experience offensive public speech in their everyday lives and what they think the law should do about it. True to the predictions of critical race and feminist scholars, and the suggestions of empirical research from related areas, sexist and racist speech has a significant impact on the daily lives of the women and minorities groups who are its targets. White men, the traditionally privileged group in our society, rarely experience offensive remarks other than begging. And even though white men see sexist and racist speech as a serious problem, they underestimate how often it happens to target groups and how deeply target groups are affected. While these patterns are not that surprising given what we already knew, what is surprising is that the overwhelming majority of my respondents—white men, white women, and people of color—see racist and sexist speech as a serious social problem but do not think the law should be deployed against it. With the exception of white men, the reasons these respondents offer do not reflect the reasoning of the courts or academic defenders of absolute freedom of speech. Rather, they reflect the experiences of different social groups both with the hierarchies of everyday life and with the law.

The deeper lesson we learn from the analysis of the official and the everyday aspects of offensive public speech is that law is an invisible foundation for the hierarchies of race, gender, and class that are enacted on the streets of American cities. Law offers an implicit license to harass women and minorities. In the courthouse and the legislature, law as interpreted by sitting judges says that harassers have a constitutional right to utter abusive comments in public, virtually no matter how harmful the remarks might be for particular individuals and groups, and virtually without regard to whether they constitute public speech in any meaningful way. In the face of this official bulwark of the law, and given a history of failed promises by legal authorities in other aspects of their lives, it is small wonder that women and minorities do not turn to law for protection from offensive public speech. It is also clear from the narratives of my respondents who have been the targets of offensive public speech that they do not effectively respond to such abuse on their own. For all the respondents' talk about autonomy and self-help, and indeed for all the discourse in academic literature about resistance to oppression, there seems to be very little actual resistance to offensive public speech. Without legal recourse, there may be no recourse at all.

In this concluding chapter I discuss the implications of my findings for debates among legal scholars on offensive public speech, for contemporary social theory, and for theories of legal consciousness.

What Happens in Public?

My observations and the narrative accounts of my respondents shed new light on what happens in public places. These data demonstrate that the public sphere is shot through with invocation of hierarchy: women are sexually harassed with surprising regularity; and people of color are the targets of racist harassment regularly and with ferocity. But how confident can we be in data drawn from only one hundred respondents from one geographic area?

We should take these findings seriously for a variety of reasons. (1) They were collected, analyzed, and presented in accordance with accepted practices for qualitative research. One hundred interviews, randomly selected, is a relatively large sample by the standards of qualitative research. While I made the same choice of depth over breadth that is the hallmark of qualitative inquiry, I consciously constructed a sample that was large enough to include significant numbers of members of different social groups. I was able perform simple statistical comparisons across these groups. (2) As I detail below, the data comport with findings by several scholars in a variety of disciplines using different methodologies. (3) The patterns in my data are very clear in many respects. Without replication, we cannot be sure they will hold across time and place. Yet they are a plausible account that may well prove robust in other contexts. These and other methodological questions are discussed at greater length in the methodological appendix, appendix A.

There is a growing body of research about being in public places. Strangers often sexually harass women in public places (Davis 1994; Duneier 1999; Gardner 1980; Gardner 1995; Kissling 1991). Comments such as those recounted in the first chapter of this book are not uncommon. People of color, both men and women, frequently are subjected to racist comments in public places (Delgado and Yun 1995; Feagin 1991; Matsuda, Lawrence, Delgado, and Crenshaw 1993; Williams 1991). Gay men and lesbians are targeted for hate speech based on sexual orientation (Garnets, Herek, and Levy 1992; Swim, Cohen, and Hyers 1998). As scholars have begun to systematically map such phenomenon (Feagin 1991; Gardner 1995; Garnets, Herek, and Levy 1992; Landrine and Klonoff 1996), it appears clear that offensive public speech is not a rare or isolated occurrence. It is a significant, ongoing aspect of public space.

Moreover, we are beginning to see that there are serious consequences of being a target of racist or sexist speech in public places. In addition to the consequences of street harassment that I document in this book—including changing the way people dress, talk, and interact—other studies report the gravity of harms produced by encounters of gender-based discrimination. Psychologists have found that women are subjected to stares, comments reflecting the belief that women are less capable than men when performing certain tasks, objectifying sexual comments, and street harassment with surprising regularity (Swim, Cohen, and Hyers 1998; Swim and Stangor 1998). Experiencing sexual objectification[1] (in various forms, including unwanted sexually suggestive speech) may lead women to engage in "self-objectification," a process whereby women internalize the outsider's view of themselves (Fredrickson and Roberts 1997). These experiences may be related to various mental health risks, including eating disorders (Noll and Fredrickson 1998). Being the target of racist speech (along with other forms of racism) is related to psychiatric symptoms and cigarette smoking (Landrine and Klonoff 1996), requires complex coping strategies (Steele

1997), and affects how African Americans think about racial discrimination (Feagin 1991). The mere invocation of race can result in "stereotype threat," which has been shown to result in academic underperformance (Aronson, Quinn, and Spencer 1998; Steele 1997; Steele and Aronson 1995).

Even more problematic than these effects of being a target of racist or sexist speech is that victims (at least of sexually suggestive speech) are conditioned to believe that they are at fault. Not only have women become accustomed to internalizing blame for their own victimization, women also are taught to see various incarnations of sexual domination as discrete and unrelated. In the minds of Americans, street harassment is not connected to rape in the same way that a burning cross is connected to racialized violence like lynching. Gender discrimination and domination all can be rationally explained (often despite reliable empirical evidence to the contrary). Women are paid less because they choose the mommy track at work. Women are date raped because they led the man on. Women are stranger raped because they fail to take proper precautions. Women are victims of domestic violence because they remained in the relationship after he showed signs that he was a batterer. Similarly, women bring on street harassment by failing to dress modestly. Or, even more insidiously, women actually appreciate these comments as forms of flattery. These societal myths are believable only if one fails to see the connection between them. These are all forms of sexual subordination that are rationalized by a particular underlying view of the world—unarticulated, taken for granted notions about gender relations.

My findings and those of other scholars show how hierarchies of race and gender are reinforced and perpetuated through offensive public speech. But what role, if any, does law play in this process?

Law and Inequality—The License to Harass

Law allows offensive public speech despite the negative consequences that follow from it. Law offers a license to harass. A license allows a harmful (or potentially harmful) behavior to continue, usually with regulation and for a price. As we come to understand the nature of the harms produced by offensive public speech it is worth asking, who pays the price? When courts apply standard First Amendment logic in this area and hold that the remedy for offensive speech is "more speech," they do three things: (1) they establish a norm; (2) they exact a price to be paid; and (3) they create a sense that such interactions are legitimate.

First, courts create a presumption in favor of all speech. This casts those who favor regulation as dissidents within the current state of the law. The justification for free speech in this country is premised on protecting the voices of the disadvantaged and minorities. Given this justification, it is politically difficult for less privileged groups to oppose First Amendment policy. The First Amendment is one area in which law celebrates its antimajoritarian stance. Yet, I found that most members of traditionally disadvantaged groups do not cite a First Amendment rationale when rejecting legal intervention into offensive public speech. Although some might insist their position is a particular version of a belief in free speech, it would require us to ignore these respondents' own words and their own account of how they construct legal authority. Instead, they oppose legal regulation for very different reasons. The First Amendment is different for different people.

Second, courts exact a price to be paid by white women and people of color when they allow offensive public speech. The "license" to harass comes at a cost that is paid by frequent targets. If begging were successfully resisted (through formal and informal mechanisms of control in the street), and if white men reported that begging was a serious social problem (which they do not), the cost could be said to be shared by different members of society. But begging is not reported by any of the groups as a serious social problem. And begging is successfully resisted by legal and nonlegal actors (city councils, policemen, merchant associations, and even individuals on the street).

Finally, by saying that offensive public speech is protected speech, with all that this conclusion implies about the relative harms and benefits of such speech and its regulation, the courts tend to normalize such interactions. While an individual target may be outraged at a comment or fearful during an interaction, they have no legitimate script for opposing such behavior in the United States. Unlike other areas of legal protection for white women and people of color, such as laws prohibiting domestic violence or employment discrimination, in this area the law denies that an actionable harm exists. Thus, the law serves as a powerful, if unseen, legitimating force that buttresses the social inequality enacted in such interactions.

OFFENSIVE OR THREATENING?

I set out to study offensive public speech in part because it is a social problem with no legal remedy. The constitution forbids the restriction of "merely offensive" speech in public places. As I delved deeper into these interactions, however, I learned that these interactions are much more complex. These data demonstrate significant and wide-ranging effects that go beyond "mere offense."

Scholars on all sides of the hate speech debate can be pleased with these findings. Those who advocate restrictions on offensive speech can point to the empirical data as proof that such interactions are experienced as troubling and having serious effects on targets. Those who advocate First Amendment protection for such speech will be reassured by the finding that most average Americans disfavor the legal regulation of offensive public speech. While these are legitimate interpretations of the data, the accounts of offensive public speech and the analysis of people's understanding of these interactions requires an analysis of threatening and offensive speech.

Restrictions on threatening speech are constitutionally permissible (*Virginia v. Black*, 2003). When constitutionally protected speech such as cross burning is done *with the intent to intimidate*, the cross burning is transformed from speech to conduct. Burning a cross, as the Supreme Court pointed out in its recent opinion, has a long history of association with racism in extreme forms including lynching. Other forms of offensive public speech probably are not as likely to be understood as threatening in the legislature or the court. The division among the justices in *Virginia v. Black* is interesting in terms of the subjective experience of "threat."

Although Sandra Day O'Connor wrote eloquently for the majority about the horrific history of cross burning in the United States, there was a split among the majority on the question of who should determine whether a cross burning was done with the intent to intimidate. Only Clarence Thomas, the Court's only African American member, was willing to say that a cross burning could be presumed to be threatening. The rest of the six-person majority concluded that the finder of fact (a judge or jury) must determine if such intent existed. This split is interesting because it comports with what these data show. Targets think about, feel, and understand these experiences differently than do nontargets.

We also have seen the courts allow restrictions on begging. This is due in part to the availability of alternative forums for begging but it also is due in part to understanding that some extreme forms of begging can be threatening.

SITUATING LEGAL CONSCIOUSNESS

What do my findings tell us about legal consciousness more generally? First, they tell us that legal consciousness varies across social groups.

Second, they elaborate on and expand Ewick and Silbey's observation that there is a greater tendency to have a resistant legal consciousness among traditionally disadvantaged groups. Third, it suggests that legal doctrine and its institutional realization can invisibly shape legal consciousness.

Ewick and Silbey tell us that there are three ways in which people interact with or think about the law (1998). Some individuals stand "before the law," respecting the law and legal authority. Others are "with the law," taking a more instrumental approach to law; these individuals use the law when and how it suits their interests. Finally, there are those who are "against the law," resisting law and legal authority. Each of the four paradigms I identify in chapter 5 as reasons for rejecting legal intervention into offensive public speech can be said to roughly approximate one of these categories.

Those who fall into the First Amendment paradigm are "before the law." They believe that limiting speech would ultimately harm society; they respect the legal system and what it currently dictates about speech. Those within the autonomy and impracticality paradigms are "with the law," but for different reasons. These people say that they do not ideologically oppose legal regulation on offensive public speech; they simply oppose legal regulation because it would be impossible to enforce (pure pragmatism) or because they think that the law would ultimately fail in its quest to aid in rectifying gender inequality (autonomy). Finally, those who fall into the distrust of authority paradigm are "against the law." They see the law as a threat to their personal interactions. They fear that laws prohibiting offensive public speech are likely to be used against those it was intended to benefit.

The paradigms correlate with race and gender. Thus, the legal consciousness of respondents varies across social groups. This kind of variation in legal consciousness should be explored in an effort to discover underlying patterns in legal consciousness. For example, Ewick and Silbey hypothesize (and this research demonstrates) that those who occupy traditionally disadvantaged social locations are more likely to have a legal consciousness that is oppositional or counterhegemonic. But what would we hypothesize about the attitudes of these groups to a reform that would improve their lives? I found that members of certain groups are apathetic toward law, even when it is proposed to remedy a social problem they view as severe.

All of those who are targets of racist and sexist public speech wish they could avoid this fate. They resist being made a target of such speech in whatever ways available to them. For women (of all races), this means avoiding certain areas and altering dress and appearance. For people of color (both men and women) it means employing a strategy to dissuade racists from making such comments. Some (mostly men) accomplish this by threatening the individual or even having a fight. Others seek to resist the imposition of the race hierarchy by ignoring the comment and thinking that the comment has nothing to do with them; it reflects on the speaker's ignorance. In each case, targets resist the imposition of these hierarchies. By asking these individuals about the use of the law to resist these categories, we learn something very interesting about law, social change, and legal consciousness. These individuals are reluctant to use the law for the reasons stated previously despite their personal commitment (occasionally even when it means risking one's own safety) to combat racism and sexism in the streets of America. These variations in legal consciousness are important because they teach us that the relationship between the individual and the social institution changes with context.

LAW AND SPEECH POLICY

How does this understanding of legal consciousness affect our understanding of the relationship between the individual, social systems of power and privilege, and law? When asked about what types of problems they face, researchers have found that, "the most frequently reported problems identified by women and racial minorities are precisely those situations that are most likely to be defined as minor, trivial, or personal (i.e., not legal matters)" (Ewick and Silbey 1998, p. 237). Racist and sexist public speech are just such problems. These forms of speech reinforce hierarchies of race and gender in society, operating with an unwritten, largely invisible license from the law. As target groups report, though, it is not a license they expect to see revoked. Nor do they expect the law to be transformed into a shield protecting the weak, or a weapon that could be successfully used to combat racism or sexism, as is the case with employment discrimination law. In a society that cherishes a legal remedy for such harms, but also cherishes free speech, this is one harm the law will not redress.

Individuals may not think there should be a law preventing offensive or even threatening speech precisely because the present doctrine of free speech is hegemonic in the courts and in the street. Indeed, there is a powerful ideology for allowing such speech that is premised on a nonmajoritarian defense of "minority opinion." Part of the rationale of free speech is that minority views (typically politically unpopular) should be allowed to be heard. The liberal legal model of the First Amendment constructs our cultural understanding in such a way that opposing free speech is opposing equality and supporting free speech, no matter how abhorrent the view expressed, is supporting equality. The data presented in this book demonstrate that this understanding is well entrenched even among those whose lived experiences do not comport with the real-world implications of such a policy.

While law plays a role in justifying offensive public speech, social hierarchies and the practices that enact them also have a life of their own. Women face discrimination in many arenas. People of color are targets of racism in a variety of forms. The state operates in the lives of those living in poverty in a variety of ways. These are the social facts. Continually being subject to unfair treatment on the basis of race or gender requires targets to adopt a variety of coping strategies. Targets tend to understand racist and sexist offensive public speech as disaggregated from larger systems of hierarchy and privilege in this country. They are isolated incidents. These interpretations allow the individual target a way to make sense of the world and regain a sense of control in the encounters. The perpetrator is an aberration; most people do not believe that about me.

Despite these rationalizations, targets of such events know that racism and sexism are pervasive and, in many circumstances, unavoidable parts of social life. In the face of racism and sexism, targets cannot always fight back. They know that sometimes they must be the ones to end such encounters by quitting a job, by accepting lower pay, or by ignoring offensive public speech. The reality of social position is not lost in such encounters. Because social position and hierarchy are pervasive, white women and people of color must accept the terms that society defines, choosing to contest inequity only some of the time. Accepting social position does not mean believing that such hierarchies are legitimate, only that they are real, pervasive, and meaningful. Accepting these "realities" sometimes means accepting inequity as a part of real life.

Law, social norms, and culture are constitutive; they mutually shape one another (Yngvesson 1988). Individuals do not clamor for laws restricting offensive public speech because such a practice seems unassailable. A real-world understanding of social norms tells us that offensive public speech is unavoidable. Law tells us that to restrict it is to condone repression. Our gender norms tell us that such speech is acceptable, either as harmless flirting or the predictable response to how women dress, behave, or the route they travel. That is, it is the victim's fault.

Moreover, with street harassment, there is no one to whom the target can "officially" complain. Unlike workplace sexual harassment, which can be the responsibility of the employer, or sexual violence, which may trigger state intervention in the form of criminal sanction, street harassment has no remedy and there is no private or state actor with authority to sanction perpetrators.

Scholars of law and society typically study social problems and law's capacity to remedy the problem. We seek to understand the ways in which law might be made to be more effective or we examine how and why law fails. Oftentimes, we study laws that seek to combat powerful social forces such as racism and sexism in various forms. Scholars may identify problems in the political process, in the courts at the trial level, in terms of victim mobilization or rights consciousness, but the underlying assumption in such scholarship is that the law has some capacity to affect social change. In the case of offensive public speech, at present, there is no basis for remedy. Indeed, law is one of many institutions and social forces that provides justification for allowing such speech. Law legitimates, rather than condemns, offensive public speech.

LAW AND SOCIAL CHANGE/MOVEMENTS

But why do we not see developing social movements around other kinds of hate speech in public places? After all, there is a civil rights movement and a woman's movement that are, in part, dedicated to the protection of individuals against dignitary harms. So why isn't racist street harassment a concern pursued in the civil rights movement? And, why isn't sexist street speech given greater prominence on the agenda of the feminist movement?

The case of street harassment demonstrates the power of a social movement backed by economically strong interests. It is not surprising that laws prohibiting begging are passed by municipalities, upheld by the courts, and enforced in the streets by the police despite the fact that targets of begging do not find the interaction very problematic. Such ordinances reflect the collective economic power of business interests. Despite efforts of social reformers to protect the interests of the homeless, including the right to ask passersby for money, municipalities wage and win restrictions on begging in the name of protecting commercial activity, including shopping, tourism, and business generally.

If offensive public speech on the basis of race and sex is as troubling as respondents report, why do we not see the development of a powerful social movement to combat racist and sexist street harassment? This is yet another arena in which Americans are not as litigious as some commentators and scholars suggest. Offensive public speech is not the kind of injury for which average citizens seek "total justice" (Friedman 1987).

Although they may not be powerful, there are emerging movements to combat street harassment. In the case of sexist street speech in New York City, the Street Harassment Project has developed.[2] This nonprofit organization encourages women to "take back the streets" from men who have too long considered the street their "turf." The organization was formed in the wake of the June 11, 2000, incident in which hundreds of men assaulted, stripped, and fondled over fifty-six women in the public space of Central Park. One of the organization's premises is that verbal street harassment often becomes assault, but the group does not seem to have an official position on the legal regulation of speech in and of itself. Rather, the organization conducts teach-ins and awareness campaigns designed to combat street harassment. With racist harassment, the "movement" has centrally been around college hate speech codes and municipal ordinances banning cross burning.

The individualized and anonymous way that offensive and threatening public speech can occur also makes it difficult to organize against. Public outrage is expressed only when such speech turns into riotous misbehavior, as in the Central Park incident or when a cross burning is performed by an organized group such as white supremacists.

The resistance of the courts to hate speech codes on constitutional grounds is part of the reason that these issues are not in the forefront of the social movements in which they could be embedded. Despite the Court's resistance to such statutes, other research demonstrates that universities and colleges continue to adopt hate speech codes (Gould 2001). In the wake of *R.A.V. v. City of St. Paul*, even before the encouragement offered in *Virginia v. Black*, cities had continued to redraft cross-burning statutes to pass constitutional muster.

These data tell us that there are more than simple structural barriers to speech reform, however. That is to say, the lack of political mobilization cannot be solely attributed to the courts' rejection of speech restrictions. Some of the reasons that people give for disfavoring legal intervention on offensive speech is related to how they understand law's ability to address certain social problems. Law defines these interactions as outside its reach. This position reinforces the trend in the postcivil rights era to treat those who would seek new forms of legal remedy as hyperlitigious and thin-skinned. It is not surprising that targets look to self-help rather than law for a solution.

Part of the attraction of studying legal consciousness is its potential for transforming the status quo. Akin to social movement theory, the hope is that if consciousness of ordinary citizens can be raised, it can transform an unjust social order. The study of legal consciousness fundamentally is the study of what comes before the political opportuni-

ties, mobilizing structures, and other conditions that can lead to powerful social movements (Meyer and Staggenborg 1996).

Systems of inequality and subordination, more broadly conceived,
certainly involve mechanisms of discrimination, racism, and sexism
that are more harmful than offensive public speech. Consider rape, domestic violence, unequal pay, and pregnancy discrimination in the
workplace for the women's movement. All of them have very real and
material consequences for women that are more serious than the dignitary harm associated with an offensive comment. They even are more
harmful than a "threat," although a threat is clearly illegal. To move
sexist street speech to the forefront of the women's movement's agenda
would be seen as silly because, to date, offensive public speech has
been seen as minor when compared to "real" problems. However,
when it is linked to these practices and seen as part of a system of
subordination that is manifest in the workplace, in the home, and now,
as we have seen, in public places, street harassment is more serious.
The real problem is racism and sexism in all of its manifestations.

Unlike these other forms of discrimination and subordination, which
often are attributed to motivations other than race and sex (and then
excused), street harassment is naked in its reference to the speaker's
race and sex. It remains one manifestation of inequality that cannot be
excused or ignored as symptomatic of something else. In the age of
formal equality, it is a reminder that racism, sexism, and class inequality are alive and well in the United States.

But how might this change if people became more aware of the nature of the problems associated with offensive public speech? Problems
associated with gender domination often seem outside the scope of
law. Laws preventing domestic violence, child abuse, and date rape all
were met with resistance on the grounds that law would not be an
effective or efficient mechanism for redressing such problems. But
eventually those understandings changed as the law adopted a more
interventionist approach.

Conclusion

The relationship between judicial doctrine, legal scholarship, the legal
consciousness of ordinary citizens, and the practical realities of offensive public speech are complex. By reviewing the doctrine and scholarship, by observing the phenomenon in the field, and by asking a sample of ordinary citizens belonging to different racial, gender, and class

groups about their experiences with such speech and their views on attempting to regulate it through the law, this research has begun to explore these links. Only by examining doctrine, theory, practices on the street, and the attitudes of different groups is it possible to understand what produces legal consciousness and the ways that law and other systems of power and privilege combine to reinforce and reinscribe systems of social hierarchy.

The results are in some ways disconcerting, in some ways reassuring for those who are concerned with the relationship between law and hierarchies of race, gender, and class in American society. They are disconcerting because I found that racist and sexist harassment are widespread problems for white women and people of color. This kind of public speech imposes significant burdens on these groups. For many, it is part of their daily existence, affecting what they wear, where they go, and how they relate to strangers. The reactions of these target groups to the problem, including the prospect of a legal remedy, also are troubling in some respects. Women tend to internalize the blame for much of the sexually suggestive harassment they experience on the street. For the most part, women oppose invoking the law as a solution because they refuse to take on the label of "victim." Or, women see the problem as so pervasive and diffuse that they doubt the law could or should try to prevent it. People of color, especially African American men, also do not favor legal intervention in the case of racist speech, because they are cynical about whether the law would really serve their interests. And, they fear that the same laws others see as protecting them may in fact be turned against them.

The results are reassuring in the sense that respondents showed realism in the face of the problems of street harassment. Scholars who look to white women and people of color as a vanguard of social change in the battle against offensive public speech may be disappointed at the rationales these groups recite, but there is reasoned wisdom in these positions. They are dubious about whether law is the proper mechanism for dealing with this unpleasant side to their life in public. Their perspectives are based on personal experience as these individuals are, in fact, the victims of racism and sexism in the streets. Rather than dismiss the attitudes of these respondents as some form of "false consciousness," misinformed, or deluded, legal scholars, advocates for social change, and sociologists should listen seriously to what they say.

We should not take too much comfort in the result that most Americans seem to agree with the present legal status of offensive public speech, however. The results do not represent a popular ratification of the legal doctrine regarding offensive public speech. Many respondents, especially women and people of color, do not adhere to the First Amendment model of street harassment. Rather, they see no viable, culturally appropriate legal mechanism for redressing these problems.

It may very well be that the policy choice we have made in favor of free speech in America is the correct one. Nonetheless, the study of offensive public speech brings to light the ways in which law works to normalize and legitimate social hierarchies of race, gender, and class, favoring the privileged in each of these types of interactions.

Appendix A

RESEARCH DESIGN

THIS STUDY of street harassment and its effects is part of a broader attempt to better understand what Ewick and Silbey call "legality," or the role of law in the everyday lives of individuals (Ewick and Silbey 1998; Sarat and Kearns 1995). I examine a particular social problem, offensive public speech, to gain insight into how ordinary people think about a phenomenon that affects their everyday lives and whether they believe law should intervene. Offensive public speech is thus a point of departure for a sociological inquiry into the legal consciousness of ordinary citizens.

Socio-legal scholars can focus on "law" when they study society. In my research I could have focused solely on attitudes about the First Amendment or civil liberties. While this is an important area of opinion research, legal attitudes are not my central concern. My purpose in conducting this research was twofold. First, I wanted to analyze offensive public speech because it is a social phenomenon that is largely invisible and unarticulated, but that may have important connections to hierarchies of race, gender, and class. Second, I wanted to understand how people think about the law as a remedy for social problems in general and with respect to offensive public speech in particular. Like other researchers of legal consciousness, I attempt to move the study of law beyond its official precincts of individuals trained in or directly affected by the law. I attempt to study the legal consciousness of ordinary citizens and how that consciousness affects their understanding of themselves and their social position. Additionally, I am interested in the link between legal elites and laypeople. Thus, my research explores legal doctrine, how doctrine is (or is not) related to what happens on the street, and how both elites and laypeople conceptualize this relationship.

Several methodological imperatives follow from this conceptualization. First, I had to study the phenomenon of street harassment and how it affects people in public places. It was critical that I devote considerable time to observing speech between strangers in public places. Second, to understand a complicated, rarely articulated thought process, it was necessary to conduct in-depth interviews as opposed to brief interviews that used only closed-ended questions to assess opinions and attitudes. To examine how average citizens evaluate the law as a remedial tool, I needed to refrain from introducing the concept of law as a possible solution until late in the interview.

Thus, my study is based on three distinct methodologies. The first is ethnography; I conducted field observations of interactions between strangers in public places. The second research method is interviews. From the field sites where I conducted the observations, I selected and interviewed one hundred subjects about their experiences with offensive public speech. The final research methodology is legal research. I examined legal opinions on offensive public speech to learn how judges understand offensive public speech. Thus I am able to compare official versions of offensive public speech with what my respondents report actually occurs in public places.

This appendix elaborates the steps taken at each phase of the empirical research process. First, I address the field observation component of the research. I then discuss how I conducted interviews.

In the Field

I conducted planned, systematic observations of interactions between strangers in public places designed to provide me with a better understanding of the nature of interactions. I spent about 120 hours in public places. During this time, I attempted to keep a low profile as a passive observer. Against my will, however, I became a target of offensive public speech on occasion (especially in the case of sexually suggestive speech). I accomplished the majority of my field observations as a passive observer, meaning that I was neither the speaker nor the target in interactions involving offensive public speech.

In each of the cities from which I selected research subjects, I spent some time observing interactions while I hid behind books in cafes or aimlessly traveled the BART (Bay Area rapid transit) train system. Throughout, I attempted to remain as unobtrusive as possible. A major drawback to nonparticipant observation is that the mere presence of the researcher changes the nature of the very things we propose to study—in my case, interactions between strangers in public places. This is less true for begging, because begging is designed to be heard by as many people as possible. Thus, my presence probably does little to deter begging. However, with race-related and sexually suggestive offensive public speech, my presence most certainly affected the interactions. One characteristic of sexually suggestive and race-related speech between strangers in public places is that it is often accomplished in such a manner that only the intended target can hear the offending remarks. Everyone is familiar with the stereotypical description of the construction worker who shouts his "compliments" to the women below for all to hear. While this scenario is certainly grounded in truth, a number of respondents say that more offensive comments, and often racist comments, are directed at individuals outside the earshot of anyone else. Speakers seem to know that these sorts of attacks and comments are socially unacceptable; they do not want people other than the intended target to hear them.

One of the major advantages of field observation is that the researcher is privy to "unfiltered" information, meaning that I was able to obtain detailed accounts of actual street interactions. Relying solely on secondhand descriptions of street interactions, such as the ones provided in an interview situation, is not enough. Respondents may downplay the story due to its graphic and degrading nature. In the alternative, respondents might embellish the bravado of their response in an interview situation in order to appear brave to the researcher. The field observations served as the basis for many of the questions I ultimately asked in the interview. I began to notice trends in responses to various forms of street speech among certain groups of individuals. I also noticed different reactions by women to sexually suggestive speech. Some women ignore and some women respond to offensive public speech, but I could not discern what made the difference between those targets who responded and those who ignored the interaction. These observations led to the interview questions that explore the factors that lead women to respond or to ignore a comment. In the section that follows, I describe the locations from which I recruited subjects for interviews.

Observation and Interview Techniques

I conducted interviews with one hundred respondents recruited from the locations in which I conducted observations. Selecting subjects from public places had several advantages. First, I knew that the people I approached were consumers of public space. That is to say, they were willing to venture into public places and have, more likely than not, been party to the interactions about which I would be asking. By going where the data are I was able to observe interactions as verification for the stories I was told in the interviews. By approaching people in person, I could establish rapport in a way that would be impossible if contact were initiated via telephone. Finally, people were less threatened being approached in a crowded public place than they might have been in some other context.

There would have been advantages to conducting a random probability sample, but there were various drawbacks that ultimately resulted in my decision to conduct a purposive sample in public places. First, I was constrained by resources available to graduate students. The costs associated with a random household survey are extensive. The sensitive nature of the questions I was asking provided another constraint. Asking subjects about experiences with offensive racist and sexist harassment in public places means speaking bluntly, using racial epithets and other offensive language, which is more successful when there is some level of rapport between the subject and the researcher. The personal connection I achieved by approaching subjects in public ultimately resulted in an open and willing attitude on the part of subjects to answer the questions I asked. Finally, although this project attempts to test theory, we know little about attitudes on offensive public speech and corresponding attitudes about law. It was necessary to pursue a more open-ended, inductive approach that might establish the basis for more conventional designs in the future. Indeed, several of the results reported here are worth exploring in a more systematic way, using a larger random sample across a wider geographic area.

Systematic Selection of Field Sites

I selected sites in a variety of locations that would ensure broad representation across race, socioeconomic status, and gender categories among subjects selected. I first chose cities and then locations within each of these cities. I used a purposive sampling approach, attempting to "select units that are 'representative' or 'typical' of the population" (Singleton and Straits 1999, p. 158). I selected cities to represent variation in population within the Bay Area. They were: the Berkeley/Oakland area; San Francisco; and Orinda, a wealthy suburb of San Francisco. Each city was selected for a particular reason.

I selected Berkeley and Oakland because of their diverse racial composition. I used Oakland to supplement the Berkeley data because I did not want to oversample people associated with the University of California, given that institution's unique history in the free speech movement. When I solicited from Berkeley, it was only in the summer months, thereby reducing the chances that I would be oversampling those with a university affiliation. During school months, I recruited in Oakland.

Berkeley has a population of 102,000 residents. Some 59% are white, 18% are African American, 15% are Asian and about 7% are Hispanic. The average household income in Berkeley is $42,902 with almost 10% of residents living below the federal poverty level (U.S. census data

1990). In Berkeley, 28% of residents have obtained a bachelor's degree and an additional 30% have a graduate or professional degree.

Oakland is similar to Berkeley. The population is larger, about 372,000 people, of whom 28% are white, 43% are African American, 14% are Asian, and about 12% are Hispanic (U.S. census data 1990). The average household income is $37,099. About 7% of residents live below the federal poverty level. Only 16% of Oakland residents have a bachelor's degree and 11% hold a graduate or professional degree (U.S. census data 1990).

Because I suspect that some of the people most offended by street speech are those who have little contact with it, I chose the town of Orinda from which to select another third of my subjects. Orinda is a suburb of San Francisco with a population of approximately 16,000. Whites make up over 90% of Orinda's residents and another 7% are Asian. Only slightly more than 1% are of Hispanic origin and fewer than 1% are African American (U.S. census data 1990). Orinda has a large number of educated residents. Of those twenty-five years and older, 38% of Orinda residents have obtained a bachelor's degree and an additional 28% also have a graduate or professional degree. The average household income in Orinda is over $106,000 and about 95% of Orindans have an income over twice the poverty level.

San Francisco is a large metropolitan city with a population of 723,000 people with quite a diverse racial composition (U.S. census data 1990). Whites make up about 47% of San Francisco's population, Asians about 29%, Hispanics 12%, and African-Americans 11%. The average household income in San Francisco is $45,663 with 6.13% of residents living below the poverty level (U.S. census data 1990). Of residents over twenty-five years of age, the highest level of education achieved is high school graduate for 18% and college graduate for 22%.

After choosing the cities, I selected two locations within each. One location was a public place such as a street and one was a location where commuters wait to utilize public transportation, such as a train station or bus stop. I tried to choose places where I thought there would be a rich source of data—places where people speak to each other. In Berkeley, Telegraph Avenue is the obvious choice. Telegraph Avenue is close to campus, and laden with panhandlers who ask for money and sometimes make sexually suggestive and racist comments to passersby. Finding panhandlers or street speech of any variety between strangers in public places in Orinda is virtually impossible. There I solicited subjects entering a grocery store. Occasionally, there would be a person collecting money for a charitable organization outside the grocery store in Orinda, but there is little interaction between strangers in public aside from polite hellos in this button-down community. In San Francisco, subjects were selected on Market Street. Like Telegraph Avenue in Berkeley, a pedestrian can hardly go five feet without being solicited for money. Sexually explicit speech is not uncommon in this location. I suspect that I would be able to make more informed comments about race-related comments in these locations as well if I were not white.

Within each city, I also chose one or more public transportation sites for observation and subject recruitment. I used the BART (Bay Area Rapid Transit) train stations in all of the cities. Public transportation sites provided numerous examples of interactions between strangers, as well as a good opportunity to solicit subjects for the interview portion of the research. Individuals standing and waiting for trains or busses were more willing to listen to my request than those walking down the street. And all people were more likely to agree to the interview if they heard my entire request.

Once the six locations were selected, I had to decide *when* to observe and solicit subjects. I wanted to vary the time of day in each location to ensure the broadest representation of subjects as possible. I went to each location at three times, rush hour (morning or evening), daytime, and night (after dark). Commuters thus are overrepresented in the rush-hour samples, retired persons and the unemployed make up much of the daytime samples, and nights were a mix of all types of people.

Selecting Subjects

The biggest opportunity for researcher bias was deciding which individuals to approach and ask if they would participate in the study. As a white woman, certain types of people are easier for me to approach. There is far less social stigma associated with approaching another young, white woman than in approaching a man, for example. In order to counteract this opportunity for bias, I employed a strategy designed to ensure that everyone within the particular location had an equal opportunity to be selected for participation and to eliminate any bias I might have in approaching strangers.

When I entered a field site, a BART station for example, I recorded the scene in my field notes. I noted the date, time of day, location and describe the people in the location. I would also describe any interactions between strangers occurring in the location. For example, at one BART station in Berkeley, there were always those preaching religion at the ticket station, with zealots asking people if they wanted a religious publication. The scene typically included several panhandlers outside the gates, who either sat quietly with signs or asked for spare change. I would spend some time observing these interactions, making notes about the types of individuals who tend to respond to or ignore these strangers addressing them. After some time observing, I would begin to solicit subjects. Even though I had not witnessed each interaction and each person's response to the public speech, I knew that every person in that BART station had recently had this sort of interaction.

In order to prevent selection bias, to guard against only approaching people with whom I felt comfortable, and to ensure that everyone in the locations had an equal chance of being selected to participate in the interview, I randomly selected subjects from among the people in the previously selected site. To determine the individuals who I would ultimately approach, I selected a number between one and six by throwing a die. I would also randomly select a side of the BART platform by flipping a coin. As an illustration, imagine I rolled the number three and that the coin toss resulted in heads. Heads represented the north side of the platform and three represented the interval of people for recruitment. I would then enter the BART station, walk to the northernmost point on the platform, and begin counting people, approaching every third individual to ask if they would be willing to participate in the research. I only breached this method three times, when the appointed individuals appeared incoherent and were frightening to me.

On the street, the method was only slightly different. I would find a street speaker, either asking for money or something and then I would walk about fifteen feet away (to his left or his right was determined by a flip of the coin) and approach those people who walked by (the interval determined by a roll of the die). I was less successful recruiting subjects on the street. People are very uncomfortable when a stranger (even a well-dressed woman) falls into step with them on the street.

When I approached potential subjects, I said, "Excuse me, could I have a moment of your time? I am a researcher at the University of California, Berkeley. I am conducting research about interactions between strangers in public places. My research consists of a brief interview. If you would like to participate, I will call you and do it over the phone at a time that is convenient for you or we could meet and do it in person. Would you be willing to participate?"

Some people I approached said yes or no right away, while others would ask me questions which I would answer. Potential subjects often wanted to know more about the topic, so I would elaborate that the research is about interactions that they might find troublesome such as aggressive panhandling. They also often wanted to know if I worked for someone or if this was my own research. As required by the University of California, Berkeley, human subjects committee, I

presented the informed consent paperwork to subjects who were willing to participate in my research and asked them to read and sign the
form. I went on to note their phone number and the time when they
wanted to be called. Whether or not they agreed to participate in the
interview, I noted the race, gender, and approximate age in order to
explore trends among individuals who refused to participate in order
to understand the representativeness of my sample. I continued such
selections until I achieved numerical goals for respondents with certain
race and gender characteristics. I oversampled white women and people of color for analytic purposes. Thus, while I randomized selections
within demographic subgroups and within strategically selected locations, this is not a random sample.[1]

I approached a total of 212 people to generate 100 interviews. Of
those 212, 11 were rejected by me in the moment because they were
minors (and my human subjects approval was based on interviewing
adults) or because they did not speak enough English to understand
my request or the consent forms. Thus, I approached 201 eligible potential respondents.

Of the 201 eligible subjects approached, 112 (56%) agreed to do the
interview. But who are those 56%? There were no significant differences by race or gender in the response of subjects approached. As
table A.1 shows, the only significant differences in response rates were
according to the city in which the subjects were recruited. Those individuals approached in the suburban areas were significantly less likely
to agree to do the interview. This is not surprising to people familiar
with Orinda and like suburbs. The affluent, mostly white individuals
who reside in this suburb seemed too busy to be bothered with my
questions.

Ultimately, I conducted 100 interviews out of 112 people who agreed
to do the interview. The 12 people who ultimately did not complete
the interview included six whose telephone numbers had been discon-
nected and six I could not reach after repeated attempts. Those with
invalid numbers might have given false phone numbers in an effort
to appear polite in the moment without having to do the interview.
Alternatively, it is possible that I may have written the numbers incor-
rectly in the public places in which I was recruiting. As a general rule,
I called willing subjects only five times. If the respondent made no effort to return my call or schedule a more convenient time to do the
interview, I abandoned them as a potential subject. Although I did not
want to give up on these six respondents, it seemed the ethical thing
to do. They were avoiding my calls, which I took to mean they had
withdrawn their consent.

TABLE A.1
Demographic Characteristics of Respondents

Race		
White	51%	(N = 51)
African American	27%	(N = 27)
Hispanic	6%	(N = 6)
Asian/Pacific Islander	16%	(N = 16)
Gender		
Male	37%	(N = 37)
Female	63%	(N = 63)
Education		
< High School Diploma	3%	(N = 3)
High School Graduate	7%	(N = 7)
Some College	36%	(N = 36)
College Graduate	37%	(N = 37)
Advanced Degree	16%	(N = 16)
Self-Educated	1%	(N = 1)
Age		
< 18 years	2%	(N = 2)
18–24	25%	(N = 25)
25–29	20%	(N = 20)
30–34	15%	(N = 15)
35–39	6%	(N = 6)
40–44	6%	(N = 6)
45–49	8%	(N = 8)
50–54	11%	(N = 11)
55–59	3%	(N = 3)
60 and over	4%	(N = 4)
City Recruited		
Orinda	24%	(N = 24)
Berkeley/Oakland	55%	(N = 55)
San Francisco	21%	(N = 21)
Total	100%	(N = 100)

Sample Bias

Most research designs are subject to questions about sample selection bias. The issue is especially problematic in the kind of site-based selection procedures I used. Although I took care not to introduce bias in the selection of the sample, it is necessary to consider how the decisions I made in the course of collecting the data may affect the results. As is the case with any research, this sample represents the area in which it was gathered. As table A.1 shows, my sample is relatively young (especially in Berkeley and San Francisco) and well educated, despite the fact that I conducted the interviews in Berkeley during the summer months so as not to include too many students in the study. Students might be atypical in several ways. In addition to being well educated and, for the most part, rather well-to-do, in Berkeley they may be greater supporters of free speech than other members of the community. And, by selecting subjects from public places, my sample is biased toward those willing to tolerate such speech; otherwise, they would not be in public places.

Additionally, as is the case with any major university, the University of California, Berkeley, has a number of programs about racism and sexism which may lead these students to be less tolerant of racism and sexism in whatever form. In the alternative, such programs could lead to a backlash in which students do not think that extra care should be taken to protect white women and people of color from racist and sexist attacks. Or, it could be biased in favor of supporters of free speech. It is difficult to know how students might bias the results.

The choice of Berkeley itself also may introduce a bias to the results. Berkeley is the home of the free speech movement. It has a long tradition of being a locus for liberal political activity. Most of those active in the Berkeley political arena are traditional liberals and supporters of civil liberties. More generally, California itself may be more politically liberal than many other parts of the country. But, it is difficult to determine the direction of this bias. There may be a high concentration of civil liberties supporters who would be hesitant to restrict offensive public speech. Or, if the people in Berkeley are politically radical, they might be *more* in favor of limiting offensive public speech because they accept the premise of critical theorists regarding equality. Of course, the study does not rest solely on Berkeley. By including Orinda and San Francisco as sites for recruiting subjects, I analyze differences in attitudes by location. Although I examined differences in results by location, none was sufficient beyond the effects of race, gender, and class to warrant discussion in this book.

Interviews

While the many hours of observation are a valuable source of data, it was essential to talk to informants in considerable depth. One goal of the project was to document and recount "life on the street." To do so, I needed to have people tell me about their experiences with street speech. They did, in fact, recount the multiple, almost constant barrage of intrusions by strangers in public places, how they felt about them, and how they responded.

My interviews were carefully designed to see where the law fits into the thinking of these subjects. I used a combination of open-ended and structured questions. By asking open-ended questions about how they deal with offensive public speech, I allowed subjects to tell me what they thought of the law and if they thought it would be a good way to solve this social problem. By leaving the legal questions until the end of the interview, I was able to see if people spontaneously mentioned the law as one possible way to solve this social problem. Thus I was able to determine the primacy of law in the respondents' analysis.

Because I called subjects at appointed times requested by the respondents, interviews took place at various times of the day, ranging from 5 A.M. to 11 P.M. Interviews ranged from about twenty minutes to ninety minutes. The pace of the interview was dictated by the number of stories about offensive public speech the subject was able to recall and willing to recount and by how willing the subjects were to discuss the regulation of speech. Some subjects had very few stories of strangers speaking to them in public places, either because it does not occur very often or because they could not recall specific instances.

The interview also varied according to the interest of the subject. Some people thought long and hard about the difficult balancing task about which I was asking. They discussed relevant principles of fairness and free speech with a great deal of thoughtfulness while others had obvious disdain of even considering limiting public speech.

The interview schedule is reproduced in Appendix B. As shown there, I began the interview by asking subjects to recall a time when someone they did not know spoke to them in a public place. By leaving the topic of the encounter to the respondent, the interview allows informants to speak first about the stories that were most memorable to them. I then went on to ask about a time when people they did not know had asked them for money in public places, followed by a question about times when people they did not know asked them for money in a way that made them feel uncomfortable or afraid. I asked a number of follow-up questions after the subject recounted their story.

If the information was not volunteered in the original telling, I asked where the subject was, where the speaker was in relation to the subject, what were the exact words used by the speaker, how did it make the subject feel, and what they thought about the interaction. I also asked what the subject did, if anything, in response to the interaction. I asked about the characteristics of the speaker, including their age, race, gender, and appearance. I then asked similar sets of questions about sexually suggestive speech and race-related speech.

One question that arises from these open-ended questions with which the interview starts is "What constitutes offensive public speech?" The answer, for purposes of this research is that offensive public speech is whatever the respondent says it is. This highly subjective standard is useful because it allows me first to determine what sorts of speech are considered problematic by individuals in public places. For example, when I asked women about times when strangers had said something to them about their appearance that they considered a polite compliment, many women indicated that no comment about their appearance is considered by them to be "polite." Allowing respondents to determine what types of comments fall into the category of offensive or problematic is the best way to discover the respondents' perceptions.

After the stories, subjects were asked a series of general questions about their experiences with these forms of public speech, including whether or not they do anything in their everyday lives to avoid such speech and whether they believe these sorts of interactions to be personal and/or social problems and of what magnitude. Up to this point in the interview, there was no mention of law or legal regulation of such speech. The rationale for not introducing the concept that this may be a problem that is or should be addressed by law is that if I did introduce this idea, it might make people conceive of offensive public speech as more of a problem than they do on an everyday basis. Additionally, I found it interesting to note how many of the subjects mentioned that they thought this sort of behavior should be legally regulated before I mentioned that idea.

The section that introduces law into the interview begins with questions about whether or not the subjects believe there are currently restrictions on offensive public speech. I then asked if they would be in favor of restrictions on offensive public speech of each variety—begging, sexist speech, and racist speech. I asked what types of restrictions they could envision. Next, I used a series of hypotheticals in which I described scenarios of offensive public speech and inquired if the subjects thought the actions I described should be legal or not. If they thought the actions should be illegal, I went on to ask them what type of punishment they thought the speaker should be subjected to.

The final section of the interview posed a series of questions designed to control for some biases I might find in the research. The answers were provided in Likert-scale format and asked about experience with the law, political affiliation and beliefs, and attitudes about other forms of speech restrictions. The interview concluded with a series of demographic questions.

Asking Hard Questions

Perhaps the two most challenging elements of my research design were approaching absolute strangers in public places and using profanity in the interviews with those kind enough to participate.

There is a certain irony in approaching individuals with whom I was unacquainted to ask them about the harms associated with interactions with strangers in public places. A number of subjects and potential subjects commented on this irony. This approach may have resulted in a particular form of bias because those individuals who are most annoyed, inconvenienced, or frightened by interactions with strangers in public places are the most likely to have rejected my advances outright. This approach might lead to a conservative bias in my results: those most likely to favor restrictions on offensive public speech might be underrepresented in the sample. I do not think that this bias is fatal, however, as it was mostly a matter of chance as to whether I approached any particular individual.

One of the advantages of approaching people in public places was that I could address individual acts of offensive public speech that I had witnessed. I could talk to a particular informant about an interaction we had both witnessed. This then provided the rapport necessary for the later interview.

It is difficult to ask questions using the words "bitch" and "nigger," and the command "suck my dick." Rapport with these respondents was established in a brief moment in which I went from being a stranger approaching another stranger and asking permission to make a follow-up phone call. In the course of the phone call, I asked subjects to recount times when strangers had said offensive things to them in public places and read hypothetical scenarios that used all of these offensive terms. Because it was important for everyone to understand exactly what type of speech was being discussed, it was necessary to use such words in the interview. Despite a warning at the initial meeting (in the informed consent paperwork), a warning at the beginning of the interview, and a warning just prior to my use of the profanity, I

could feel respondents' discomfort at the introduction of these words
into the interview.

Choice of Measures

Throughout the book where data are presented, I discuss each individual measure when I present results. But it is useful to offer some general comments about the selection of measures for further reflection. One of the fundamental questions for this research is "Are people in favor of restricting offensive public speech?" I asked a number of open and closed-ended questions to attempt to answer this question. With various constructions of this question, the answers change.

Social scientists have long recognized that how questions are constructed can seriously affect responses (Babbie 1997). My results reflect this. I found that levels of support for restrictions on offensive public speech vary widely depending on the way the questions are presented. It depends on what questions are asked and how respondents think about the issues. There is high support for restrictions on "speech" in the form of burning a cross. Similarly, there is high support for restrictions on "speech" that borders on or crosses over into the category of threat. Nonetheless, in general, people are reluctant to restrict speech. Even as subjects answered "yes" to some questions about restricting speech, they were voicing the concerns that I elaborate in detail in chapter 4.

The categories of "in favor of" and "in opposition to" the regulation of offensive public speech are contingent and shift as my questions become more specific. Thus, it is possible, using one form of the question to argue that people generally disfavor the legal regulation of offensive public speech. In the alternative, using answers to other questions, it seems quite plausible to argue that most people support the legal regulation of offensive public speech. The closed-ended questions provide a useful yet muddled picture regarding attitudes about limiting offensive public speech.

These seemingly contradictory answers present a dilemma for the researcher. By using a combination of open and closed-ended questions, I am able to provide a more thorough and accurate answer to the question "Are people in favor of limiting offensive public speech?" The answer emerges through the discourses about regulation provided in response to the open-ended questions toward the end of the interview about law. And, although there is some support for restricting speech, in general, people oppose the legal regulation of offensive public speech.

The only way to gain a more precise understanding of these attitudes is through the use of free response format questions. The decisions subjects made in response to the fixed choice questions I posed are not opinions that can be accurately revealed through the use of a format that limits their options. Indeed, a number of subjects refused or at least resisted giving firm answers to the questions when I asked if they thought certain forms of offensive public speech should be regulated by law.

Ewick and Silbey say that legality is a process (1998). The fact that responses about making certain behaviors illegal changes quite dramatically in response to changes in behavior, and context reflects the character of legal consciousness. To understand the process that occurs in the minds of individuals, the researcher must allow the subject to reveal herself and to think out loud about these issues. When the answers to these questions are analyzed, the picture becomes more clear. This approach allows me to explore subtle distinctions between forms of speech, as well as between speech and actions.

The best argument that people favor the use of law to limit offensive public speech comes from the extreme hypotheticals that I presented to subjects toward the end of the interview. For each hypothetical situation, I asked respondents if they thought the scenario I described should be legal or illegal. For begging, the extreme hypothetical read, "You are on a public street and a man you do not know asks you for money. When you refuse or ignore him he shouts at you and follows you for about one block making repeated requests. Should this be legal or illegal?" A slight majority, 54%, thought this should be illegal. For sexually suggestive speech, the extreme hypothetical read, "A woman is walking on a public street when a man she does not know shouts, 'Suck my dick!' to her. Should this be legal or illegal? About two-thirds, 66%, thought this behavior should be illegal. The extreme hypothetical for race-related speech was as follows: "An African American man is walking on a public street when a white man yells 'Nigger' at him. Should this be legal or illegal?" Under half, only 42%, thought this behavior should be prevented by law.[2]

In these more extreme cases, an average of 54% favor legal restrictions. Of course, 54% represents an important number because it is a majority and from a political standpoint, that has a certain significance. However, the answers to these closed-ended questions belie ambivalence about law as a mechanism for restricting any sort of speech—offensive or otherwise. Even as halting affirmative responses were marked on the code sheet, I began asking people about their reluctance.

The reluctant "yes" responses provided an excellent opportunity to inquire about the almost universal hesitation on the part of respondents for limiting speech. My interviews offered both subtle and explicit indications that many Americans doubt the wisdom of using law to regulate speech, although they express different reasons for those doubts. The closed-ended questions provide an interesting measure of how people think on this topic when forced to choose between "yes" and "no" after giving the matter only a few minutes of thought. There are careful and important calculations made in the minds of individuals when asked about laws regarding speech. The respondents' reservations would be evident to even the most obtuse researcher. Respondents changed their answers in the course of the interview after giving matters more thought.

Open-ended or free-response questions allow respondents to provide complex answers that detail their logic and thought process (Singleton and Straits 1999, p. 281). Given my interest in better understanding legal consciousness—that is, the way that individuals think about the law and legal processes in relation to their own lives—it makes sense to rely more heavily on the open-ended questions. They are more appropriate measures when the aim of the research is to understand the "basis on which opinions are founded, the depth of respondent's understanding . . . or the intensity with which respondents hold opinions" (Singleton and Straits 1999, p. 283). Because the aim of this research is theory building more so than hypotheses testing, I ultimately relied more on the free-response questions than closed-ended questions. Closed-ended or fixed-choice questions are traditionally thought to be adequate to assess attitudes on subjects about which respondents have formed an opinion (Singleton and Straits 1999, p. 283). It is likely that in the case of the First Amendment, people hold strong opinions but they have not really had many opportunities to articulate the basis for those opinions. Thus, while the closed-ended questions provide insight into a small snapshot of respondents' thinking, it is not the whole picture.

CONCLUSION

Research design must be motivated by the theoretical questions the researcher seeks to pursue. Because I am interested in building theory, understanding the ways in which individuals think about the law in relation to social problems generally, and with respect to offensive public speech in particular, it was essential that I include open-ended questions. Moreover, because there is a lack of documentation about the magnitude and nature of street harassment as a social phenomenon, it is important to include the ethnographic component to the research as well. It is the combination of observation, in-depth interviews, and structured questions that allowed me to explore the context for attitudes about speech and the thought processes of respondents. Furthermore, by including all types of people in the sample, I am able to make systematic comparisons across groups.

QUESTIONNAIRE

FIRST, I would like to, with your permission, ask if I could tape record this interview.

I also want to reinforce that all of your answers will be kept confidential and no individual will be identified in the final project.

My research is about interactions between strangers in public places. Some of the types of interactions we may talk about today are ones that you might find offensive. You may or may not have experienced all of the forms of street speech that I will ask you about. I would like to start by asking you about times when strangers have spoken to you in public places. By public I mean the street, the sidewalk, on public transportation, in a park, or anywhere else that is public.

1. Can you think of a time when you were in a public place and someone you did not know said something to you? What did they say? (ask questions a–h below)

2. Can you think of a time when you were in a public place and a person who you did not know asked you for money? Tell me about that time. (*Prompt*: Why don't you tell me about the last time?)

3. Can you think of a time when you were in a public place and someone you did not know asked you for money in a way that made you feel uncomfortable or afraid? (ask questions a–h below)

4. Can you think of a time when you were in a public place and someone you did not know said something to you about your appearance that was meant to be complimentary?

5. Can you think of a time when you were in a public place and someone said something to you about your appearance or something that you considered to be particularly sexually suggestive or explicit? (ask questions a–h below)

6. Can you think of a time when you were in a public place and someone you did not know said something to you on account of your

race? (*Prompt*: Why don't you tell me about the last time?) (ask questions a–h below)

7. Can you think of a time when you were in a public place and someone you did not know said something to you on account of your race that was particularly aggressive or offensive?

ABOUT EACH STORY

a. Where were you when the person said that? What was that person like? Male or female? Race? Age? Anything else that you remember?

b. How did you respond to that?

c. How did you feel when they said that to you? *Prompt*: Were you afraid? Angry? Embarrassed? Annoyed?

d. Did you think about the incident after it occurred? What did you think about it?

e. Did you tell anyone else about it? What was their reaction? Did that change how you felt about the event?

f. Did you feel safe in that location before the incident occurred? After?

g. If you had to say, how many times in the last week would you say something like this has happened to you? In the last month? In the last year?

h. Do you do anything in your everyday life to avoid these sorts of interactions? What do you do? Do you ever:
   i. change the route you take?
   ii. change the time of day you might go a particular place?
   iii. avoid certain places to avoid this type of interaction?
   iv. attempt to change your appearance to avoid these sorts of interactions?
   v. wear accessories such as sunglasses or a Walkman to avoid these sorts of interactions?

i. When you are asked for money, do you usually give them money? Why or why not?

j. Are their certain types of people who you are more likely to give money to? What are they like? Why is this so?

8. Can you think of a time when *you* have spoken to a stranger on the street? What did you say?
   a. What was the response of the person to whom you were speaking?
   b. Was that the response you expected?
   c. Where were you? Where was the person you were speaking to?
   d. Why did you say that?

If They Can Only Think "In General," Ask

a. What is a type of question you are likely to ask?

b. How do you determine who you might ask?

c. Are there any other factors such as you location or the time of day that play into your calculation of deciding whether or not to ask?

9. My research focuses mainly on three types of interactions: begging, sexually suggestive comments, and race-related comments. I am interested in how frequently you think these sorts of interactions occur. I'll ask you to answer the next few questions using a scale of every day, often, sometimes, rarely or never.

a. If you had to guess, how frequently are you asked for money in public places?

Every day, often, sometimes, rarely or never?

b. If you had to estimate, how often do you think women hear "polite" remarks about their appearance from strangers in public places?

Every day, often, sometimes, rarely or never?

c. If you had to estimate, how often do you think men hear "polite" remarks about their appearance from strangers in public places?

Every day, often, sometimes, rarely or never?

d. If you had to estimate, how often do you think women hear offensive, vulgar, or sexually suggestive remarks from strangers in public places?

Every day, often, sometimes, rarely or never?

e. if you had to estimate, how often do you think men hear offensive, vulgar, or sexually suggestive remarks from strangers in public places?

Every day, often, sometimes, rarely or never?

f. If you had to estimate, how often do you think people of your race hear remarks about their race from strangers in public places?

Every day, often, sometimes, rarely or never?

g. If you had to estimate, how often do you think people of other races hear remarks about their race from strangers in public places? (feel free to distinguish among races)

Every day, often, sometimes, rarely or never?

10. My research focuses mainly on three types of interactions: begging, sexually suggestive comments, and race-related comments.

I would like to know which, if, do you consider to be a problem for you?

a. Is begging a problem for you? Why?

b. Are sexually suggestive or explicit comments a problem for you? Why?

c. Are race-related or racist comments a problem for you? Why?

d. Which, if any is the biggest problem for you and why?

e. Which is the least of a problem for you? Why?

11. I am also interested in which, if any of these sorts of interactions you consider to be a social problem.

a. Do you consider begging to be a social problem? Why?

b. Do you consider sexually suggestive or explicit comments to be a social problem? Why?

c. Do you consider race-related comments to be a social problem? Why?

d. Which, if any is the biggest social problem? Why?

e. Which is the least of a social problem? Why?

12. Do you think that your attitude toward strangers who speak to you on the street has changed over time? If so, why? Was there a particular incident in your life that led to the change? Or was it a gradual change?

FOR ALL SUBJECTS (LAW)

I am also interested in whether or not people think that these sorts of interactions should be restricted, either by law or by any other mechanism.

13. Again, just to remind you, my research focuses on begging, sexist and racist remarks made in public places.

a. Do you think it is legal to ask strangers for money in public places?

b. Do you think it is legal to make sexist remarks to strangers in public places?

c. Do you think that it is legal to make racist comments to strangers in public places?

Now I would like to ask you about your views on whether or not these comments *should* be legal or illegal.

14. Begging

a. Do you think there should be any kind of legal limitation on asking strangers for money in public places? What kinds and why?

b. Would you be in favor of:

    i. programs that attempt to limit asking strangers for money by encouraging people to buy tokens that the homeless can use for food?

    ii. legal limitations on begging that restrict begging after dark?

    iii. legal limitations on begging by location (such as within twenty feet of an ATM or in front of stores)?

15. Sexually Suggestive Remarks

a. Do you think there should be any kind of legal limitations on sexually explicit speech in public places? Why or why not?

b. Would you be in favor of:

    i. public education programs to attempt to limit this sort of speech? Why or why not?

    ii. restricting sexually suggestive speech in certain locations? Why or why not?

    iii. restricting sexually suggestive speech at certain times of day, such as after dark? Why or why not?

16. Race-Related Remarks

a. Do you think there should be any kind of limitations on race-related speech between strangers in public places? Why or why not?

c. Would you be in favor of:

    i. public education programs to attempt to limit this sort of speech? Why or why not?

    ii. restricting race-related speech in certain location? Why or why not?

    iii. legally restricting race-related speech at certain times of day, such as after dark? Why or why not?

REGULATION ISSUE FOLLOW-UPS

a. It is difficult to enforce lots of laws, but they are on the books because we think they are important. Is this just not important? Or is there something about regulating this kind of conduct that is particularly troublesome in your mind?

b. Is there anything else that society should do about this? What?

FIRST AMENDMENT FOLLOW-UPS

a. You mentioned the First Amendment or freedom of speech. What do you mean by that? How do your ideas about free speech affect the way you think about this behavior?

b. What principle is that supposed to protect?

c. What sorts of speech do you think might be limited that you think should not be?

Now I would like to read you some brief scenarios and ask what you think about the legality or illegality of each. These scenarios are based on observations of interactions in public places and you may find some of the words to be offensive. I apologize if you find them offensive, but I believe it is important to understand how people think about offensive public speech and whether or not it should be limited.

I will read you a number of scenarios and for each I will ask you to decide if you think the action should be legal or not. I will provide you with a range of options for each scenario. You can tell me if you think the action should be legal or should be illegal. If you think it should be illegal, I will ask you if you think the speaker should be subjected to an infraction (like a ticket), civil liability (the harmed individual could sue for money), or criminal punishment. If you think it should be criminal, I will ask you if you think the punishment should be jail time or something less such as probation and education.

17. Begging
a. You are on a street and a man, apparently homeless, is sitting on the sidewalk with a sign that requests money. He is not blocking your way. Should this be legal?

b. You are on a public street and a man, apparently homeless, is standing with a sign and shaking a cup and asking passersby, "Spare change?" Should this be legal?

c. You are on a public street and a man, apparently homeless, shouts, "How about some money?" When you refuse or ignore him, he follows you for about one block, making repeated requests. He does not touch you or block your path. Should this be legal?

d. You are on a public street and a man, apparently homeless, shouts, "How about some money?" When you refuse or ignore him, he follows you for about 1 block, making repeated requests. He also touches you and blocks your path. Should this be legal?

18. Now for sexually suggestive comments. I know you may not have been subjected to them, but I am interested in your opinion as to whether or not these sorts of comments should be legal or illegal.
a. A woman is walking on a public street and a man politely says, "You look lovely today." Should this be legal?

b. A woman is walking on a public street and a man whistles, catcalls, and shouts, "Looking good!" Should this be legal?

c. A woman is walking on a public street and a man says, "Nice tits!" Should this be legal?

d. A woman is walking on a public street and a man says, "Come suck my dick!" Should this be legal?

e. A woman is walking on a public street and a man says the same thing and he touches her shoulder. Should this be legal?

f. Now, let's suppose that a male coworker says the same thing to a female coworker. Should this be legal?

g. Now, let's suppose that a male boss says the same thing to a female employee. Should this be legal?

19. Now for the race-related comments. Again, although you may not have personally been the target of these sorts of remarks, I am interested in your opinion as to whether or not you think these sorts of actions should be legal or illegal.

a. An African American man is walking on a public street and a white person says, "Hey brother!" Should this be legal?

b. An African American man is walking on a public street and a white person quietly says, "Nigger!" to him. Should this be legal?

c. An African American is walking on a public street and white person shouts loudly, "I'm gonna get you nigger." Should this be legal?

d. A White person, without trespassing, manages to burn a cross in the front yard of an African American's home. Should this be legal?

20. Those are all of the scenarios, but with them in mind, do you think the target's reaction to the remark should have any bearing on whether or not the remarks are illegal or, should certain actions be illegal regardless of whether or not the target finds them to be a problem?

21. Legal Experience
a. Have you ever been sued (how many times?)
b. Have you ever filed a criminal complaint (how many times?)
c. Have you ever met with a lawyer?

I am also interested in whether or not people's general attitudes about law affect the way they think about the issue of offensive public speech, so I would like to read you a series of statements about the law and I will ask you to say if you *strongly agree, agree, have no opinion, disagree, or strongly disagree.*

22. There are too many lawyers for the good of the country.

23. People too often try to use the law for selfish reasons.

24. Stronger laws are needed to guarantee fair treatment for women in employment and education.

25. Stronger laws are needed to guarantee fair treatment for women in general.

26. Stronger laws are needed to guarantee fair treatment for minorities in employment and education.

27. Stronger laws are needed to guarantee fair treatment for minorities in general.

28. There are too many laws about things that the government has no business regulating.

29. Public authorities should have power to require manufacturers to put warning labels on music CDs and videos that indicate the presence of obscene material.

30. Public authorities should have power to remove obscene material from music CDs and movies.

31. Public authorities should have power to limit pornography that presents women in demeaning positions or as objects of violence.

32. Public authorities should have power to limit pornography that presents children.

33. Is there anything else that I have not touched on that you think is important regarding public speech and whether or not it should be limited?

Now I would like ask you some general questions about yourself.

34. Are you male or female?

35. What is your age?

36. What do you consider your race to be?

37. Would you tell me about your education background?

38. Could you tell me a bit about your current job if you have one? (full-time/part-time)

39. Do you usually think of yourself as a Democrat, a Republican, or an Independent? Do you vote?

40. What town do you live in?

41. What religion, if any, are you? Do you practice?

42. Is there anything else about offensive public speech that you would like to say or have you thought of any other incidents of offensive public speech that you encountered that you would like to tell me about?

43. Do you have any questions for me?

Thank you very much!

NOTES

CHAPTER ONE
INTRODUCTION

1. In addition to offensive speech, subjects of color reported being pushed, slapped, glared at, and spat upon due to their race, while women of all races reported being groped and fondled by strangers in a sexual manner while in public. Although this research focuses on offensive public *speech*, these assaults are noteworthy. Assaults often are preceded by offensive public speech. The threat of assault plays a role in how targets understand such interactions, even when they involve "only" speech.

CHAPTER TWO
LAW AND POWER IN SIDEWALK ENCOUNTERS

1. Despite the American perception that free societies require "free speech," prohibitions on hate speech exist in Austria, Belgium, Brazil, Canada, Cyprus, England, France, Germany, India, Israel, Italy, Netherlands, and Switzerland. 2002.

2. *Young v. New York City Transit Authority,* 903 F.2d 146 (2d Cir.), cert. denied, 498 U.S. 984 (1990) (holding that begging and panhandling could be prohibited in the New York City subway system because the subway system is not a public place for purposes of First Amendment analysis. (See below for more discussion of *Young*).

3. *Gresham v. Beterson,* 225 F.3d 899 (7th Cir., 2000) (upholding a city ordinance on panhandling as a reasonable time, place, and manner restriction using the *Perry* standard).

4. *Smith v. Ft. Lauderdale,* 177 F.3d 954 (11th Cir., 1999) (upholding order of summary judgment in favor of city's ordinance restricting begging, soliciting, and panhandling on the beaches using the *Perry* standard).

5. *Greater Cincinnati Coalition for the Homeless and Charles Godden v. Cincinnati,* 56 F.3d 710 (6th Cir., 1995) (denying standing to Godden, a beggar cited with an infraction on the basis of the ordinance).

6. *Blair v. Shanahan,* 775 F. Supp. 1315 (N.D. Cal. 1991) (striking down state statute criminalizing aggressive panhandling. *Blair* suffers a complex subsequent history in which portions of the opinion were vacated, but not the decision as to the unconstitutionality of the statute on First Amendment grounds).

7. *Loper v. New York City,* 999 F.2d 699 (2d Cir., 1993) (striking down a law which prohibited loitering for the purposes of begging throughout all of New York City).

8. In *Gresham*, the parties stipulated that the ordinance in this case was con-tent-neutral because it was justified without reference to the content of the speech and with reference to the state interest of keeping the sidewalks clear and passable. The stipulation meant that the court did not rule on the issue.

9. I do not mean to essentialize the scholars in either camp. Both the tradi-tional scholars and the critical race scholars, at times, respond to developments in the arguments put forth by members of the other group.

CHAPTER THREE
EXPERIENCING OFFENSIVE PUBLIC SPEECH

1. The questionnaire appears in appendix B.

2. Because the sample was not randomly selected, it is important to re-member that the frequency of instances of offensive public speech cannot be generalized to a larger population such as Americans or even citizens of the San Francisco/Bay Area. I have, however, taken great care to reduce the possi-bilities of bias in selecting the sample. For more on sample selection, see ap-pendix A.

CHAPTER FOUR
OFFENSIVE PUBLIC SPEECH AS A PERSONAL
PROBLEM, SOCIAL PROBLEM, AND SUBJECT FOR LEGAL INTERVENTION

1. This number comes from a question that appears prior to the discussion of any hypothetical situations in the interview and reads, "Would you be in favor of laws prohibiting the types of speech I have asked you about today?"

2. These numbers come from questions 10–14. They read, "Would you be in favor of laws to restrict begging?" "Would you be in favor of laws that restrict sexually suggestive speech between strangers in public places?" and "Would you be in favor of laws that restrict race-related speech between strangers in public places?" I inquired about both criminal and civil liability for offensive public speech. Where I report percentages of people who "favor the legal regu-lation of offensive public speech," I refer to people in favor of any type of legal restriction. When respondents indicated they may favor the legal regulation of speech, I asked, "Should that be an infraction, like a ticket with a fine? Or, should there be civil liability for that, meaning the target could sue the speaker for money? Or, should there be criminal punishment for that, meaning the speaker would have jail time or probation?"

3. The questionnaire appears in its entirety in appendix B.

4. Table 4.4 reports including the over sample of people of color. Because the sample is not completely random, and is not weighted, they may be overly suggestive. Presentation is meant for comparison purposes.

5. This is an indexed variable, meaning that I asked respondents a number of questions about their attitudes regarding law and legal intervention. The questions were in Likert scale form: responses were: strongly agree, agree,

have no opinion, disagree, or strongly disagree. Questions number 22, 23, 24, 25, 26, 27, and 28 make up this scale (See appendix B). The statements were, "There are too many lawyers for the good of the country"; "People too often try to use the law for selfish reasons"; "Stronger laws are needed to guarantee fair treatment for women in employment and education"; "Stronger laws are needed to guarantee fair treatment for women in general"; "Stronger laws are needed to guarantee fair treatment for minorities in employment and education"; "Stronger laws are needed to guarantee fair treatment for minorities in general"; and "There are too many laws about things that the government has no business regulating."

6. The questions that went into this index were numbers 29 through 32 (See appendix B). They read, "Public authorities should have power to require manufacturers to put warning labels on CDs and videos that indicate the presence of obscene material," "Public authorities should have power to remove obscene material from music CDs and movies"; "Public authorities should have power to limit pornography that presents women in demeaning positions or as objects of violence"; and "Public authorities should have power to limit pornography that presents children." I eliminated question number 32 from the index because there was not sufficient variation in responses.

7. I inquired about both criminal and civil liability for offensive public speech. Where I report percentages of people who "favor the legal regulation of offensive public speech," I refer to people in favor of any type of legal restriction. When respondents indicated they may favor the legal regulation of speech, I asked, "Should that be an infraction, like a ticket with a fine? Or should there be civil liability for that, meaning the target could sue the speaker for money? Or should there be criminal punishment for that, meaning the speaker would have jail time or probation?"

CHAPTER FIVE
ORDINARY CITIZENS' VIEWS ON THE LEGAL REGULATION OF STREET SPEECH

1. Ideas about how individuals conceive of justice and what is normatively just have long been the subject of theoretical debate and some political theorists claim that law's legitimacy is derived from principles of fairness, equality, and justice Fuller 1964; 1975. Only recently has empirical research turned to the question of that how people think about the law. One important strand of this work develops theories about procedural fairness and substantive justice Lind and Tyler 1988; 1990.

2. These data provide a way to test the Ewick and Silbey framework, but the data collection and analysis were conducted prior to the release of their most recent book (1998, P.167). I describe four general orientations toward law, while they identify three. Although I use my own terms to describe the orientations, my findings generally complement Ewick and Silbey's. The similarities in orientations to law are particularly interesting, given that my subjects were recruited from a different geographic location and were presented with very different legal issues from those used by Ewick and Silbey.

3. Chapter three analyzes women's perception that being made the target of sexually suggestive street speech is within their control.

Chapter Seven
License to Harass

1. "Sexual objectification occurs whenever people's bodies, body parts, or sexual functions are separated out from their identity, reduced to the status of mere instruments, or regarded as if they were capable of representing them" (Fredrickson et al., 1998).

2. See www.streetharassmentproject.org.

Appendix A
Research Design

1. In the analyses that follow, I emphasize comparisons across race and gender and limit the statistical analysis to simple chi-square tests for differences across groups. Given the size of the sample, the results should be seen as suggestive in a statistical sense and worthy of examination in larger sample designs.

2. There were two more extreme hypothetical scenarios for race-related speech. One involved a burning cross which was largely not thought of as speech by the respondents and 88% were in favor of laws restricting that behavior. Additionally, there was a hypothetical that read, "An African-American man is walking on a public street when a white man shouts, 'I'm going to get you, Nigger!' at him. Should this be legal or illegal?" A number of subjects felt (probably correctly) that such a statement is a threat and would therefore already be prohibited by law.

CASES CITED

Abrams v. United States, 250 U.S. 616 (1919)

Blair v. Shanahan, 775 F. Supp. 1315 (N.D. Cal. 1991)

Chaplinsky v. New Hampshire, 315 U.S. 568, 86 L. Ed. 1031, 62 S. Ct. 766 (1942)

Cohen v. California, 403 U.S. 15, 29 L. Ed. 2d 284, 91 S. Ct. 1780, (1971)

Consolidated Edison Co. v. Public Service Comm'n, 447 U.S. 530, 65 L. Ed. 2d 319, 100 S. Ct. 2326 (1980)

Corry v. Stanford University, No. 740309 (Cal. Super. Ct. Feb. 27, 1995)

Doe v. University of Michigan, 721 F. Supp. 852 (E.D. Mich. 1989)

Greater Cincinnati Coalition for the Homeless v. City of Cincinnati, 56 F.3d 710 (6th Cir. Ohio 1995)

Gresham v. Peterson, 225 F.3d 899, (7th Cir. Ind. 2000)

Hague v. CIO, 307 U.S. 496, 83 L. Ed. 1423, 59 S. Ct. 954 (1939)

Hill v. Colorado, 530 U.S. 703, 719, 147 L. Ed. 2d 597, 120 S. Ct. 2480 (2000)

Loper v. New York City Police Dep't, 999 F.2d 699 (2d Cir. N.Y. 1993)

Madsen v. Women's Health Ctr., 512 U.S. 753, 129 L. Ed. 2d 593, 114 S. Ct. 2516 (1994)

Perry Education Ass'n v. Perry Local Educators' Ass'n, 460 U.S. 37, 74 L. Ed. 2d 794, 103 S. Ct. 948 (1983)

R.A.V. v. City of St. Paul, 505 U.S. 377, 112 S. Ct. 2538, 120 L. Ed. 2d 305 (1992)

Schaumburg v. Citizens for Better Environment, 444 U.S. 620, 63 L. Ed. 2d 73, 100 S. Ct. 826 (1980)

Smith v. City of Fort Lauderdale, 177 F.3d 954 (11th Cir. Fla. 1999)

The UWM Post, Inc. v. Board of Regents of University of Wisconsin System, 774 F. Supp. 1163 (E.D. Wis. 1991)

Virginia v. Black, 155 L. Ed. 2d 535, 123 S. Ct. 1536 (U.S. 2003)

Ward v. Rock against Racism, 491 U.S. 781, 105 L. Ed. 2d 661, 109 S. Ct. 2746 (1989)

Young v. New York City Transit Authority, 903 F.2d 146 (2d Cir.), cert. denied, 498 U.S. 984, 112 L. Ed. 2d 528, 111 S. Ct. 516 (1990)

REFERENCES

Abel, Richard L. 1998. *Speaking Respect, Respecting Speech*. Chicago: University of Chicago Press.

Albiston, Catherine R., and Laura Beth Nielsen. 1995. "Welfare Queens and Other Fairy Tales: Welfare Reform and Unconstitutional Reproductive Controls." *Howard Law Journal* 38:473.

Aronson, Joshua, Dianne M. Quinn, and Steven J. Spencer. 1998. "Stereotype Threat and the Academic Underperformance of Minorities and Women." In *Prejudice: The Target's Perspective*, edited by J. K. Swim and C. Stangor. San Diego: Academic Press.

Babbie, Earl. 1997. *The Practice of Social Research*. Cambridge: Cambridge University Press.

Bobo, Lawrence D. 1999. "Prejudice as Group Position: Microfoundations of a Sociological Approach to Racism and Race Relations." *Journal of Social Issues* 55:445–72.

Bourdieu, Pierre. 1977. *Outline of a Theory of Practice*. Cambridge: Cambridge University Press.

———. 1987. "The Force of Law: Toward a Sociology of the Juridical Field." *Hastings Law Journal* 38:805–53.

Bowman, Cynthia Grant. 1993. "Street Harassment and the Informal Ghettoization of Women." *Harvard Law Review* 106.

Bumiller, Kristin. 1988. *The Civil Rights Society: The Social Construction of Victims*. Baltimore: Johns Hopkins University Press.

Butler, Judith. 1997. *Excitable Speech: A Politics of the Performative*. New York: Routledge.

Cain, Patricia A. 1989. "Feminist Jurisprudence: Grounding the Theories." *Berkeley Women's Law Journal* 4:191.

Chevigny, Paul. 1988. *More Speech: Dialogue Rights and Modern Liberty*. Philadelphia: Temple University Press.

Collins, Patricia Hill. 1990. *Black Feminist Thought: Knowledge, Consciousness, and the Politics of Empowerment*. New York: Routledge.

Comaroff, Jean, and John Comaroff. 1990. *Of Revelation and Revolution: Christianity, Colonialism, and Consciousness in South Africa*. Chicago: University of Chicago Press.

Conley, John M., and William M. O'Barr. 1998. *Just Words: Law, Language, and Power*. Chicago: University of Chicago Press.

Curran, Barbara A. 1977. *The Legal Needs of the Public: The Final Report of a National Survey*. Chicago: American Bar Foundation.

Darian-Smith, Eve. 1999. *Bridging Divides: The Channel Tunnel and English Legal Identity in the New Europe*. London: University of California Press.

Davis, Diedre. 1994. "The Harm That Has No Name: Street Harassment, Embodiment, and African-American Women." *U.C.L.A. Women's Law Journal* 4.

Delgado, Richard. 1993. "Words That Wound: A Tort Action for Racial Insults, Epithets, and Name Calling." In *Words That Wound: Critical Race Theory, Assaultive Speech, and the First Amendment*, edited by C.R.L. Mari J. Matsuda, Richard Delgado, & Kimberle W. Crenshaw. Boulder, Colo.: Westview Press.

Delgado, Richard, and Jean Stefancic. 1994. "Hateful Speech, Loving Communities: Why Our Notion of 'A Just Balance' Changes So Slowly." *California Law Review* 82.

———. 1997. *Must We Defend Nazis? Hate Speech, Pornography, and the New First Ammendment*. New York: New York University Press.

Delgado, Richard, and David Yun. 1995. "'The Speech We Hate': First Amendment Totalism, the ACLU, and the Principle of Dialogic Politics." *Arizona State Law Journal* 27:1281.

Downs. 1985. *Nazis in Skokie: Freedom, Community, and the First Amendment*. Notre Dame, Ind.: University of Notre Dame Press.

Duneier, Mitchell. 1999. *Sidewalk*. New York: Farrar, Straus, and Giroux.

Duneier, Mitchell, and Harvey Molotch. 1999. "Talking City Trouble: Vandalism, Social Inequality, and the 'Urban Interaction Problem.'" *American Journal of Sociology* 104:1263–95.

Engel, David M., and Barbara Yngvesson. 1984. "Mapping the Terrain: 'Legal Culture,' 'Legal Consciousness,' and Other Hazards for the Intrepid Explorer." *Law and Policy* 6:299–307.

Epstein, Edward. 1995. "Homelessness No. 1 Problem, S.F. Voters Say." P. A1 in *San Francisco Chronicle*, October 30.

———. 1998. "Muni, Homelessness Send Brown's Ratings Skidding." P. A1 in *San Francisco Chronicle*, November 17.

Ewick, Patricia, and Susan Silbey. 1992. "Conformity, Contestation, and Resistance: An Account of Legal Consciousness." *New England Law Review* 26:731–49.

———. 1998. *The Common Place of Law: Stories from Everyday Life*. Chicago: University of Chicago Press.

Fagan, Kevin. 1994. "Berkeley Finding Vouchers Work: Program to Help Homeless Being Used More and More." Pp. A21 in *San Francisco Chronicle*, November 24.

Feagin, Joe R. 1991. "The Continuing Significance of Race: Antiblack Discrimination in Public Places." *American Sociological Review* 56:101–16.

Fiss, Owen. 1986. "Free Speech and Social Structure." *Iowa Law Review* 71.

Frankel, Bruce, and Maria Puente. 1994. "Cracking Down, Cleaning Up; Big Apple Wants New Appeal." P. 4A in *USA Today*. New York, July 7.

Fredrickson, Barbara L., Tomi-Ann Roberts, Stephanie M Noll, Diane M. Quinn, and Jean M. Twenge. 1998. "That Swimsuit Becomes You: Sex Differences in Self-Objectification, Restrained Eating, and Math Performance." *Journal of Personality and Social Psychology* 75: 269–84.

Fredrickson, Barbara L., and Tomi-Ann Roberts. 1997. "Objectification Theory: Toward Understanding Women's Lived Experiences and Mental Health Risks." *Psychology of Women Quarterly* 21:173–206.

Friedman, Lawrence M. 1987. *Total Justice: What Americans Want from the Legal System and Why*. Boston: Beacon Press.

Fuller, Lon. 1964. *The Morality of Law.* New Haven: Yale University Press.

Gabel, Peter. 1981. "Reification in Legal Reasoning." *Research in Law and Sociology* 3.

Gale, Mary Ellen. 1990. "Reimagining the First Amendment: Racist Speech and Equal Liberty." *St. John's Law Review* 65.

Gardner, Carol Brooks. 1980. "Passing By: Street Remarks, Address Rights, and Urban Women." *Sociological Inquiry* 50.

———. 1995. *Passing By: Gender and Public Harassment.* Berkeley and Los Angeles: University of California Press.

Garnets, Linda, Gregory M. Herek, and Berrie Levy. 1992. "Violence and Victimization of Lesbians and Gay Men: Mental Health Consequences." In *Hate Crimes: Confronting Violence against Lesbians and Gay Men*, edited by G. M. Garnets and K. T. Berrill. Newbury Park, N.J.: Sage Publications.

Glendon, Mary Ann. 1991. *Rights Talk: The Impoverishment of Political Discourse.* New York: Free Press.

Goffman, Erving. 1959. *The Presentation of Self in Everyday LIfe.* Garden City, N.Y.: Doubleday.

———. 1963. *Behavior in Public Places.* Glencoe, Ill.: Free Press.

———. 1971. *Relations in Public.* New York: Basic Books.

Gould, Jon B. 2001. "The Precedent That Wasn't: College Hate Speech Codes and the Two faces of Legal Compliance." *Law and Society Review* 35:345–92.

Harris, Angela P. 1990. "Race and Essentialism in Feminist Legal Theory." *Stanford Law Review* 42:581–616.

Hershkoff, Helen, and Adam S. Cohen. 1991. "Begging to Differ: The First Amendment and the Right to Beg." *Harvard Law Review* 104.

Herz, Richard. 1994. "No Homeless People Allowed: A Report on Anti-Homeless Laws, Litigation, and Alternatives in Forty-nine United States Cities." National Law Center on Homelessness & Poverty, Washington D.C.

"Homeless Aid: Fountain Yields Change for Charity." 1994. P. J6 in *Los Angeles Times*. Santa Monica, October 9.

Kissling, Elizabeth Arveda. 1991. "Street Harassment: The Language of Sexual Terrorism." *Discourse & Society* 2.

Landrine, Hope, and Elizabeth A. Klonoff. 1996. "The Schedule of Racist Events: A Measure of Racial Discrimination and a Study of Its Negative Physical and Mental Health Consequences." *Journal of Black Psychology* 22:144–168.

Lawrence, Charles. 1990. "If He Hollers Let Him Go: Regulation of Racist Speech on Campus." *Duke Law Journal* 1990.

Lederer, Laura, and Richard Delgado. 1995a. "Introduction." in *The Price we Pay: The Case against Racist Speech, Hate Propaganda, and Pornography*, edited by L. Lederer and R. Delgado. New York: Hill and Wang.

———. 1995b. "The Price We Pay: The Case against Racist Speech, Hate Propaganda, and Pornography." New York: Hill and Wang.

Lind, Allan E., and Tom R. Tyler. 1988. *The Social Psychology of Procedural Justice.* New York: Plenum.

MacKinnon, Catharine. 1987. *Feminism Unmodified: Discourses on Life and Law.* Cambridge: Harvard University Press.

MacKinnon, Catharine. 1989. *Toward a Feminist Theory of the State*. Cambridge: Harvard University Press.

———. 1993. *Only Words*. Cambridge: Harvard University Press.

Madriz, Esther. 1997. *Nothing Bad Happens to Good Girls: Fear of Crime in Women's Lives*. Berkeley and Los Angeles: University of California Press.

Matsuda, Mari J., Charles R. Lawrence, Richard Delgado, and Kimberle Williams Crenshaw. 1993. *Words That Wound: Critical Race Theory, Assaultive Speech, and the First Amendment*. Boulder, Colo.: Westview Press.

McCann, Michael. 1994. *Rights at Work: Pay Equity Reform and the Politics of Legal Mobilizations*. Chicago: University of Chicago Press.

———. 1999. "Review of *The Common Place of Law: Stories from Everyday Life*, by P. Ewick and S. S. Silbey." *American Journal of Sociology* 105:238–40.

McCann, Michael W., and Tracey March. 1996. "Law and Everyday Forms of Resistance: A Socio-Political Assessment." *Studies in Law, Politics, and Society* 15.

McCloskey, Herbert, and Alida Brill. 1983. *Dimensions of Tolerance: What Americans Believe about Civil Liberties*. New York: Russell Sage Foundation.

Meiklejohn, Alexander. 1948. *Free Speech and Its Relation to Government*. New York: Harper Brothers Publishing.

Merry, Sally Engle. 1990. *Getting Justice and Getting Even: Legal Consciousness among Working-Class Americans*. Chicago: University of Chicago Press.

Meyer, David S., and Suzanne Staggenborg. 1996. "Movements, Countermovements, and the Structure of Political Opportunity." *American Journal of Sociology* 101:1628–60.

Neuman, Elena. 1994. "Attitudes Hardening toward the Homeless; As Public Gets More Fed Up, Cities Respond with Tougher Laws." P. A7 in *Washington Times*. Washington, D.C., March 2.

Nielsen, Laura Beth. 1999. "License to Harass: Offensive Public Speech, Legal Consciousness, and Hierarchies of Race, Gender, and Class." Ph.D. Dissertation Thesis, Jurisprudence and Social Policy, University of California, Berkeley.

———. 2000. "Situating Legal Consciousness: Experiences and Attitudes of Ordinary Citizens about Law and Street Harassment." *Law and Society Review* 34:201–36.

Noll, Stephanie M., and Barbara L. Fredrickson. 1998. "A Mediation Model Linking Self-Objectification, Body Shame, and Disordered Eating." *Psychology of Women Quarterly* 22:623–36.

Note. 1993. "The Demise of the Chaplinsky Fighting Words Doctrine: An Argument for Its Internment." *Harvard Law Review* 106.

Post, Robert. 1990. "Racist Speech, Democracy, and the First Amendment." *William and Mary Law Review* 32.

———. 1993. "Meiklejohn's Mistake: Individual Autonomy and the Reform of Public Discourse." *University of Colorado Law Review* 64.

Poverty, National Law Center on Homelessness and Poverty. 1996. "Mean Sweeps: A Report on Anti-Homeless Laws, Litigation, and Alternatives in Fifty United States Cities." National Law Center on Homelessness and Poverty, Washington, D.C.

————. 1999. "Out of Sight—Out of Mind: A Report on Anti-Homeless Laws, Litigation, and Alternatives in Fifty United States Cities." National Law Center on Homelessness and Poverty, Washington, D.C.

Rubin, Jeffrey W. 1996. "Defining Resistance: Contested Interpretations of Everyday Acts." *Studies in Law, Politics, and Society* 15:237–60.

Ryan, Mary P. 1990. *Women in Public: Between Banners and Ballots.* Baltimore: Johns Hopkins University Press.

Sarat, Austin. 1990. "The Law Is All Over: Power, Resistance, and the Legal Consciousness of the Welfare Poor." *Yale Journal of Law and Humanities* 2.

Sarat, Austin, and Thomas R. Kearns, eds. 1995. *Law in Everyday Life.* Ann Arbor: University of Michigan Press.

Scott, James C. 1990. *Domination and the Arts of Resistance: Hidden Transcripts.* New Haven: Yale University Press.

Silbey, Susan, and Austin Sarat. 1987. "Critical Traditions in Law and Society Research." *Law and Society Review* 21.

Singleton, Royce A., and Bruce C. Straits. 1999. *Approaches to Social Research.* 3rd ed. New York: Oxford University Press.

Spelman, Elizabeth V. 1988. *Inessential Woman: Problems of Exclusion in Feminist Thought.* Boston: Beacon Press.

Steele, Claude M., 1997. "A Threat in the Air: How Stereotypes Shape Intellectual Identity and Performance." *American Psychologist* 52:613–29.

Steele, Claude M., and Joshua Aronson. 1995. "Stereotype Threat and the Intellectual Test Performance of African-Americans." *Journal of Personality and Social Psychology* 69:797–811.

Stouffer, Samuel A. 1992. *Communism, Conformity, and Civil Liberties: A Cross-Section of the Nation Speaks Its Mind.* New Brunswick, N. J.: Transaction Publishers (Originally published by Doubleday and Co.) 1955.

Strossen, Nadine. 1995. *Defending Pornography: Free Speech, Sex, and the Fight for Women's Rights.* New York: Scribner's.

Sullivan, John L., James Piereson, and George E. Marcus. 1982. *Political Tolerance and American Democracy.* Chicago: University of Chicago Press.

Swim, Janet K., Laurie L. Cohen, and Lauri L. Hyers. 1998. " Experiencing Everyday Prejudice and Discrimination." In *Prejudice: The Target's Perspective,* edited by J. K. Swim and C. Stangor. San Diego: Academic Press.

Swim, Janet K. and Charles Stangor. 1998. "Introduction." in *Prejudice: The Target's Perspective,* edited by J. K. Swim and C. Stangor. San Diego: Academic Press.

Thompson, E. P. 1975. *Whigs and Hunters: The Origin of the Black Act.* London: Allen Lane.

Tsesis, Alexander. 2002. *Destructive Messages: How Hate Speech Paves the Way for Harmful Social Movements.* New York City: New York University Press.

Tushnet, Mark. 1984. "An Essay on Rights." *Texas Law Review* 62:1363.

Tyler, Tom R. 1990. *Why People Obey the Law.* New Haven: Yale University Press.

Unger, Roberto. 1985. *Law in Modern Society: Toward a Criticism of Social Theory.* New York: Free Press.

Volokh, Eugene. 1992. "Freedom of Speech and Workplace Harassment." *University of California Law Review* 39:1791.

Wells, Aliena. 2002. "Berkeley Cares." www.berkeleycares.org.

West, Robin. 1987. "The Differences in Women's Hedonic Lives." *Wisconsin Women's Law Journal* 3.

White, Lucie. 1990. "Subordination, Rhetorical Survival Skills, and Sunday Shoes: Notes on the Hearing of Mrs. G." *Buffalo Law Review* 38.

Williams, Patricia J. 1991. *The Alchemy of Race and Rights.* Cambridge: Harvard University Press.

Yngvesson, Barbara. 1985. "Law, Private Governance, and Continuing Relationships." *Wisconsin Law Review* 1985:623–46.

———. 1988. "Making Law at the Doorway: The Clerk, the Court, and the Construction of Community in a New England Town." *Law and Society Review* 22:409–48.

consciousness raising, 153, 177. *See also* legal consciousness research

Consolidated Edison v. Public Service Commission (1980), 21

content-based restrictions on public speech, 21; and begging, 25; and cross burning, 26

content-neutral restrictions on public speech, 21, 30; and begging, 23, 25; court disagreement over what constitutes, 26

Corry v. Stanford University (1995), 23

counterspeech as response, 117, 134–35, 164; as burden on disadvantaged groups, 135, 165; courts holding "more speech" as proper remedy, 134–35, 170–71; to racist speech, 141; to sexist speech, 148–50. *See also* overt acts of resistance

court rulings, 18–25, 167; effectiveness in producing social change, 126; on hate speech codes, 177; on "more speech" as proper remedy, 134–35, 170–71; on types of forums, 21; on types of restrictions on public speech, 21–23

court system burdened by enforcement, 121–24

criminal behavior directed at women, 44–47

critical feminist scholars. *See* feminism

critical legal theorists on free speech, 29, 38

critical race theorists: on effects of racist speech, 16, 17, 67, 167; on free speech and social hierarchies, 29–30; on resistance, 138, 144; on targets' likelihood to support regulation of speech, 86–87

cross burning, 24, 25–26, 84, 172, 177

cynicism about law. *See* distrust of authority paradigm for opposing legal regulation of offensive speech

date rape, 120, 170, 178

Delgado, Richard, 30, 40, 86

democratic values and free speech, 8, 12, 29, 171, 174

denial by target of sexist speech, 156, 159

detailed calculus for being in public, 6, 39, 55–65; and appearance/dress of women, 60–61; and assessment of speakers/potential speakers, 63–65; and begging, 56–57; and body lan-

guage of women, 59–60; and racist speech, 65–66; and routes chosen by women, 61–63; and sexist speech, 57–65, 114–15, 150

disadvantaged groups: burden of counterspeech on, 135, 165; and free speech rights, 10–12, 112, 171; legal orientation of, 129. *See also* social class

distrust of authority paradigm for opposing legal regulation of offensive speech, 2, 10, 105, 106, 106t5.1, 124–27, 128, 133, 173, 179–80

Doe v. University of Michigan (1989), 23, 27

domestic violence, 36, 57, 170, 178

domination theory, 34–35, 136

doxa of assumptions that shape individual's world view, 33–34

dress of women. *See* appearance/dress of women

Duneier, Mitchell, 31, 32, 33

educational level and willingness to support civil liberties, 11, 90t4.5, 92–93

education of offensive speaker, seen as purpose of response, 74, 123, 141–42, 144

education programs for panhandlers, 164

enforcement: burdening the courts, 121–24; difficulties of enforcing in the street, 119–21; police interactions with African American men, 125

equal protection. *See* Fourteenth Amendment

escape plans of women, 58. *See also* detailed calculus for being in public

Ewick, P., & S. Sibley, 7, 9, 37, 99–101, 106–7, 128, 137, 173, 181

eye contact between women and strangers, 59

false consciousness, 130–31, 179

Feagin, K., 40

fear and ignoring offensive speech, 146–47, 160, 165

feminism: antivictimization feminism, 117; and blaming victim, 36; on effects of sexist speech, 11, 16, 17, 67, 167, 176–78; and social change, 131; on women's role in the home, 57

fighting words, 23, 27

fights: minority members feeling challenged to, 52, 80, 141; prevention of, as rationale to regulate offensive speech,